TREATISE
on RIGHT
and WRONG

TREATISE
on RIGHT
and WRONG

· H · L · MENCKEN ·

OCTAGON BOOKS

A DIVISION OF FARRAR, STRAUS AND GIROUX

New York   1977

Reprinted 1977
by special arrangement with Alfred A. Knopf, Inc.

OCTAGON BOOKS
A DIVISION OF FARRAR, STRAUS & GIROUX, INC.
19 Union Square West
New York, N.Y. 10003

Library of Congress Cataloging in Publication Data

Mencken, Henry Louis, 1880-1956.
    Treatise on right and wrong.

    Reprint of the 1st ed. published by Knopf, New York.
    Bibliography: p.
    Includes index.
    1. Ethics—History.   2. Ethics.   I. Title.
BJ71.M5   1977   170'.9   76-54778
ISBN 0-374-95579-4

Manufactured by Braun-Brumfield, Inc.
Ann Arbor, Michigan
Printed in the United States of America

PREFACE

*This book is a sort of companion volume to my
" Treatise on the Gods," and follows the same general
plan. As I tried to make plain in the former, there is no
necessary connection between religion and ethics, but
all the same they have been associated in the thought
of mankind for many centuries, and so my inquiries
into the embryology, physiology and pathology of the
one led me almost inevitably into an investigation of
the natural history of the other. My reading in the subject has been going on since my nonage, but I do not
pretend to be a professor of it, and all I presume to do
here is to present some unearthings of fact that have
interested me, and to add a few reflections and rumina-
tions upon them.*

*There is a certain amount of rambling in my expo-
sition, as there was in " Treatise on the Gods." I do not
offer a systematic text, and there is no need for one,
for many of a high excellence already exist. But it has
seemed to me that what has interested me, whether it
be important or trivial, may also interest other persons, and so I have gone down a number of side tracks,
and tried to show what is at the end of them. In particu-*

[v]

lar, I have given rather more attention than is usual to the moral ideas and practices of so-called uncivilized peoples, for there is instruction in them, and only too often they are passed over loftily. Naturally enough, civilized men have got much further in their moral speculations than savages, but it is a mistake to think that savages have neglected the subject, or that the problems before them are too elemental to be worth attention, either relatively or absolutely.

Most treatises on ethics give a great deal of space to attempts to define such concepts as right and wrong, good and evil, moral and immoral, sin and virtue. I avoid that labor because it appears to me to be useless, and turn for support to Matthew Arnold, who says in "Literature and Dogma": "Conduct is really, however men may overlay it with philosophical disquisitions, the simplest thing in the world. That is to say, it is the simplest thing in the world as far as understanding is concerned; as regards doing it is the hardest thing in the world." Here we are concerned with understanding rather than with doing, and I assume that the definitions of the aforesaid terms cherished by my readers will be sufficiently close to my own to enable them to follow me. They will discover as they go on, if they do not know it already, that I have a great dislike for metaphysics, and I apologize to them in advance for the few excursions into that pseudo-science that

PREFACE

necessity has forced upon me. These will be found mainly in the passages dealing with Free Will, and they may be avoided by the tender without much damage to my argument.

Most works on moral science have been written by men who were not only inclined to metaphysics but also infected more or less by the messianic delusion. I think I may honestly plead not guilty to the second count as well as to the first. I believe with Henry Sidgwick that " the predominance in the minds of moralists of a desire to edify has impeded the real progress of ethical science," and so I have not added any hortatory purpose, at least consciously, to that " disinterested curiosity " which he so eloquently advocates. Later on, in a smaller work, I plan to publish a few practical conclusions about human conduct, arrived at by induction from the observed practices of ordinarily decent men. Here I confine myself to setting forth a few common facts, and to criticizing as amiably as possible the theories hatched by other men, either on their own motion or under inspiration from the powers and principalities of the air.

That ethics deserves to be ranked among the sciences I verily believe, in spite of Aristotle. Its frequent pollution by theology should not be permitted to disguise the fact that, at bottom, it deals with realities — indeed, with some of the most solid realities confronting

PREFACE

mankind. *There is no getting away from its problems, and there is no denying some of its fundamental postulates. Its corpus of ideas has been enriched by the enforced and unbroken thinking of the whole human race since the dawn of reason. Only too often, finding this thinking painful, man has tried to get rid of it by retreating behind what he has been pleased to accept as mandates of the Most High, who knoweth all things and cannot err. But the mandates themselves, coming into conflict with his baser nature, have only beset him with fresh problems, and forced him into new and ever more painful cogitation. Thus he can't escape, and in all probability he will never reach the end of his agony, for ethical dilemmas of novel and embarrassing character throng upon him at every step along his weary road. But if he can't dispose of them altogether, he can at least tackle them in a free and enlightened spirit, forgetting what the vague gods ordain, and concentrating upon what mere man is able to do, and in fact does. If my book has any thesis, it is that this essentially scientific approach is really possible.*

H. L. M.

Baltimore,

February 9, 1934.

CONTENTS

TREATISE
on RIGHT
and WRONG

I

The Nature and Origin of Morality

1

Children come into the world without any visible
understanding of the difference between good and bad,
right and wrong, but some sense of it is forced upon
them almost as soon as they learn the difference between light and dark, hot and cold, sweet and sour.
It is a kind of knowledge that seems to be natural and
essential to all creatures living in societies, and it
shows itself in many of the lower animals quite as well
as in human beings. To be sure, they do not appear to
formulate a concept of evil *per se*, and certainly they
know nothing about the highly metaphysical abstrac-
tion that mankind calls sin, but many species are well
acquainted with concrete acts of wickedness, and punish them severely. Theft and adultery are familiar
examples. A dog will pursue and, if it can, castigate
another dog which steals its bone, and an ape will try
to kill any bachelor intruder which makes too free
with its wives. This sharp and often bloody discrimina-
tion between *meum* and *tuum* is to be observed not
only in mammals, but also in animals of lower orders, including birds, insects and even fishes. Much

[1]

of the uproar that goes on among sparrows and star-
lings is caused by conflicts over property rights, and
everyone has seen two goldfishes in a globe fighting over a speck of food, with one claiming it and
trying to gobble it and the other seeking to make off
with it.

A German popular naturalist, Dr. Theodor Zell, has
gone to the length of writing a treatise called " Moral
in der Tierwelt " (Morality in the Animal World),
in which he argues that many species, especially
among the social insects, entertain not only the somewhat negative idea of vice but also the positive idea of
virtue. The ants, he says, are better citizens than the
members of any known human society, for they never
go on strike. If the workers of a given colony should
quit work their queen would starve, and each of them
would enjoy thereby the democratic privilege of as-
piring to her power and circumstance, but they never
cease to feed her so long as any food is obtainable.
Thus they are true patriots, and show a luxuriant development of that loyalty to the established order
which is put so high among the virtues by human beings. It appears also, sometimes in curious forms,
among rather more complex but still untutored and
infidel creatures. Thus we are told by travelers that
certain monkeys have a great aversion to a brother
who, on being taken by men, lives contentedly in captivity, and that they try to kill him when they can get
at him. They seem to feel, however dimly, that he has

repudiated a solemn obligation to the tribe, and they punish the crime as men might.

Here it may be argued that such acts and attitudes in the lower animals are purely instinctive, and that it would be irrational to dignify them by calling them moral. But to that it may be answered that the motives and impulses lying behind many of the moral concepts of human beings seem to be instinctive in exactly the same sense, and almost to the same extent. No teaching is required to induce a baby to recognize a given rattle as its own; all the power of pedagogy must be devoted to inducing it to surrender its property on demand. Nor is there any reason to believe that the various manifestations of sexual rivalry among men are any nobler in origin than those observed among apes or dogs; the whole tendency of an advancing culture is to obliterate them, not to nourish them. In the days when anthropology was a pseudo-science chiefly cultivated by missionaries there was a belief that the lower races of men had no morals at all — that they yielded to their impulses in a naïve and irrational manner, and had no conception whatever of property rights, whether in goods or in women, or of duties, whether to their gods or to their fellow men. But it is now known that savages are really rather more moral, if anything, than civilized men. Their ethical systems, in some ways, differ from ours, just as their grammatical systems differ, and their theological and governmental systems, but even the most primitive of them submit unquestioningly to complicated and onerous duties and taboos, and not only suffer punishment willingly when the Old Adam lures them into false steps, but also appear to be tortured by what, on higher levels, is called conscience — to the extent, at times, of falling into such vapors of remorse that they languish and die.

Primitive man, in this respect as in others, seems to have been much like the savages of today. At the time when we get our first vague glimpse of him, lurking in the dark of his spooky caves, he was already a family man, and hence had certain duties, rights and responsibilities. We know, of course, very little about him, but we are at least reasonably sure that he did not habitually share his wife with all comers, or kill and eat his children, or fail in what he conceived to be his duty to the gods. To that extent, at least, he was a moral agent, and as completely so as any Christian. Later on in human history, when men discovered the art of writing and began to record their thoughts and doings for posterity, they devoted almost as much time and energy to setting down their notions of right and wrong as they gave to recording their prodigies and glories. In the very first chapter of the collection of hoary documents which we call the Bible there are confident moral mandates, and similar ones are to be found in the ancient books of every other people. The earliest conquerors and despots of whom we have any news seem to have regarded themselves, precisely like their colleagues of today, as the heralds of an ethical enlightenment, and every one of them was apparently just as eager as the celebrated Hammurabi to be known as " the king of righteousness."

In the world that we now live in the moral sense seems to be universally dispersed, at all events among normal persons beyond infancy. No traveler has ever discovered a tribe which failed to show it. There are peoples so primitive that their religion is hard to distinguish from a mere fear of the dark, but there is none so low that it lacks a moral system, elaborate and unyielding. Nor is that system often challenged, at least on the lower cultural levels, by those who lie under it. The rebellious individual may evade it on occasion, but he seldom denies its general validity. To find any such denial on a serious scale one must return to Christendom, where a bold and impatient reëxamination of the traditional ethical dogma has followed the collapse of the old belief in revelation. But even in Christendom the most formidable critics of the orthodox system are still, as a rule, profoundly moral men, and the reform they propose is not at all an abandonment of moral imperatives, but simply a substitution of what they believe to be good ones for what they believe to be bad ones. This has been true of every important iconoclast from Hobbes to Lenin, and it was preëminently true of the arch-iconoclast Nietzsche.

His furious attack upon the Christian ideal of humility and abnegation has caused Christian critics to denounce him as an advocate of the most brutal egoism, but in point of fact, he proposed only the introduction of a new and more heroic form of renunciation, based upon abounding strength rather than upon hopeless weakness; and in his maxim " Be hard! " there was just as much sacrifice of immediate gratification to ultimate good as you will find in any of the *principia* of Jesus.

The difference between moral systems is thus very slight, and if it were not for the constant pressure from proponents of virtues that have no roots in ordinary human needs, and hence appeal only to narrow and abnormal classes of men, it would be slighter still. All of the really basic varieties of moral good have been esteemed as such since the memory of mankind runneth not to the contrary, and all of the basic wickednesses have been reprehended. The Second Commandment preached by Jesus (Mark xii, 31) was preached by the Gautama Buddha six centuries before Him, and it must have been hoary with age when the Gautama Buddha made it the center of his system. Similarly, the Ten Commandments of Exodus and Deuteronomy were probably thousands of years old when the Jewish scribes first reduced them to writing. Finally, and in the same way, the Greeks lifted their concept of wisdom as the supreme good out of the stream of time, and if we think of them today as its

[6]

inventors, it is only because we are more familiar with their ethical speculations than we are with those of more ancient peoples.

The five fundamental prohibitions of the Decalogue — those leveled at murder, theft, trespass, adultery and false witness — are to be found in every moral system ever heard of, and seem to be almost universally supported by human opinion. This support, of course, does not mean that they are observed with anything properly describable as pedantic strictness; on the contrary, they are evaded on occasion, both by savages and by civilized men, and some of them are evaded very often. In the United States, for example, the situations in which killing a fellow human being is held to be innocent are considerably more numerous than those in which it is held to be criminal, and even in England, the most moral of great nations, there are probably almost as many. So with adultery. So, again, with theft, trespass and false witness. Theft and trespass shade by imperceptible gradations into transactions that could not be incommoded without imperiling the whole fabric of society, and bearing false witness is so easy to condone that bishops are sometimes among its most zealous practitioners. But despite this vagueness of moral outline and this tolerance of the erring the fact remains that all normal and well-disposed men, whether civilized or uncivilized, hold it to be axiomatic that murder, theft, trespass, adultery and false witness, in their

cruder and plainer forms, are anti-social and immoral enterprises, and no one argues seriously, save
maybe in time of war, when all the customary moral
sanctions are abandoned, that they should be counte-
nanced. When they are perpetrated in a naked manner, without any concession to the ancient and in-
eradicable feeling against them, they are viewed with
abhorrence, and the guilty are severely punished.

2

But if the fundamental moral ideas of all peoples
are thus pretty much the same — and they tend toward that identity on the side of the virtues almost as
often as on the side of the vices — the nature of the
authority which men put behind them differs considerably from time to time and place to place. No one
glancing through the Nicomachean Ethics can fail to
see at once that the sanctions which seemed apposite
and persuasive to Aristotle were not the sanctions
which appeared nearly four centuries later in the
Beatitudes. To Aristotle " the moral activities " were
" purely human," and the business of defining and
estimating them was a matter for philosophers, not
for priests. He scoffed at the idea that the gods could
be either moral or immoral in the human sense, and
believed that the only thing men and women could
learn from them was their serenity. To him, as to
Socrates, virtue was mainly a function of wisdom, and

[8]

the chief means of attaining it, and happiness with it, was " some form of contemplative activity."

But to Jesus it was simply obedience to the will of Yahweh, and the way to it ran through an humble and a contrite heart. There was, to Him, no merit in wisdom, not even in moral wisdom, but only in submission. The thing to do was to follow faithfully the precept of Yahweh, the tribal protector of the Jews and the pattern of all goodness, and to carry out in the trusting manner of a little child such of his special mandates as could be intercepted and interpreted. Thus the ethical doctrine of Jesus was based almost wholly upon supernatural commands, many of them arbitrary and unintelligible, and the surmises and experiments of human reason had little if anything to do with it. To this day the system that He founded, despite the adept use of casuistry by its defenders, remains fundamentally contemptuous of reason, and some of its characteristic principles — for example, its exaltation of poverty, chastity and obedience — have yet to be squared with a sound social philosophy. But to Aristotle reason was everything and the will of the gods nothing. If he could not justify a given article of conduct on purely logical grounds he was inclined to reject it.

There is yet a third way to account for ethical ideas, and that is by the device of laying them to the inherent nature of man. From this point of view neither revelation nor reason has any validity: the moving force is a body of impulses and habits that stretches back to the infancy of the race, and is at least in some part an inheritance from pre-human ancestors. Perhaps Aristotle alluded to it darkly when he spoke of " moral qualities that are thought to be the outcome of the physical constitution "; it did not get much attention, however, until the Earl of Shaftesbury stated it clearly in his " Inquiry Concerning Virtue or Merit " (1699), and it was not studied seriously until the time of Darwin.

In Darwin's first great work, " The Origin of Species," he depicted life on earth as a merciless struggle for survival, and left scarcely any room in the picture for moral restraints. This neglect seriously incommoded some of his disciples, for it was plain that such restraints existed, and not only on the human level; thus they were compelled to look for them outside what Huxley called " the cosmic process," which is to say, in some extra-natural realm. Any such necessity, to men of their generally skeptical cast of mind, was bound to be embarrassing, for the only extra-natural realm conveniently at hand was that of the Judæo-Christian Yahweh, which they were certainly not eager to enter. After they had sweated and panted over this dilemma for twelve long years Darwin came to their rescue with the celebrated fourth and fifth chapters of " The Descent of Man." It was these chapters, even more than anything in " The Origin of Species," which gave him the evil name among Christians that he still enjoys in Arkansas. For in them he laid the whole moral passion of man, even in its loftiest forms, to what he called, perhaps somewhat loosely, instinct, and brought forward evidence tending to show, as he thought, that the same moving force was present in many of the lower animals.

Its genesis he sought in the structure and evolution of the family. Below a certain level, as everyone knows, nothing resembling the family exists. The adult creatures lay their eggs and then go about their business; the young come forth fully able to fend for themselves. But as one comes up the scale the young appear at earlier and earlier stages of their development, until finally they are born quite helpless. Their helplessness naturally requires that they be helped, and this help commonly comes from their mothers, with their fathers sometimes lending a hand. Thus the family appears in the world, and within its fold, according to Darwin, the social instincts develop. The parent animal, having learned to perform services for its young, to take pleasure in their company, and to feel sympathy for them, cannot well remain completely indifferent to the young of other adults, or to those adults themselves. And the young, having learned to trust to their parents for aid, and to sport and play with their brethren, grow up with an amiable attitude toward other individuals.

Darwin added cautiously that " these feelings and

services are by no means extended to all the individuals of the same species, but only to those of the same
association "; nevertheless, once they exist there is
no psychological impediment to a gradual extension
of their range. He believed that, in man, three things
have contributed to that extension, and so created the
great body of moral sentiments, *i.e.,* of impulses to
positive benevolence and negative restraint. The first
is the development of human intelligence, which en-
ables man to weigh his conflicting instincts, and urges
him to yield oftenest to those which give him the most
durable satisfaction. The second is the appearance of
language, which causes a common opinion to form,
and a sense of the common good. The third is habit.
Darwin argued that these factors were sufficient to account for all the essential phenomena of morality,
even the highest. We shall look into his ideas at greater
length in Chapter II.

3

The lines between the three fundamental moral
theories, of course, are not sharply drawn, and it is
quite possible for a given moralist to found his system upon two of them, and even upon all three. Thus
Aristotle, though he believed firmly that all ethical
problems could be worked out by a purely intellectual
process, almost like problems in algebra, could yet
admit that " some moral qualities " might be " the

outcome of the physical constitution " and that others might have " a close affinity in many respects with the passions," which are plainly irrational; moreover, like most other Greek philosophers of his time, he had not quite divested himself of a sneaking belief in the gods, and in consequence he occasionally discussed ethics in terms of their probable desires. In the same way Darwin, besides making intelligence almost as important in his system as instinct, confessed that " the reverence or fear of the gods or spirits " must also be considered by every professor of morals — if not because such beings actually exist, then at least because multitudes of men believe that they do, and act upon that belief in daily life.

Contrariwise, not many moral theologians of any dignity halt their exposition with a bald statement of what the gods command. Always they make some effort to prove that it is in accord both with human reason and with what they conceive to be the eternal nature of man. Or nearly always. In the Christian moral system, as we now know it, a few elements remain that cannot be rationalized, but have to be accounted for on the ground that Yahweh's mind is so much superior to the human mind that certain of its mandates must be forever inscrutable to man (" How unsearchable are his judgments, and his ways past finding out! "), but such wholly unfathomable mysteries are not numerous. In the main, theologians profess to know precisely why this or that ordinance was issued by the gods, and precisely what it is intended to achieve. Knowing such things, in fact, is their principal business in the world. They are specialists in penetrating the impenetrable, or they are nothing.

As a practical matter, all moral systems of any complexity gather in virtues and wickednesses based upon each of the three sanctions — the theological, the logical and the biological. In the Christian system, for example, one act may be forbidden on the ground that it is repugnant to God, another on the ground that it is in contempt of sound reason, and a third on the ground that it does violence to the nature of man. Acts belonging to the first category decrease in number and importance as belief in revelation decays, but enough of them survive to condition, to some extent, our everyday thinking on moral matters, and even to color our secular jurisprudence.

A familiar example is blasphemy. There is obviously nothing in the nature of man to interdict it (even theologians, in fact, recognize that the impulse to it is a natural " weakness "), nor is there any impediment to it in reason, save maybe on grounds of taste and decorum, for if it is logical for a believer to call upon his gods for help, then it is equally logical for him to abuse them roundly (as is the habit of Italian peasants and African cannibals) when they mock his faith by failing him. What gives blasphemy a bad name in Christendom is simply the Third Commandment, supported by such glosses as Leviticus xxiv, 16 and Mark

III, 29. There is never any complaint about it from non-believers; on the contrary, they commonly esteem it, at least in its more seemly forms, as an effective weapon against both the general piety and their own inherited qualms. When one hears of a concerted effort to put it down — as by the organization of Holy Name Societies among Catholics — it always appears that the chief appeal is to revelation unadorned: the thing is evil simply because Yahweh frowns upon it. And when there is a civil prosecution, as still sometimes happens, notably in the English-speaking countries, it is always evident that the animus behind it is theological rather than legal. In other words, the prohibition of blasphemy is what the anthropologists call a taboo. It is a survival from the day when our savage forebears feared not only to irritate their gods, but even to name them.

In the index to my copy of the Nicomachean Ethics I can find no reference to the offense; if Aristotle mentions it in his text I have forgotten the passage and can't find it. It had, indeed, little terror for the speculative and realistic Greeks, and when they accused anyone of it, as in the case of Socrates, it was only to give a pious flourish to the bill of charges against an unpopular man, condemned before he was heard. The Romans, though their moral sanctions were less purely metaphysical than those of the Greeks, had no specific law against blasphemers, and no apparent abhorrence of them. If they were proceeded against at all, it was simply as disturbers of the public order. Nor is there anything against them in the sanctions of the post-Darwinian moralists, save in so far as their acts break the peace, and thus outrage the social instinct. " It is to the Jewish and Christian Law," says Dr. W. F. Geikie-Cobb, a learned English patrologist, " that we have to look for the creation of the offense of blasphemy." And Law, of course, is here used in the sense that Jesus understood it, as a synonym for a divine mandate, or, as an anthropologist would say, for taboo.

But not many true analogues of the prohibition of blasphemy survive in the civil codes of civilized countries. Even among professing Christians there is a tendency to neglect and reject whatever has no other authority behind it than the command of Yahweh, published by his amanuenses of the Old and New Testaments. Thus Protestants in general are very careless about resorting to the sacraments, though failure to do so is still a mortal sin to Catholics. Nor do they pay any noticeable heed to what Catholic moral theologians call the " supernatural precepts " — faith, hope and charity —, or to the Catholic ordinances for fasts. Both Catholics and Protestants long ago put the Tenth Commandment on the shelf, and both, relying upon various passages in Paul's epistles (and conveniently forgetting Matthew v, 17–18 and Luke xvi, 17), ignore the whole of Leviticus.

Even the Jews, including the most orthodox among

them, have discreetly edited the Law. They still observe the sacrament of circumcision and they still respect the taboos on eating pork, oysters, eels, shrimp,
crabs, lobsters and clams, and butter or milk with
meat, but they no longer feast on locusts, beetles and
grasshoppers (Leviticus XI, 22), just as they no longer
execute witches (Exodus XXII, 18), or stone an ox that
gores a man (*ibid.* XXI, 28), or bar him "that is
wounded in the stones, or hath his privy member cut
off," from the synagogue (Deuteronomy XXIII, 1).
According to the Catholic moral theologians, McHugh
and Callan, the Mosaic Law was handed down " when
experience had proved that knowledge is not sufficient to make men virtuous," and was abrogated when
further experience showed that " external observance
is not sufficient for holiness." The Jews accept the first
half of this, but not the second: they still think of
themselves as bound by the Law. But it grows more
and more vague to them as year follows year, and
many of them, exposed to the growing skepticism of
Christendom, scarcely know what it is. More than
once I have greatly astonished a Jewish friend by as-
suring him that he was perfectly free, under Yahweh,
to dine upon June bugs.

4

But though in the law of today and in morals properly so called the sanctions of revelation are thus in

decay, the sanctions of reason are still powerful. That this is the case is largely and perhaps mainly due to Greek influence. The bold and beautiful speculations of the Greek moralists have reached us in two ways — first, indirectly (but on the purely legal side, only the more patently) through the Roman Law, the foundation of most of the civil law and of much of the ecclesiastical law of Europe; and secondly, directly, through St. Paul, the Scholastic philosophers of the Middle Ages, and the intellectual revolutionaries of the Renaissance. It is a commonplace that Paul was a thoroughly Hellenized Jew, and it is easy to see that his celebrated twelfth chapter of Romans owes almost as much to the Stoics and to Aristotle's definition of the high-minded man as it owes to the Beatitudes. The whole New Testament, as we have it today, was written originally in Greek, and practically all of the Early Fathers wrote either Greek or Latin.

Now, a language, manifestly, is not merely a series of words; it is also the overt embodiment of a system of ideas, a way of looking at things. No man bred to Greek could have written the Pentateuch, and no man bred to its Hebrew could have written the Pauline Epistles. Thus the early Christians, whether they lived in the territory that had been Greek down to 146 B.C. or elsewhere in the wide empire of the all-conquering Romans, were exposed constantly to the impact of Hellenic ideas, either at first or at second hand. The naïve view of Jesus (Matthew xxii, 37–40) that the whole Law could be reduced to two simple principles, both based on the Decalogue, did not long survive Him; indeed, it was probably challenged in His presence by " one of them which was a lawyer." Other lawyers appeared soon enough — a long procession of them, culminating in the immortal Buzfuz, Tertullian (*c.* 160–220) — and by the end of the Second Century moral jurisprudence had become a highly secularized and academic science, with quite as much of speculation in it as of revelation. The Fathers, of course, did not forget the Gospel mandates, nor did they overlook the continuing aid that the Holy Spirit could give to weak and stumbling mortals: they believed with Paul that It interceded on high " with groanings which cannot be uttered," soliciting not only the boon of grace, but also that of light and leading. But they also discussed right and wrong from a purely philosophical standpoint, and laid down their contradictory conclusions with great assurance.

In consequence, some of the principal articles of the moral code prevailing in Christendom today are quite without support in revelation, and were unknown to either the Jews or the early Christians. Consider, for example, the virtues which enter principally into the character of what we now call a good citizen. These virtues certainly do not come out of the Bible, for the Jews of the great days, despite what is observed in their descendants today, had a low view of industry and an even lower view of thrift, and were almost devoid of the banal sentimentalities which now pass under the name of patriotism. Their loyalty was to Yahweh rather than to the state or the community, and they were ever ready to defy and overthrow their rulers, and to make war upon their brethren. In brief, their moral system was that of separatists and individualists, impatient of every secular restraint and disdainful of all hard and continued social effort. They originated as a tribe of desert nomads, and their point of view remained that of nomads to the end of their bloody chapter.

Work, in their eyes, was not the glorious privilege it has come to be in our highly socialized society, but an unmitigated curse, laid upon Adam for his sins, as the pains of parturition were laid upon Eve for hers. "Because thou hast . . . eaten of the tree, . . . in the sweat of thy face shalt thou eat bread." This concept of work as expiation eventually made it more or less tolerable, but it never became anything properly describable as pleasant. The Jews always laid great stress — rare in their time and place — upon the Sabbath's function as a day of rest: " in it thou shalt not do any work, thou, nor thy son, nor thy daughter, thy manservant, nor thy maidservant, nor thy cattle, nor thy stranger that is within thy gates." This rest was the righteous and highly appreciated reward of piety: by serving God assiduously they escaped at least a seventh part of the burden of work. Almost always, in the Old Testament, that burden is bracketed with sorrow, as in Psalms XC, 10. If " the sleep of a laboring man is sweet," then it is only because his work is done. There is no subjective stimulation in it, and no durable good. " As he came forth of his mother's womb, naked shall he return to go as he came, and shall take nothing of his labor."

The idea that wealth can be a good in itself, that there is a mystic virtue in accumulating it by hard work and self-denial — this was as foreign to the thinking of the Jews as it was to that of the Greeks. A rich man, to them, was almost always a villain; in fact, he was the favorite villain, next to the idolator, of their moral homilies. Are there occasional friendly words, in Proverbs, for the " man diligent in his business "? Then Dr. James Henry Breasted tells us that they are only borrowings from an ancient Egyptian book, the Wisdom of Amenemope (c. 1000 B.C.) — and that with them, and from the same source, came dire warnings that diligence might be easily carried too far. Did Solomon, to whom Proverbs is traditionally (but falsely) ascribed, counsel his son to emulate the laborious ant? Then Solomon himself was a money-grubber, and hence, by Jewish theory, a suspicious character. When we get into the New Testament we find him held up in contemptuous contrast to the lilies of the field, which " toil not, neither do they spin." Jesus had two rich followers, Zaccheus of Jericho and Joseph of Arimathæa, but the former was induced to give half of his goods to the poor and the latter did not

appear until after the Crucifixion. The general view of
wealth that He entertained is too well known to need
recalling. Preaching, as He did, the imminent end of
the world, He could imagine no valid reason for pil-
ing up property, and in His system of ethics there was
thus no room for the virtues of Babbitt. " Verily, I
say unto you that a rich man shall hardly enter into
the Kingdom of Heaven. And again I say unto you, It
is easier for a camel to go through the eye of a needle
than for a rich man to enter the Kingdom of God."
Many other familiar echoes of the Tenth Commandment will come to mind: " Lay not up for yourselves
treasures upon earth. . . . The deceitfulness of riches
. . . choke[s] the Word, and it becometh unfruitful.
. . . Ye cannot serve God and Mammon." And even
more plainly and uncompromisingly there is this:

*Take no thought for your life, what ye shall eat, or what
ye shall drink; nor yet for your body, what ye shall put on.
. . . Behold the fowls of the air: for they sow not, neither
do they reap, nor gather into barns; yet your heavenly Father feedeth them. Are ye not much better than they?*

As for Paul, he saw in opulence only a ticket to
Hell. " They that will be rich," he wrote to Timothy,
" fall into temptation and a snare, and into many foolish and hurtful lusts, which drown men in destruction
and perdition. For the love of money is the root of all
evil." Here the counsel of Jesus is supported, as is so
often the case with Paul, by the dicta of the Greek

philosophers and their Roman followers. Both Greeks and Romans — with the exception, perhaps, of a few Stoics — viewed work much as the Jews did: as no more, at its best, than an unpleasant sacrifice to the gods for their somewhat grudging mercies. In the Golden Age men knew nothing of it, as Hesiod tells us. The Italian *Kulturkritiker*, Adriano Tilgher, in his " Homo Faber," recalls the fact that the Greek word for work, *ponos*, came from the same root as the Latin word for sorrow, *poena*. He says that the failure of the Greeks to apply some of their scientific discoveries was largely due to their disdain of labor, worldly enterprise, and the accumulation of property. They even had a certain contempt for artists; cutting statues and raising buildings, they thought, were not vocations for free men, but for slaves. Aristotle, always seeking a golden mean, allowed that riches might be useful on occasion, if only as a stimulus to liberality and justice, but he saw no virtue in the bare act of accumulating them, and he thought that they were unnecessary to most of the higher emprises of man. The seeker after wisdom (which to him, as to Confucius, was the highest good that could be imagined) " needs no external apparatus; on the contrary, worldly goods may almost be said to be a hindrance to contemplation."

The Romans, being a far less idealistic people than the Greeks, with no great love of wisdom, took a rather more friendly view of wealth, but they had rigid views about the means of getting it. Work, in itself, was disgusting to them, and they resigned it to slaves whenever possible. The two really respectable ways of accumulating money among them were by cultivating the land and by engaging in what we now call Big Business, but the latter was esteemed only because, in Tilgher's phrase, it led to " honorable retirement into rural peace as a country gentleman." For ordinary thrift and diligence the Romans had only contempt. Shopkeepers and common traders were clowns to them, and workingmen were scarcely human.

5

The early Christian Fathers, when the hope of the Second Coming faded at last, had to fit their moral system to the realities of a disturbed and exigent world, and so the counsels of Jesus were delicately revised. In particular, some thought had to be given to the ever-approaching and always menacing morrow, and in consequence the accumulation of goods began to take on a certain respectability. But the notion that work could be a good in itself was still far off. To Augustine (354–430), as to the Jews, it remained a kind of sacrifice — if not an actual expiation for sin, then at least a device for reducing temptation. He believed that all monks should be compelled to work, for it wore them out and took their minds off lubricity and other evil concerns. But when it came to laymen he was somewhat vague: they were in duty bound to share their gains with the poor, but they were apparently not in duty bound to labor and save.

It was not until the Middle Ages, when society in Europe began to reorganize itself very painfully on a commercial basis, that a general obligation to work began to be heard of. St. Thomas Aquinas (c. 1226–74) preached it as a corollary to his doctrine of fixed and immovable social classes. It was the duty of certain lowly orders of men to labor diligently, as it was the duty of the noble and learned to cultivate the humanities, spread the True Faith, and smite the infidel. But there was no revelation in this, and not much theology. Thomas, as always, spoke thunderously *ex cathedra,* but he spoke as a sociologist rather than as a theologian. In other words, his theory was simply a logical deduction from the social necessities of his time. Work was inescapably needful in a world in which money was becoming more and more important, and it thus had to be endured. But thrift was yet somewhat dubious. The first duty of a man who happened to accumulate a great deal of wealth was to spend it — a large part of it on the poor, but a part of it also on that conspicuous waste which was one of the major social phenomena of the age. A prince who showed caution in this department was held in low esteem, and likewise a prelate. Most of the great cathedrals were built, not primarily to the glory of God, but in gorgeous proof of the liberality of archbishops.

TREATISE ON RIGHT AND WRONG

As the Middle Ages flowed into the Renaissance and sustained work became ever more necessary to the well-being of a rapidly changing society, it naturally became more and more virtuous. But the Catholic theologians granted it their approval, one suspects, only under harsh economic compulsion: in their hearts they apparently still cherished the old Christian view of it as burdensome and painful, and when they praised it roundly it was chiefly as penance. It remained for the heretic, Martin Luther, to discover that the thing was laudable in itself. He was the true inventor of the modern doctrine that there is something inherently dignified and praiseworthy about labor — that the man who bears a burden in the heat of the day is somehow more pleasing to God than the man who takes his ease in the shade. Here, as in other directions, he gave an eager theological ratification to the economic revolution that was going on around him, and could not be stayed. He was the champion of the new masters of Europe, the *bourgeois* men of business, against its old masters, the soldiers and priests. These men of business needed willing laborers, and the easiest way to make them willing was to convince them that by working hard they were serving and gratifying God.

But even Luther was suspicious of the mere capitalist, as opposed to the *entrepreneur*, and in his early sermons he denounced the taking of interest in terms recalling the philippics of the early Christian Fathers.

Later on, facing a tide that he could not stem, he prudently modified his position, and his final doctrine granted that taking rent for the use of land was pleasing to God, provided the charge did not run beyond 5% of the value. He held also that it was moral to recover from a borrower if the lender lost a chance of profit by making the loan, or if he had to borrow himself to replace what he had lent. But he never went the whole way: to the end he had grave doubts about certain kinds of investments. His great contribution to latter-day Christian ethics did not lie in this hazardous and dubious direction: it was his invention of the dignity of work. " With him," says Tilgher, " the German word *Beruf,* meaning profession, took on a religious color which it was never to lose, and which from German passed into all the analogous words of Protestant countries. Profession and vocation or calling became synonymous. Luther placed a crown on the sweaty forehead of labor."

The incomparable Calvin went a step further. To Luther there was still a certain validity in the medieval doctrine that a man should be content in that station to which a righteous and omnipotent God had been pleased to call him, but Calvin rejected it flatly. Instead, he declared for the up-and-coming man, the go-getter, the rebel against caste and condition, and with him for the whole gospel of success, until lately so vastly esteemed in all the more enlightened nations. No true believer, he was willing to grant, could ever be quite sure whether God had destined him for Heaven or for Hell, but meanwhile it was a pretty good sign that Heaven was the goal if the candidate prospered on this earth, rising from a low place to a higher. Thus industry and enterprise, under the influence of Calvinism, took on the appearance of Christian virtues, or, at all events, of signs that the Christian virtues were concurrently present, and with them went the accumulation of goods. By 1758 it was possible for Dr. Samuel Johnson to say, forgetting the whole history of moral theology before Luther, that " to be idle and to be poor have always been reproaches." It became a kind of sin to lack worldly ambition, to disdain hard effort and its rewards.

This doctrine has been under heavy fire in late years, but there is little evidence that it has been shaken. It lies at the heart of all the new non-Euclidean theologies — for example, Bolshevism and Fascism —, though they reject certain of its traditional implications. They are all hot for labor, and reserve their worst anathemas for those who seek to shirk it. Says the Charter of Labor of the Italian Fascists: " Work in all its forms, intellectual, technical, manual, is a social duty." To which the Constitution of the U.S.S.R. replies in sonorous antiphon: " The Union of Socialist Soviet Republics declares labor to be the duty of all citizens." Nor is the accumulation of goods denounced *per se*, even by the Bolshevists. They struggle frantically to achieve it, and dream gorgeous dreams of a Golden Age when every citizen will have his large and equal share. All forms of Socialism, indeed, whether of Russian ferocity or American mildness, lay heavy stress upon the powers and joys of wealth, for all of them are alike founded on the idea that every human value of any significance is simply a function of material estate and status. If they propose to rob the rich it is only to enrich the poor. In none of them is there the slightest trace of Jesus's fear of laying up treasures upon earth.

Holy Church, in the face of this tide, shows a considerable vacillation and discomfort, as one discovers on examining two recent encyclicals, the *Rerum novarum* of Leo XIII, dated May 15, 1891, and the *Quadragesimo anno* of Pius XI, dated May 15, 1931. There is some discreetly loose thinking in both of these documents, as there always is in papal pronunciamentos. The former, though it praises the early Christians as " industrious and laborious " and says that " there is nothing to be ashamed of in seeking one's bread by labor," yet speaks of labor itself, following Genesis III, 17, as " the painful expiation of sin." Again, though it defends private property vigorously, it yet warns the rich that they are, in the eye of the Church, only trustees for the benefit of the poor, and quotes with approval the scathing denunciation by Jesus in Luke VI, 24–25. The second encyclical is equally dubious about the new gospel. A good part of it is devoted to a laborious explanation of Leo's defense of private property, and there is a return to the Thomistic doctrine that men should be content in " the position assigned to them by Divine Providence." Here Holy Writ plainly supports Thomas and Pius.

6

It would be easy to multiply examples of such conquests of revelation by reason: modern Christendom, indeed, has become far more Greek than Hebraic, and even its theologians constantly subordinate the letter of the divine law to the needs and notions of an increasingly skeptical and contumacious society. The thing runs both ways — in favor of acts that were interdicted by the prophets, and against acts that they regarded as quite virtuous. As a specimen of the former the taking of interest has just been mentioned briefly; as a specimen of the latter the holding of slaves comes to mind at once.

Who it was that first denounced slave-holding as immoral is not known, but there is little reason to believe that he was a Christian theologian. The institution broke down less because there were moral objections to it than because, in the long run, it turned out to be unworkable economically. The theory that it was wicked was scarcely more than an afterthought. Unfortunately, the process whereby, in Europe, the slave acquired the relative freedom of the serf was too long and tortuous to be traced in detail here; suffice it to say that it was simply a function of the process whereby the old Roman society broke up, just as the subsequent liberation of the serf was a function of the decay of feudalism. So long as the *pax romana* prevailed it was possible to work slave labor safely and (at least according to the ideas of the time) profitably, but when the Empire began to go to pieces and barbarian adventurers arose to challenge the rights and prerogatives of the provincial magnates the latter could no longer sit in pleasant security on their estates, watching their slaves sweat, but had to arm themselves and take to the field. Many of them never came back, and those who did often found their human chattels flown or in rebellion. Moreover, it was no longer possible to obtain fresh supplies from abroad. The time was one of dreadful chaos — as Ferdinand Lot says, " a truly accursed period " — , with property in jeopardy everywhere, and every man for himself. Naturally enough, the lowly made the best of the general demoralization. They flocked to that master-brigand who offered them the easiest terms, and helped him to fight for land — his own or some other's. Thus the slave became the *colonus,* who could not be sold save with the land, and the *colonus* gradually developed into the early medieval *villein,* a man still bound to the soil but with many inalienable rights.

With the rise of feudalism, which consolidated and extended the power of the stronger brigands, there was a reaction, and at certain times and in certain places the *villein* returned to substantial slavery. But feudalism itself was under heavy pressure from the start, not only from the nascent monarchies but also and more especially from the burghers of the towns, and in consequence it could never make that slavery either complete or durable. So early as the Twelfth Century, six hundred years before Lord Mansfield's celebrated decision of 1772, giving freedom to every slave who set foot on English soil, many of the imperial cities on the Continent had set up the same rule — for example, Bremen in 1186, and Vienna and Ratisbon in 1230. This fact, together with the gradual decline of latifundia and the reorganization of the whole economic order on a trading basis, made it hard to hold slaves and unprofitable to work them, and the *villein* was put upon the path to emancipation. It was not until the Revolution of 1789 that he was legally liberated from his last disabilities in France, and not until 1810 that complete liberation followed in Prussia, but for many centuries before that time he had been very far from a slave.

Genuine slavery, when it was revived in the Fifteenth Century, was reserved for the heathen, who, as heretics, had no rights. They came mainly from Africa, which the Portuguese began to explore in 1415, and not many of them were ever landed on European soil. It was not until 1511 that the trade in them got to be of any importance, and then they were all shipped to the Spanish colonies in America. The English, at the start, were chary of the business; indeed, Queen Elizabeth rebuked Sir John Hawkins for taking 300 Guinea Negroes to Hispaniola (now Haiti) in 1562, and even went to the length of hinting that God was displeased. But by 1631 an African Company was chartered for the express purpose of carrying blacks from Guinea to the West Indies, including the British islands this time, and thereafter, until 1807, the English were prime movers in the trade. They probably hauled at least four-fifths of the multitudes of poor savages who were brought before 1776 to what is now the United States. When they gave up slaving at last it was mainly because Yankee entrepreneurs were gobbling most of its profits.

But once they had got out, they proposed, characteristically, to put down the trade by force, as an offense to international morals, and pressed an agreement to that end upon the other Powers. Inasmuch, however, as they claimed in the same breath the right to search any and all suspected vessels on the high seas, the other Powers were naturally mistrustful, and it was not until 1841 that Austria and Prussia, the first to sign, were induced to do so. France, as a maritime nation, hung back, and so did the United States. It was the American Civil War, as every schoolboy knows, that finally broke the back of the slave trade, and with it of slavery in Christendom. But there were slaves in Porto Rico until 1873, in Cuba until 1880, in Brazil until 1888, and in the Philippines until 1902 — all pious countries, long under the wing of Holy Church. And there are slaves to this day in Liberia, which was established more than a century ago as a Christian refuge for fugitive black bondmen from the United States, and has been under the special care of the Methodist hierarchy since 1847.

It never seems to have occurred to the law-givers of the Old Testament that slavery was immoral. They made rules for regulating and humanizing the institution (Exodus xxi, 2–11, 20–21, 26–27), and they denounced the faithful when those rules were broken, which seems to have been very often (Jeremiah xxxiv, 8–22), but they never thought to prohibit it. The Jews, even in their great days, remained in all essentials a pastoral and frontier people, and among such peoples slavery never becomes as important, either economically or socially, as it is in denser and more complicated societies; thus the Jews had fewer slaves than the Egyptians and Babylonians, and worked them less savagely. Nevertheless, their laws on the subject were certainly brutal enough. A Jew could sell his own children into slavery, or let a creditor take them in payment of a debt. A creditor could make a slave of a bankrupt debtor, and sell him to another. And any poor man could be enslaved in return for food and lodging, though he had to be liberated, if he survived, at the next year of jubilee, which came every fifty years.

It was not uncommon for a man to be seized by enemies and sold to a traveling slave-trader, who shipped him to Babylon or Egypt: the case of Joseph and his brethren will be recalled. In theory, every slave who was a Jewish citizen had to be liberated at the end of six years' service, but in practice he was often detained indefinitely. If he had married while in bondage, his wife and children belonged to his master, and could not go with him. If he was incautious enough to protest, " I love my wife and my children," a hole was bored in his ear with an awl and he became a slave forever. A master was permitted to punish his slaves by beating or otherwise, but he had to be somewhat careful, for one that lost either an eye or a tooth in the process was liberated forthwith. It was unlawful to beat a slave to death, but only in case death followed the beating within " a day or two." What the punishment was is not clear: Exodus simply says that " he shall be surely punished." If the slave died after two days there was no punishment at all, " for he is his money " — that is, the loss of the slave's cash value was sufficient.

The slaves of the Jews seem to have been mainly captives from half-savage desert tribes (Leviticus xxv, 44–46), and in consequence they were seldom fit for anything better than domestic service or farm work. One hears nothing in the Old Testament of the slave physicians, engineers, sculptors and even philosophers who were so common among the Greeks and Romans. Not infrequently the Jews circumcised their slaves, and the latter then acquired the right to join in the celebration of the Passover, and, presumably at least, all the other special privileges which belonged to a slave who was also a Jew. Slavery continued among the Chosen People long after Biblical days; indeed, they were the chief slave-traders of the Mediterranean region in the Middle Ages, and dealt impartially with Christians and Moslems. From the time of Constantine onward there were objections to their owning Christian slaves, but they seem to have gone on doing it. The Talmud and the lesser codes are full of curious rules for the regulation of slave-holding. Any slave who escaped to Palestine became free — an anticipation by many centuries of the decision of Lord Mansfield. If a master hung phylacteries on a slave, or let him read so much as three verses of the Law in the synagogue, or bade him exercise any other power or function that was only possible to a Jew, the slave went free. Every slave had a right to be circumcised if he so desired, and when it was done his place in the community was a relatively honorable one — a good deal below that of born Jews, of course, but higher than that of intruding *Goyim.* It was the duty of a master " to be merciful to his slave, not to make his yoke heavy nor to distress him, not to multiply complaints and anger against him, but rather to speak gently to him and lend a kindly ear to his grievances."

7

The early Christian Fathers never got much beyond this humane but unprotesting attitude. They could find nothing in the New Testament which categorically condemned slavery, and there was little to that effect in the public opinion of their time. Perhaps they were sometimes a bit disquieted by Paul's doctrine of equality before God (Galatians III, 28; Colossians III, 11), but if so they managed to meet its demands, not by proposing the liberation of slaves, but simply by admitting them to the sacraments. Paul himself, indeed, had scarcely gone further; he seemed to believe that there was as clear and as inescapable a difference between freeman and bondman as between Jew and Greek. In Ephesians VI, 5 we find him urging " servants " (Ballantine and Goodspeed, in their modern speech versions of the New Testament, make the word " slaves," a better translation) to be " obedient to them that are your masters in the flesh, with fear and trembling, in singleness of heart, as unto Christ," and in I Peter II, 18 he adds " not only to the good and gentle, but also to the froward." Moreover, in the Epistle to Philemon we actually discover him returning a runaway slave, Onesimus, to the latter's master, and addressing that master as " our dearly beloved and fellow laborer." Philemon, a rich man of Colossæ, seems to have owned many slaves, yet Paul writes to him of " thy love and thy faith which thou hast toward the Lord Jesus," and says that " the bowels of the saints are refreshed by thee."

This toleration becomes all the more remarkable when one remembers that many of the first converts to the new Evangel were slaves. " Nearly all the names of the Christians whom Paul salutes in his Epistle to the Romans [xvi, 3–15]," says Paul Allard in the Catholic Encyclopedia, " are servile *cognomina*." Slaves were baptized without question, and before the end of the Second Century some of them had suffered martyrdom for the faith, but it was generally held by the most esteemed canon lawyers of the time that they could not be ordained without the consent of their masters. Nevertheless, so early as the last years of the First Century a slave managed to become deacon, priest, bishop and Pope (Evaristus, *c.* 99–107). Fifty years later there was another slave Pope, Anicestus, and in the early part of the Third Century yet another, Calixtus I. Some authorities even add a fourth, Pius I (*c.* 140–154).

All the principal early Fathers, with the possible exception of St. Gregory of Nyssa, seem to have let slavery go virtually unchallenged. Origen reproached some of his flock for having too many bondmen, but he apparently did not advocate their manumission. Clement of Alexandria, Tertullian and Justin Martyr counselled their kindly treatment, and St. Jerome reminded the faithful, following Paul, that all men were equal in the sight of God, but Cyril of Jerusalem argued that slavery was natural and probably good, and the mighty Augustine, as one reads in " De Civitate Dei," regarded it as a just punishment of sin. With the dawn of feudalism in the West the chief dignitaries of the Church became feudal barons, always in fact and often also in name, and as such they held slaves and serfs and freely bought and sold them. Gregory the Great was the largest slave-owner of the Sixth Century.

In the Ninth Century some reformer proposed that fugitive slaves be given a right of sanctuary in the churches, but this was refused, and they were returned to their masters. If, however, a slave undertook to join a monastic order, his servitude was suspended for the duration of his stay in the monastery. But, as we have just seen, he could not, without his master's consent, be ordained as a secular priest, and this disability, I believe, still survives in Catholic canon law. The Council of Saragossa, in 593, made it obligatory for a bishop or abbot to enfranchise any of his slaves who showed a religious vocation, but other councils forbade enfranchising those who did not. In general, the slaves of the bishops and religious houses seem to have been treated humanely. They had to work in the demesne but three days a week; the rest of their time was their own. The Church also permitted and encouraged them to marry, a right which had been denied to them by Roman law. To the Romans sexual intercourse with a slave woman was as inert and meaningless a matter, legally speaking, as it was in the Southern American States before the Civil War, but St. John Chrysostom, always eager to discover new sins, denounced it as adultery.

Catholic historians make much of the fact that the Church busied itself, after the Third Crusade, with the liberation of Christians held by the Moslems, and point with pride to the Trinitarian Order, founded for the purpose in 1198, which ransomed or otherwise rescued 90,000 such captives during the three centuries following, including no less a personage than Cervantes. The Mercedarians, devoted to the same humane end, are said to have brought home nearly 500,000 between 1218 and 1632. But it is conveniently forgotten that these worthy brethren gave all their attention to Christians enslaved by the heathen, and had none left for the Christian slaves of Christians. Nor is there much point in showing that Pius II denounced slavery as a great crime (*magnum scelus*) in 1462, for by that time it was almost extinct in Europe. Nor in showing that Pius VII urged the Congress of Vienna to suppress the American slave trade in 1815, for England had passed laws against it in 1807, and John Jay had tried to have it proscribed by the Treaty of Paris in 1783. The men who really launched the long agitation which finally disposed of slavery in Christendom were, in the main, not Christians at all, save maybe in name. The demand that it be put down was a product of the Eighteenth Century enlightenment, and the great hero of the movement, Granville Sharp, was a lay reformer who also devoted himself to urging the reform of Parliament, freedom for the American colonies, home rule for Ireland, and the abolition of the naval pressgangs. Certain Quakers had preceded him, but they were officially heretics and had little influence, even in their own sect; after the Mansfield decision he was joined also by a few advanced and somewhat *déclassé* clergymen of the Establishment, notably John Wesley. But the real foundations for the abolition of slavery were laid by men quite innocent of theology — Adam Smith, Edmund Burke and the poet Cowper in England, Necker in France, and Benjamin Rush, Jefferson, Franklin, and the French *emigré*, Anthony Benezet, in America.

During the long and impassioned contest between Southern slave-owners and Northern Abolitionists in the United States, the former, says an ecclesiastical historian, the Rev. Leonard D. Agate, " managed to get the Christian Church, as a whole, on their side." In Hermann Eduard von Holst's " Constitutional and Political History of the United States " this is made more sweeping; the American churches, says von Holst, were " the bulwarks of slavery," and defended not only its basic morality but also some of its most villainous abuses. " The question was put to the Savannah River Baptist Association," says James Ford Rhodes, " whether in the case that slaves were separated, they should be allowed to marry again. The answer was in the affirmative, because the separation was civilly equivalent to death, and the ministers believed 'that in the sight of God it would be so viewed.' " Nor were all of these apologists for the " peculiar institution " Protestants; there were also many Catholics among them — for example, the celebrated Monsignor John England, first Bishop of Charleston, S. C., editor of the first Catholic newspaper in the United States, and the first Catholic cleric ever to be invited to address Congress. He was a bitter foe of Nullification, and yet, as Edward Westermarck tells us, he " undertook in public to prove that the Catholic Church had always been the uncompromising friend of slave-holding." In this position he was upheld by the great moral theologian, Jean-Baptiste Bouvier, whose " Institutiones Theologicæ " was used as a text-book in nearly all the Catholic seminaries of the United States during the middle years of the last century. So late as 1888, indeed, Pope Leo XIII wrote to the bishops in Brazil, denouncing the slaves who were in revolt there, and declaring truthfully that " the Church has always condemned such unlawful efforts, and through her ministers applied the remedy of patience."

One must say again for these defenders of what the whole of Christendom now abhors that revelation was manifestly on their side, not to mention the authority of the most eminent of the early Fathers. In the end, their Abolitionist opponents — mostly Unitarians or

Quakers, and hence under theological odium — were reduced to rejecting the plain letter of the Old Testament as null and void. It was thus that they got rid of Exodus XXI, 4, just as their Prohibitionist successors of yesterday got rid of I Timothy v, 23 and John II, 1–11. The more liberal of the pro-slavery clergy, influenced by Paul, were ready to admit, with Bishop England, that slaves had souls, and that, at least after baptism, they enjoyed equality before God, but the majority seem to have viewed the doctrine somewhat doubtfully, as Moslems view the analogous theory about the souls of women. At all events, the pastors of the Protestant Episcopal Church, — the dominant Christian organization among the gentry of Tidewater, where the density of slaves was greatest — , were not eager to take the baptized black folk into their own communion; instead, they handed them over to itinerant Methodist and Baptist evangelists, who filled them with the barbaric theology which still inflames and impoverishes Aframerica. These evangelists, like their heirs now in practice in the Southern mill-towns, were careful to preach nothing offensive to the ruling oligarchy; in consequence, they laid every stress upon those counsels of Paul which urged slaves to be loyal and obedient in this life, and trustful about a gaudy reward *post mortem*. When emancipation came at last, it came again, for the second time in Christian history, not out of moral theology, but out of the insensate evolution of political and economic forces. If that evolution got any direction from human volition, the impulse came mainly from the damned.

8

It is astonishing, indeed, how few of the more modern moral postulates have their primary sanction in revealed religion. If the civilization of the past two centuries may be said to have had any ethical bias at all, it has surely run against the exercise of irrational and oppressive authority and the infliction of needless pain. True enough, the Christendom of today is often grossly unfaithful to its own ideal, in this field as in others, but one seldom hears that ideal formally questioned, save maybe by the more preposterous variety of politicians. Not many really enlightened men would venture to deny that freedom is a good in itself, or that cruelty is an evil. Even in the midst of wars there is a persistent and not always vain effort to make war less bloody and brutal, and in times of peace the liberation of the individual is constantly advocated and often forwarded, and save under pressure of frank reaction, recognized and admitted to be such, he is more and more safeguarded against the operation of inimical natural and social forces.

Such phenomena as Bolshevism and Fascism may seem, on the surface, to work against this tendency, but at the bottom of them one always finds the idea, however mistaken it may be, that they move toward the common goal, and will some day reach it. A hundred years ago, in most Christian countries, women were still infants in the eyes of the law, children got little if any protection from the state, and animals had no rights at all. Obviously, there has been a tremendous change, and the end is not yet. But that change owes almost nothing to Christian theology, and very little to specifically Christian charity. On the contrary, it is the product of a purely secular movement, based upon reason rather than upon religion, and to a large extent the official forces of Christianity have opposed it vigorously, and are still opposing it today. Such consent as they accord to it is only a grudging consent, wrung from them after a long and bitter struggle.

The gradual emancipation of women, perhaps the most revolutionary social event of modern times, gets no support from the Christian Scriptures, nor from any of the accepted glosses thereon. To the ancient Jews a woman, at best, was simply an inferior sort of man — inferior, and not a little sinister. She had a long list of dull and onerous duties, ranging from high-pressure childbearing to cooking, spinning, weaving, tailoring and the care of the family vines (Proverbs xxxi, 13–24), but almost no rights. The curse of Eve was upon her; she was the eternal temptress, and hence to be regarded warily. Her subordination in marriage was almost complete: " thy desire shall be to thy husband, and he shall rule over thee." If her husband suspected her of adultery, even though he had no evidence, he could subject her to a cruel and ignominious trial by ordeal (Numbers v, 12–31); if she made a vow, even to Yahweh, he could " disallow " it and make it " of none effect " (*ibid.* xxx, 6–15); he could divorce her by his own free act, for any reason or no reason at all (Deuteronomy xxiv, 1–4); and he was free to affront her with concubines, few or many, all quartered in her house. Finally, if he died, she had to marry his brother, that the family line might be carried on. Jesus dissented sharply from this barbaric attitude toward women. He apparently held them in high regard, and was not averse to having them among His following. In particular, He objected to the Jewish divorce law, which ran wholly against the wife, and in Matthew xix, 3–9 we find Him fencing with the Pharisee canon lawyers upon the subject, and laying down the principle that there should be no divorcing her save for her adultery. Moreover, His compassion covered women of the street as well as virtuous wives, and He seized every opportunity to show it, as we read in Luke vii, 37–50 and John viii, 3–11.

But in Paul, the real founder of dogmatic Christianity, there was not much compassion for human frailty, and it is to him that Christian moral theology has always looked for light and leading, not to Jesus. At his hands the counsel of Jesus to the Disciples in Matthew xix, 10–12 became converted into the fantastic doctrine, still cherished by orthodox Christianity, that there is something inherently illicit and degrading in all sexual relations, and that marriage is no more, at best, than a sorry necessity, born of human weakness. The thesis of Jesus is not as clear as it might be; nevertheless, its general drift is plain enough. He had just been maintaining, in His argument with the Philistines, that a wife's adultery was the only morally justifiable ground for divorcing her, and the Disciples, who had heard Him, complained that this greatly limited a prerogative that Jewish husbands had long enjoyed, and thus made it " not good to marry." Jesus's answer was that, whether marriage was good or not, abstention from it was feasible only to three classes of men, all of whom He called eunuchs — those " so born from their mother's womb," those " made eunuchs of men," *i.e.* by castration, and those " which have made themselves eunuchs for the Kingdom of Heaven's sake." The difference between this doctrine and that set forth by Paul in I Corinthians VII, 1–9 is manifestly abysmal. Jesus regarded marriage as natural and laudable, and saw voluntary chastity as something possible only to a small and highly devout minority of men, but to Paul chastity was the normal state and marriage no more than a poor compromise with the Old Adam, tolerable only because it could give fornication a certain cover of regularity and decency. " It is good for a man not to touch a woman. . . . I would that all men were even as I myself. . . .

But if they cannot contain, let them marry: for it is better to marry than to burn."

Such being Paul's view, it is not surprising that he tried to keep women in a safely subordinate place in his new Church, for it must be remembered that, according to the almost unanimous opinion of his place and time, they were ordinarily the aggressors in sexual matters. This opinion still prevails throughout the Levant and is an essential doctrine of Moslemism; it has always kept a good deal of authority, indeed, in Christianity, and by a curious irony it has got of late some powerful support from infidel psychologists. To it the Levantines of Paul's time added the belief that women were inferior to men both mentally and spiritually — in Aristotle's phrase, incomplete or mutilated men. It is thus no wonder that Paul ordained that they "learn in silence with all subjection," and conduct themselves "with shamefacedness and sobriety," and that he forbade them tartly to "usurp authority over the man [I Timothy II, 9, 11, 12], . . . forasmuch as he is the image and glory of God, but the woman is the glory of the man" (I Corinthians XI, 7).

Paul owed a great deal to women. Like any other travelling evangelist he looked to their piety for his entertainment, and whenever he preached they seem to have turned out in large numbers. In Romans XVI he mentions a half a dozen by name, and in grateful terms — Phebe, Priscilla, Aquila, Junia, Julia and Mary. He was thus constrained to grant that they had

[48]

souls, and to accord them that same equality before God which he accorded to slaves (Galatians III, 28). But subject, of course, to the same serious limitations. They were no more to resist the inferiority which God had laid upon them than slaves were. As the daughters of Eve, who was deceived by the serpent, they were upon an inescapably lower level than the sons of Adam, who " was not deceived." Thus they were " commanded to be under obedience," and to " keep silence in the churches," and to refrain from teaching elsewhere, and to go softly and humbly all their days, " not with braided hair, or gold, or pearls, or costly array."

This Pauline view of women has colored all subsequent Christian thinking upon the subject. It never occurred to the early Fathers that a woman had any rights comparable to those of a man, and neither did it occur to the great medieval doctors of the Church, or to the Reformers. To Luther as to St. Thomas Aquinas the female sphere embraced only *Kirche, Küche und Kinder*. When, on February 10, 1880, Pope Leo XIII issued his celebrated encyclical, *Arcanum divinæ sapientiæ*, he gave over a good part of it to reiterating formally the doctrine that " the husband is the ruler of the family and the head of the wife " — that " the husband ruling represents the image of Christ, and the wife obedient the image of the Church." Forty years later, on December 31, 1930, Pope Pius XI sought to soften this somewhat by holding that " the wife obedient " was not bound to " obey her husband's every request if not in harmony with right reason or with the dignity due to a wife " and that she " should not be put on a level with those persons who in law are called minors," but he prudently refrained from defining either reasonable requests or wifely dignity. Instead, he solemnly ratified, with the inconsistency which is one of the privileges of infallibility, " both the primacy of the husband with regard to the wife and children, the ready subjection of the wife, and her willing obedience, which the Apostle commends " [in Ephesians v, 22–23]. The Apostle, naturally, is Paul, and this is the text: " Wives, submit yourselves unto your own husbands, as unto the Lord. For the husband is the head of the wife, even as Christ is the head of the church." To which v. 24 may be added: " Therefore as the church is subject unto Christ, so let the wives be to their own husbands in everything."

The emancipation of women thus owes nothing to organized Christianity. Its true origin is to be sought, as a Catholic historian, Father Augustine Rössler, C.SS.R., honestly says, in the French Revolution, a predominantly anti-Christian movement. Its first advocates were the atheistic Marquis de Condorcet and his disciples, the two furies, Theroïgne de Méricourt and Olympe de Gouges. It was a pamphlet by the latter, " Déclaration des Droits de la Femme et de la Citoyenne " (1791), that inspired Mary Wollstonecraft's epoch-making " Vindication of the Rights of

Women " (1792). Later on the agitation remained mainly in the hands of skeptics — for example, Robert Owen, John Stuart Mill and George Holyoake. The Christian clergy everywhere and of all sects — though there were a few exceptions — were on the other side: they could not forget their master, Paul. Nor did they confine themselves to protesting against giving women the vote: they also opposed every other variety of enfranchisement, whether legal, social or economic. The English bishops, roaring in the House of Lords, were solidly against every proposal to give their wives and daughters the free use of their own money, their own labor and their own persons. And the Scotch Presbyterian pastors, standing firmly upon Genesis III, 16, denounced James Y. Simpson's introduction of chloroform in obstetrics as wicked and against God, and were silenced only when the ingenious Simpson — a Scotsman, and hence a born theologian — had back at them with Genesis II, 21.

To this day, as everyone knows, the Catholic clergy, despite what should be the humanizing effects of mariolatry, still hold out stoutly against a woman's right to decide how many children she will bring into the world, and against liberating her from her husband on any ground whatsoever, no matter how intolerable her marriage may be, and even against saving her from a cruel and needless death in childbed, when the choice is between her life and the child's. What the general attitude of Holy Church is you may discover by reading the aforesaid Father Rössler's article, "Women," in the Catholic Encyclopedia: he simply cannot conceal his Pauline indignation that the women of today are not content to remain in the humble station to which Yahweh condemned them after the Fall, remembering always that their " true home is in a world beyond the grave."

But we shall look into these matters more particularly in the chapter on the Christian moral system. For the present it is enough to observe that if it has come to be a principle of civilized morals that oppressing and exploiting women is somehow ignoble and immoral — that they have inalienably, and ought to have, precisely the same right to life, liberty and the pursuit of happiness that men have — , then that principle has been established in the world, not by any resort to Christian revelation, but by a frank appeal to reason. The sanction behind it is as purely and exclusively rational as the sanction of free speech and free thought.

9

So is the sanction behind many another salient article in the code of civilized man — for example, that against the exploitation of children, that against cruelty to animals, that against bloody and merciless punishments, that against the arbitrary and tyrannical exercise of political power, even that against lying.

The counsel of Jesus in the matter of filial duty and

the rights and prerogatives of parents left His immediate followers in considerable confusion. Though He
assured them that He had not come to " destroy the
Law or the prophets," but to " fulfil " them, He yet
preached a strange and disquieting rebellion against
the Fifth Commandment: " If any man come to me,
and hate not his father, and mother, . . . he cannot
be my disciple [Luke xiv, 26]. . . . For I am come
to set a man at variance against his father, and the
daughter against her mother, and the daughter-in-law
against her mother-in-law [Matthew x, 35]." Paul
tried heroically to embrace this heresy, but it was too
much for him, and so we find him reverting to sound
Jewish doctrine in Colossians iii, 20: " Children, obey
your parents in all things," and in Ephesians vi, 2–3:
" Honor thy father and thy mother, which is the first
Commandment with promise, that it may be well with
thee, and thou mayest live long on the earth." Paul,
indeed, was a sound enough scholar in the Law to
know that the heretical words of Jesus in Matthew x,
35 came from Micah vii, 6, and that Micah had used
them, not with approval, but in indignation, to describe the wickedness of his time. The Jews exacted
the most rigid obedience from their children, and allowed them few if any rights. In their more spacious
and barbaric days they were quite willing to sacrifice
even their first-born to Yahweh, and in their decline
they clung to a parental authority which fairly
matched the stern *patria potestas* of the Romans. A

Jewish father was a sort of Yahweh in little — as Philo Judæus said, " a visible god."

The growth of the theological concept of the Fatherhood of God naturally guided the early Church toward Paul and the Old Testament prophets rather than toward Jesus. As Yahweh gradually assimilated the characters and habits of mind of a human father, every human father took on some of the privileges and attributes of Yahweh. The likeness between the two was constantly stressed in the patristic literature, and came to a dogmatic statement in the celebrated *Catechismus Romanus* of the Council of Trent (1566). A medieval Christian father had almost the same rights over his offspring as those enjoyed by a Jewish or Roman father of a thousand years before him. The state never interfered with his government of his household, and public opinion did not interest itself. Nor did the Church commonly meddle — that is, so long as he brought his children to the sacraments.

To the credit of the early Fathers it should be said that they were unanimously against infanticide, which met with little serious challenge among the Greeks and Romans (Plato and Aristotle, indeed, both defended it), and that one of them, Lactantius, induced the Emperor Constantine to prohibit it. But it should be added that this prohibition was quickly followed by a law permitting anyone who found and brought up an abandoned baby to make a slave of it, and that the Fathers were a great deal less interested in succoring the living infant than in saving its soul by baptism. When, in the early Middle Ages, hospitals and other refuges for the helpless began to be established, the Christian charity of Holy Church covered the young as well as the old, and Europe saw the beginnings of that long career of sacrifice and devotion which is one of the true glories of Christianity. But the battle for justice to children, as opposed to mere charity, was fought mainly on other fronts. It had its origin, like the struggle for the enfranchisement of women, in a purely secular movement, which appeared with the Renaissance, took on momentum in the iconoclastic Eighteenth Century, and came to fruition only in our own time. " The influence of Christianity in the protection of infant life," says Lecky, in his " History of European Morals," " though very real, may be, and I think often has been, exaggerated."

The dumb brutes owe a little more to revelation, but not much. The ancient Jews, sharing that feeling of kinship with the domesticated animals which is always marked in pastoral tribes and seems to have been widespread in antiquity, treated their cattle humanely. They were forbidden by Moses to " muzzle the ox when he treadeth out the corn," they were commanded to lift up the ass that had fallen by the wayside, and they had to share the Sabbath day of rest with all their beasts. They sacrificed living animals to Yahweh, but there appears to have been no more cruelty in the process than in that of the butcher. The Egyptians and

Assyrians were equally humane, and so were the Greeks. Most of the Greek philosophers had something to say about the moral duty of kindness to animals, and some of them, notably Porphyry and Seneca, went to the length of denouncing the eating of animal flesh. Unfortunately, this position, under the influence of Pythagoras and his school, was commonly grounded upon a belief in the transmigration of souls, from man to beast and back again, and so the early Fathers opposed it vigorously, for that belief, which was widely held during the first few centuries, menaced Christian theology almost as seriously as the hypothesis of biological evolution menaces it today. The Fathers carried their opposition so far that they arrived at the doctrine that the lower animals were mere mechanisms, with no rights whatever, and the latter half of this doctrine remains official in the Catholic Church to our own day.

Downright and deliberate cruelty, of course, is not inculcated, but the consideration which discourages it, as Thomas Aquinas says in his " Summa Contra Gentiles," is not concern for the animals but fear that mistreating them " may result in loss to the owner " and that " anyone, by exercising cruelty toward brutes, may become cruel also toward men." A recent moral theologian of the Latin rite, Father Charles C. Miltner, puts the matter with shocking plainness. Animals, he says, " are not capable of suffering moral injury, for, not knowing rights, they cannot be unwilling that they be violated. Moreover, whoever has rights has duties. . . . But animals cannot be said to have duties, hence neither have they any rights." Father Miltner, I suppose, excludes babies from the category of animals. But how they manage to know their rights, and what, precisely, their duties are — these questions he somewhat inconveniently neglects to discuss.

10

All this, I hope, is sufficient to show that revelation, as a moral sanction, has serious limitations. The Christian theory is that the Bible is a complete guide to conduct, but that theory is constantly breaking down in the face of experience, as is the corresponding Moslem theory about the Koran. Open any handbook of Christian ethics that you choose, whether Catholic or Protestant, and you will find that it gives almost as much attention to what the learned author calls natural law as to what he calls divine law, and that this natural law, on inspection, turns out to be a neat compound of the reason of the Greeks and the social instinct of Darwin. As Fathers McHugh and Callan say in their " Moral Theology," it arises partly from man's " rational nature " and partly from his " very nature " — in other words, partly from his reason and partly from his instinct. The same authorities boldly put it above revelation: it " has precedence," they say, " over the positive law, divine or human."

Thus the unqualified divine mandate, "Thou shalt not kill," has, in practice, certain qualifications, and the conscientious Christian is permitted to decide, with the aid of his reason, what they are. But in those areas wherein the Commandment is supported by the natural law it takes on an immovable rigidity, and even the Divine Lawgiver may not grant a dispensation from it. "God cannot command," say Fathers McHugh and Callan, "the killing of a person who has the right to life." It should be added that the rev. moralists, after laying down this somewhat startling proposition, hasten to add that He may nevertheless get round the difficulty by deciding *ex cathedra,* and apparently quite arbitrarily, who has "the right to life": thus "the command to Abraham to kill his son was not a dispensation from the law against murder." But here we get into casuistry, and had better haul up.

A somewhat clearer statement of the case for reason, and with it, *per vias rectis,* for natural law, is made by another Catholic authority, Father J. T. Barron, S. T. D., who argues that even revelation can have no validity save it be supported by evidence. "Before I can use the teachings of the Catholic Church as a criterion of truth," he says, "I must be assured of (and therefore have evidence for) these facts: (1) that God exists; (2) that He has made a revelation; (3) that this revelation is embodied in the teachings of the Church." If this be true in gross it must be true in detail, and so we arrive, perhaps, at an understanding of the process whereby Catholic moralists have come to reject certain of the plain injunctions of Holy Writ, *e.g.*, against taking interest, eating shellfish, and suffering witches to live, and to invent and credit to Omnipotence others that are plainly not in it, *e.g.*, against slavery, the *patria potestas*, suicide, contraception, and divorce. Their general position seems to be that though God undoubtedly made a revelation it was incomplete, and in some parts ill-advised, and that it is thus subject to enlightened revision. This doctrine is by no means modern. If Jesus did not actually state it, then He at least acted upon it (*cf.* Mark x, 4–9), and His example was quickly followed by Paul, and by all of the most esteemed seers and soothsayers of the early Church.

The business has continued in full blast into our own unhappy time, as every connoisseur of moral endeavor must have observed. Whenever there is a war the Sixth, Eighth, Ninth and Tenth Commandments are formally suspended, and with them the Beatitudes, and no louder howls for blood and loot are heard than those which issue from the larynxes of Christian and Jewish *Geistliche*. The movement in the opposite direction also goes on constantly — that is, there is a continuous enrichment of revelation by the divinations of living prophets. The Abolitionists who raged in the Northern United States between 1831 and 1861, though they could find absolutely nothing against slavery in the Bible, nevertheless set up the doctrine that Yahweh was teetotally (if secretly) opposed to it, and that strange doctrine quickly gained adherents in the churches which gave them ear, and became, in the end, a cardinal article of faith. It was on this ground, in fact, that Yahweh was elected honorary chairman of the Republican National Committee in 1864 — a position he still holds.

As we have seen, the real objection to slavery was not theological at all, nor even ethical, but purely economic and political, and the final war upon it was carried on mainly by persons of no visible Christian passion, *e.g.*, William Lloyd Garrison, a printer and hence a suspicious character; John Brown, a horsethief and border ruffian; Abraham Lincoln, a village atheist with a taste for the indelicate; and Ulysses S. Grant, a drunkard galvanized into genius by the smell of blood. But once a general feeling had got abroad that holding blacks in servitude was evil, moral theology came to the aid of economic pressure with corroborative revelation, and presently the two sets of experts in the Divine Will, North and South, were engaged in a furious combat. In 1844 the Methodist brethren of the South, encouraged in their fidelity to Holy Writ by what they regarded as enlightened self-interest, parted formally from the Northern heretics, and a year later the sub-Potomac Baptists followed. These schisms still survive, but in late years the opposing factions have been drawn together by a new and equally dubious revelation regarding Prohibition.

In conclusion, I emphasize again that no moral system of any complexity and refinement is ever grounded upon one sanction alone — that all of them tend to gather in the three sanctions of instinct, of reason and of revelation, and to seek support for a given article in all three. Thus, though the more advanced Christian nations have lost their old innocent faith in Yahweh, they have yet retained the ways of thinking that that faith implanted in them, and it strikes no one as unnatural that the Supreme Court of the United States should speak respectfully of the Divine Will, and that even birth controllers and other such heretics should dispute gravely as to what it is. Contrariwise, it does not seem unnatural that even the most pious Moslems should condition their confidence in the Koran with certain logical reservations. Their moral system, as Seymour Vesey-Fitzgerald says in his " Mohammedan Law," is the tightest ever heard of, for " the claims of divine revelation are all-embracing, and preclude the acceptance of new streams of legal thought." Nevertheless, Moslem moralists are well acquainted with the doctrine of *zarurat*, or necessity, which justifies even a gross neglect of Allah's ordinances to save life, and the oldest school among them, the Hanafi, holds flatly that " with a change of times the requirements of the law change."

But if such change is admitted to be inevitable, it is yet resisted very stoutly, and as long as possible. The triple sanctions are never thought of as three ways of escape from the moral bastile, but as three locks upon the door. They bind far more often than they loose. In our own time we have seen a steady fall in the authority of revelation, and large numbers of highly enlightened men and women now reject it altogether. But as it has lost ground its old advocates have turned with great diligence and ingenuity to the sanction of reason, and in more than one instance they have found it even more potent than revelation. Perhaps it is destined, in its turn, to be overthrown too: reason, indeed, has always been notorious for its unhappy faculty of devouring itself. If so, then the sanction of instinct, in some form or other, will probably be heaved into the breach, or maybe a fourth sanction, so far unimagined, will be invented, with a fifth and a sixth following after, and so on *ad infinitum.*

II

Its Evolution

1

All moral systems of any practical importance in the world assume that the will of man is free, and that it is thus rational and equitable to reward him when he does what is currently regarded as good, and to punish him when he does what is called evil. Take that assumption away, and both secular government and ecclesiastical authority would lose one of their chief excuses for being, and the good order which holds human society together would be gravely imperiled. But it should be added at once that no moral system regards this freedom as, under all circumstances, quite complete: there remains invariably an area in which the will is thought of as at the mercy of hostile forces, whether internal or external, congenital or environmental. Though a man may know precisely what his right course of action is, and be eager to follow it, it is generally recognized that he may be unable to do so, for his passions may overcome him from within or adverse pressure from without. No one, certainly, could be supposed to harbor a more resolute will to virtue than a novice in a convent, fled but yesterday from the snares of the world to the arms of the Divine Bridegroom; nevertheless, Holy Church, taught by its infallible head, accepts the axiom that even this most innocent damsel, try as she will, cannot keep her feet on the narrow path without an occasional slip, and so it provides for periodical examinations of her conduct by a prudent confessor, himself a veteran of many such slips, and for the reinforcement of her conscience by measures both natural and supernatural.

The study of the massive and instructive phenomenon of sin always causes moral theologians to harbor larger and larger doubts of the freedom of the will, and some of the most talented of them, notably Augustine, Luther and Calvin, have been close to throwing it overboard altogether. How, indeed, is it to be reconciled with the omniscience and omnipotence of God, that first postulate of all revealed religion? If He knew that I was going to put in this evening at work upon the present ribald book, to the scandal of the True Faith and the menace of souls, then why didn't He divert me to some more seemly labor? It is impossible to imagine, at least in the light of that True Faith, that He didn't know what I was up to, and equally impossible to imagine that He couldn't stop me. *Ergo,* He must shoulder at least a part of the blame for my sin, and will cut a sorry figure if He undertakes to punish me for it in Hell.

But this, of course, is going a great deal further

than any really discreet moral theologian ever lets himself go. Before he comes to the point of putting the whole blame upon God he always transforms the divine omniprescience into something considerably less sweeping, usually with a disarming metaphysical name, and thereby makes room for free will. The Catholic Molinists, for example, split it neatly into three parts, *simplex intelligentia, scientia visionis* and *scientia media,* none of them capable of precise definition: thus the question is disposed of by making it unintelligible to the vulgar. And thus, despite His infinite wisdom and awful powers, God is left free to be surprised, disappointed, grieved or indignant, and man is left free to sin, and to be roasted for it throughout eternity. This concession, I fancy, gives some pain to the theologians in their rôle of logicians, but as practical pastors they make it with good grace, for making it is absolutely essential to their business. Take away the idea of free sinning, freely arrived at, and revealed religion ceases to be a going concern.

The secular philosophers proceed in the other direction, but they arrive at substantially the same position. Their problem is not to find a precarious foothold for free will under the universal shadow of God, but to keep it within plausible evidential bounds. The ideal savage, immersed as he is in his animistic naïveté, sees will in everything that moves and in many objects that do not, and can scarcely imagine it curbed and circumscribed in man, the lord of creation. If A kills B, even though it be by plain inadvertence, A must pay the ordained penalty: either his own life or a heavy indemnity. The will, in other words, is assumed from the act; there is no legal difference between the most deliberate premeditation and what we would call mere chance. But this ideal savage and his jurisprudence exist only as abstractions in the more romantic sort of anthropology books. In the real world even the most primitive tribes think of free will with certain reasonable reservations. Homicide under one set of circumstances is felt to differ materially from homicide under another, and the concepts of the unintentional, the excusable and the compulsory creep in. Thus, R. F. Barton, in his treatise on the law prevailing among the Ifugao headhunters of Northern Luzon, shows how those simple folk distinguish between slaying by *gulad*, or free intent, and slaying without it. He says:

Suppose that in the chase a number of hunters have surrounded a wild boar. The boar charges one of them. The man leaps backward, and at the same time draws back his spear to throw it at the boar. In so doing, he stabs a companion behind him with the shod end of the spear handle. . . . No fine is assessed.

Here we have the specific and obvious absence of will cancelling the general assumption that it is there. It may be cancelled similarly by proof that the murderer was insane, or " so drunk as to have utterly lost his reason." But carelessness, as with us, is assumed formally to be willed.

Suppose that a number of men are throwing at a target with their spears. A child runs in the way, and is killed. One-half the usual fine . . . is assessed, on the ground that the thrower was careless in that he did not make sure before he threw the spear that such an accident could not occur.

These same Ifugao recognize that there is a natural conflict between the moral sense and the emotions, and that the latter, on occasion, may reach such intensity as to be irresistible. Thus they do not exact the penalty for murder of a man who, taking his wife and a paramour *in flagrante*, kills either one or both of them, for they understand that his sudden anger may very well sweep away all philosophical restraints, and make a mock of his will. This recognition of the havoc that emotion wreaks upon the process of free choice is widespread among primitive peoples, and so is recognition of what Edward Westermarck calls general intellectual disability, whether transient or permanent. It would be hard to find a tribe which holds lunatics to strict legal account for their doings, though many tribes kill them on theological or sanitary grounds, and it would be just as hard to find a tribe which punishes children as it punishes adults. The fact that a boy of eight (as Sir Roland Wilson tells us in his history of English law) was hanged for arson in Eighteenth Century England would horrify an African Bushman even more than it horrifies a present-day Englishman. The Chinese, whose jurisprudence, in many ways, is more enlightened than our own, except the very old from punishment as well as the very young, for they know that when senility sets in, the will begins to decay, and that at advanced ages the individual is almost as irresponsible as in infancy.

Much of the evidence upon which careless compilers of anthropological books base their theory that primitive peoples recognize no limitation upon the freedom of the will shows a confusion between ordinary crime and violations of taboo. The latter are not crimes in the common sense, but a species of misfortune, for a sane man would hardly commit them voluntarily, and the penalties which they carry are analogous to the restraints and disabilities which we inflict upon a person gone dangerously insane or come down with smallpox or leprosy. The man who has violated a taboo is a walking arsenal of evil magic, and hence a menace to all who may come into contact with him. He must get rid of this magic by some act of expiation, and if that act is beyond his own resolution then he must be taken in hand by the secular power, lest the whole community suffer from great evil. In exaggerated cases even his life may be forfeited. It naturally makes little difference whether his offense was voluntary or involuntary, for the effects upon him and upon the community are the same in both cases. This point of view is set forth clearly in Leviticus v, 15–19, wherein we find rules as to what is to be done " if a soul commit a trespass, and sin *through ignorance,* in the holy things of the Lord." In brief, the offender is directed to bring a ram to the priest, who will " make an atonement for him " by sacrificing it. " It is a trespass offering: he hath certainly trespassed against the Lord " — though quite unintentionally.

Among many primitive peoples shedding blood is itself a violation of taboo: thus there is nothing irrational in their belief that one who sheds it should be purged by some sort of enforced unpleasantness, even though he be innocent of wrongdoing under their ordinary law. This concept is frequently encountered in barbaric legal codes. The Koran, for example, requires a believer who has accidentally slain another believer to liberate a believing slave, or, if he has no slave, to fast for two consecutive months (IV, Women, 92). " But whoso slayeth a believer of set purpose, his reward is Hell forever." Many other unwitting offenses, by invading the mysterious prerogatives and dignities of the gods, may also involve violations of taboo, *e.g.,* using forbidden words through ignorance or inadvertence, eating forbidden fruits or meats by mistake, uncovering accidentally the nakedness of a parent (Genesis ix, 20–27), or destroying or damaging a sacred building. Under the Salic Law, says Westermarck in " The Origin and Development of the Moral Ideas," one who set fire to a church by chance was " treated with great severity," though there was no penalty for the like destruction of any other house. "The action of taboo," explains F. R. Jevons in his "Introduction to the History of Religion," "is always mechanical. The intentions of the taboo-breaker have no effect upon the action of the taboo." And no relation to the question of free will.

2

So much for the rough approximations of practical men, eager only to preserve the public peace in this world and to placate the inscrutable gods in the next, even at the cost of incidental error and injustice. But the problem whether the will of man is really free has not only a practical aspect, but also a purely scientific aspect, and that scientific aspect has engaged the attention of the learned since the most remote times. I can recall very few professional philosophers, whether ancient or modern, who have not wrestled with it at some length; indeed, it has given the fraternity a harder tussle than any other question of their trade, save only, perhaps, that of the nature of knowledge. I wish I could add that their struggles have disposed of all doubt and misgiving upon the subject, but that would be going a great deal too far. The essential mystery remains quite as mysterious as it was in Plato's time, and the long debate over it has only served to divide philosophers into warring schools, and to break up many of those schools into warring factions. The line that runs through the grove of Athene, separating the believers in free will from the believers in determinism, does not coincide with any of the smooth curves of division on other matters. Instead, it is a wild zigzag, following a path all its own. Not only do Christians and heathen differ diametrically about the will, but also Christians and Christians, and heathen and heathen.

Most of the early Fathers, and especially Tertullian, Origen and Irenæus, seem to have had no doubt that every man was the complete master of his own acts, but when Augustine began to preach the revolutionary doctrines of grace and original sin this primitive certainty disappeared, and there ensued a dispute which raged into the Middle Ages and even beyond. How could a man be called free and held responsible if the Old Adam was in him, seducing and corrupting his will, and what real significance could be attached to sin if the grace of God could wipe it out? These questions were hard to answer, and Augustine did not answer them with any noticeable clarity, but he was a man of such tremendous force of character that he gradually beat down the disposition to ask them, and by the year 418 his vague and often contradictory pronunciamentoes on the subject, though they still baffled logicians, were made official by the Council of Carthage. Various dissenters, however, continued to challenge him, and one of them, an Irishman named Pelagius, gained such a following, especially among the learned, that Popes and councils had a hard time putting him down. Pelagius's arguments are worth a great deal more attention than they get today, for they show clearly that grace and original sin on the one hand and free will on the other are essentially irreconcilable.

The eminent St. Thomas Aquinas (*c.* 1226–74) swallowed the Augustinian hodge-podge without gagging, but his chief rival, Duns Scotus, found it hard to reconcile free will and original sin, and inclined toward free will. The ensuing Catholic theologians, in the main, followed Aquinas without looking into the matter too particularly, and he was showered with honors and titles (*Doctor Communis, Doctor Angelicus, Princeps Scholasticorum,* and so on), and finally, in 1323, canonized, whereas Scotus had to be content with the single (and somewhat ironical) dignity of *Doctor Subtilis.* But when Martin Luther, in his " De Servo Arbitrio " (1524), came out with a thunderous ratification of Augustine, laying heavy stress upon his obvious whittling away of free will, Rome found itself in a position of considerable embarrassment, and when the Council of Trent met in 1545 to liquidate the Reformation it was persuaded to offer truce and compromise to the Scotists.

This compromise took the form of a declaration (I quote the paraphrase of a recent Catholic historian) that " the free will of man, moved and excited by God, can by its consent *coöperate* with God," and that,

though " weakened and diminished by Adam's fall,"
it is " yet not destroyed in the race." Here we have a
plain evasion, and in their attempts to give it plausibility the Roman theologians have had to resort to
many another, *e.g.*, the metaphysical logomachy of
the Molinists (or Jesuits), referred to a few pages
back, and the rival teaching of the so-called Thomists
(or Dominicans), who hold that God " premoves "
man to act " freely," and may thus inflict just punishment for an evil choice, but that, being omniscient,
He can foresee exactly how any given man will act.
The Protestant brethren are confused and divided in
the same way, and quarrel much more openly. Some
of them tend to follow Erasmus, who was an implacable believer in free will, and others remain more or
less faithful to Luther, who denounced it as a " fic-
tion." The Presbyterians, in this matter, are all Lutherans, but many of the Lutherans are Erasmians.

The same lamentable lack of accord is to be found
among the heathen, old and new. The most ancient
Greeks inclined toward determinism: they saw the
life of man as something wholly at the mercy of the
implacable fates. In the tragedies of Sophocles and
Æschylus human destiny is depicted as inscrutable
and irresistible. Socrates held that virtue and knowledge were the same, and that a man of wisdom was
inescapably impelled to good actions: that it was psy-
chologically impossible for him to do wrong. His disciples, in general, followed him, but Plato seems to

have had some doubts, and they moved him in the direction of free will. Aristotle went even further. In the third book of his Nicomachean Ethics one finds a long discussion of human conduct, leading to the unequivocal if somewhat banal conclusion that " if we are unable to trace our acts to any other origins than those within ourselves, then acts of which the origins are within us themselves depend upon us, and are voluntary."

Aristotle admits, of course, that in many cases the origins of an act are not in the will, for the agent may be forced into acting by external compulsion or misled into it by ignorance. (A plain echo, here, of Socrates.) Moreover, " the irrational feelings are just as much a part of human nature as the reason," and so even the wisest man may succumb to his vagrom desires and emotions, and do evil. (Here Aristotle departs from Socrates.) But in normal situations " it is manifest that man is the author of his own actions." This cautious acceptance of free will made a profound impression in Greece, and tended to upset the old innocent determinism. It not only had a persuasive influence upon such later sages as Epicurus, Carneades and Plotinus, otherwise so widely at variance; it also colored the popular philosophy, and greatly reinforced those ideas of political liberty which were in the air of Athens.

But Aristotle's triumph was not complete, nor did it last. The Stoics, harking back to Socrates, favored a kind of fatalism that was ameliorated by a belief in the potency of wisdom. They taught that a man's ultimate fate was determined by powers beyond him, but that he was still capable of a certain amount of self-control, and that this self-control could be augmented by knowledge. They thus came into conflict with the Epicureans, who preferred pleasure to abnegation, and were all for free will. With the decay of Greece the conflict was transferred to Rome, and there the Stoics seem to have had the better of it. The Epicureans, to be sure, found eminent recruits among the poets, notably Horace and Lucretius, for poets, as professional improvers of the universe, are commonly hearty believers in free will (" I am the master of my fate! I am the captain of my soul! "), but the Stoics were more successful with sober and reflective men, for example, Epictetus and Marcus Aurelius, and until Rome succumbed to Christianity the majority of educated Romans seem to have been more or less deterministic in principle. But the question, of course, was never settled, and there were intelligent men in each camp to the end.

That division continues. " Thinkers of the most diverse moral systems," says Donald Mackenzie, " are indiscriminately found on both sides of the discussion." On the side of determinism the authorities commonly range Bacon, Hobbes, Hume, J. S. Mill, Schopenhauer, T. H. Green, Priestley, Spencer, Condillac, Schleiermacher, Schelling and Hartmann, on the side of free will Kant, Locke, Jonathan Edwards, Lotze, Fichte, Hegel, Berkeley, Reid, Hamilton, Martineau, Fechner, Royce, William James, Driesch, F. C. S. Schiller and Bergson, and in the dubious middle ground Descartes, Malebranche, Leibniz and Nietzsche, to mention only the most notable. I have omitted the name of Spinoza because both sides make noisy claim to him. Perhaps Descartes should be put among the advocates of free will; perhaps among the determinists. Leibniz opposed what he took to be the reckless determinism of Spinoza, but is himself set down by a recent authority on Spinoza as " to all intents and purposes a thorough-going determinist." Where Nietzsche is to be placed I don't know, though I have read him attentively for many years. His theory of eternal recurrence is plainly pure determinism, but on the other hand he devoted most of his writings to exhorting human beings to convert themselves, by a process of sheer willing, into something that they were clearly not.

3

Nietzsche's dichotomy is so common among philosophers that it is almost the rule. Even the most convinced determinists among them yet speak of the will, on occasion, as if it were free, and even the most ardent libertarians are constrained to admit, once they descend from theory to fact, that the freedom they believe in is anything but complete. Thus the problem continues to be debated as it was in Aristotle's day, and the solution seems as far off. Neither the libertarians nor the determinists can prove their case in the simple, dispassionate, unanswerable way in which a physical fact is proved — say, the circulation of the blood, or the revolution of the earth around the sun — , for the evidence they rely on is enormously complicated, frequently very dubious, and always obviously incomplete. As a consequence they are forced, willy nilly, to resort to dogmatism, and that dogmatism gains nothing in cogency by the circumstance that it is usually either theological or metaphysical. On reading what even so lucid a writer as Aristotle has to say about the will one recalls inevitably Dugald Stewart's verdict upon the theological argument for predestination: " There is a fallacy here somewhere, but the Devil himself can't find it! " When one turns to the less gifted sages of modern times confusion becomes intolerably confounded, for most of them are not only loose thinkers but also bad writers. Thus the inquirer wanders hopelessly in a maze of gratuitous premises and unintelligible conclusions, and comes out in the end precisely where he went in.

The moral philosophers themselves, despairing of reaching an agreement or even of framing the problem in terms satisfactory to all hands, have often sought to get rid of it by proving it to be meaningless, either on metaphysical or on common sense grounds. A shining exponent of the former process is the Frenchman,

Henri Bergson, who discusses the matter at length in his " Time and Free Will." He begins by arguing that the human mind can deal with time only by converting it into a kind of space. We think of it in retrospect, he says, as having unrolled much as a scroll unrolls, *i.e.*, continuously, but in truth it is a succession of disjointed and unrelated " qualitative changes," each quite unlike any of the others. The free act has to occur during one of these changes: it can take place only " in time which is flowing, not in time which has already flown." *Ergo*, it thus lies beyond reach of the reason, which can deal only with relations, and in order to bring it to heel we must make use of intuition, which tells us that " freedom is a fact," and that " among the facts which we observe there is none clearer." " All the difficulties of the problem, and the problem itself," says Bergson, " arise from the desire to endow duration [*i.e.*, time] with the same attributes as extensity [*i.e.*, space], to interpret a succession by a simultaneity, and to express the idea of freedom in a language into which it is obviously untranslatable." From all this he argues that we can neither prove nor disprove, by any process of logic, that the will is free: we must simply accept its freedom at the prompting of intuition. " Freedom is the relation of the concrete self to the act which it performs. This relation is indefinable, just because we *are* free." The argument, it must be apparent, is really only an elaborate begging of the question. Bergson locks up that question in a neat metaphysical box, and then assumes complacently that he has disposed of it. The mind, unconvinced, continues to grapple painfully with both time and free will.

The common sense effort to get rid of the puzzle is best exemplified, perhaps, by the Englishman, Henry Sidgwick. He begins by differentiating between the capacity to form a judgment as to the morality of a given act, and the capacity to either perform that act or refrain from performing it. The latter, he argues, may be diminished in various obvious ways without diminishing the former at all. Thus even the most ardent libertarian may " accept as valid, and find it instructive to contemplate, the considerations which render it probable that he will *not* choose to do right in any particular circumstances." And even the most ardent determinist, though bound in conscience to take neither credit nor blame for his acts, may yet feel a considerable satisfaction when they are good and an aversion akin to remorse when they are evil. " In all ordinary cases, therefore," says Sidgwick, " it does not seem to me to be relevant to ethical deliberation to determine the metaphysical validity of my consciousness of freedom . . . unless the affirmation or negation of [it] somehow modifies my view of what it would be reasonable to choose to do if I could so choose." But this also is a begging of the question. Sidgwick simply tries to get rid of the problem whether the will is free by pushing it aside as unimportant, and then diverting attention to, and afterward delicately evading, the problem whether the mind is free. Thus we get nowhere.

What, really, is to be said about the matter? Alas, not much. As far back as the days of Zeno the Eleatic, who, according to Plato, was " a man of forty " when Socrates was still " very young," the essential problem was treated as a riddle, which is to say, as a jest. Once Zeno caught a servant stealing from him, and gave the fellow a beating. " But it was predetermined," protested the servant, who had done some listening while his master wrangled with Socrates and Parmenides, " that I steal." " Very well," answered Zeno, " but it was also predetermined that I beat you." However we approach the question, our reasoning is bound to run in some such circle. Let us imagine, for example, a man who, in fear that his will is not free, resolves to protect it against immoral pressure and suggestion by immersing himself in a monastery. Obviously, he is much less likely, living there, to succumb to either evil companions or the Old Adam within him than if he remained outside, and went into practice as a lawyer or a policeman. But equally obviously, his decision to enter the monastery was itself an act of free will, or of " something else of the same name," and if, in point of fact, he did not enter willingly, but was kidnapped by the right rev. abbot, then it was an act of free will by the abbot.

If we proceed in the other direction we come to

much the same dilemma. Let us assume that our fugitive from sin went into the monastery in a manner wholly voluntary — that both in his own sight and in that of the spectators his entrance was an act of pure will. But was it so in fact? Wasn't he impelled to it, on the one hand, by the wickedness of the world, an external agency, and on the other hand by his yearning to be saved? And wasn't his yearning to be saved mainly a product of influences quite beyond his volition — his inherited cast of character, the accidents of his early training (especially in theology), his unsatisfactory experiments with sin, the circumstances of his immediate environment? And if not, could he have made himself, by any effort of the will, as secure against sin outside? We must answer the last question in the negative; it is so answered, indeed, by definition. Therefore, we must admit that in even so resolute an enthusiast for virtue there was insufficient strength, in the will alone, to attain it — that the will in itself was fundamentally impotent, and could function in a given way only in the presence of favorable circumstances, most of them external to it.

4

I have dismissed Sidgwick as begging the question, but though he undoubtedly does so in his conclusion, there is a considerable significance in his effort to differentiate between freedom of the mind and freedom of the will. A great many libertarians think that they have proved the latter when they have only offered evidence for the former. That the mind is substantially free, at least in its normal state, must be assumed as a kind of metaphysical necessity, for if we argue that it is not free then we argue that our opinion to that effect is not a reasoned opinion at all, but simply an inevitable product of forces over which we have no control, and which we can scarcely comprehend. We are, of course, well aware that our ideas are often conditioned, and even wholly determined, by our appetites and passions or by pressure from our environment, but though we accept this fact as practically true, we are yet convinced, and no doubt rightly, that there are times when the mind can overcome all such influences, however powerful, and operate wholly on its own. Every man remembers to his sorrow occasions when his wayward passions corrupted his thinking, but he also remembers occasions when sober reflection opposed and even overcame his passions. In the areas which passion does not commonly enter, the freedom of the mind, or, at all events, of the enlightened and disciplined mind, appears to be so nearly complete that its remaining infirmities are of little consequence. A man does not reach the conclusion that $\pi = 3.141592+$ by a passionate process, or by any other sort of compulsion, whether within him or without, and having reached that conclusion, he does not feel himself bound, nor, in fact, *is* he bound, to hold it in the face of plain disproof. There is, in all such matters, a very close approach to absolute freedom. What a man thinks is not determined by the state of his liver, or by his sex life, or by the law of the land, but by his reason alone.

When we come to the moral realm there is manifestly less freedom, for moral concepts are usually emotions before they are thoughts, and we are very apt to let our hearts lead our heads. But even here, as Aristotle long ago pointed out, the head that is led may still hold itself sufficiently aloof to play with ideas of escape, and to condemn its own bondage. Thus even the most abandoned rogue may be convinced that his villainies are wicked and ought to be punished, and even the most virtuous man is free to think of adultery, robbery and murder as agreeable adventures, unfortunately impossible to him because of his fear of the police. The Freudians, behaviorists and other such psychological revolutionists, for all their talk about conditioned reflexes, irresistible complexes and the domination of the unconscious, really do no appreciable damage to this freedom, for they deal mainly, and perhaps only, with either infantile or pathological states, in which the mind is admittedly operating badly, and is hence easily overborne by irrational compulsions. A really healthy adult mind is as innocent of complexes as a healthy body is innocent of fevers. Its judgments, only too often, may be false, but that is no proof that they are not substantially free.

When one comes to the will, as opposed to the mind, there is apparent at once a much larger uncertainty. We undoubtedly have an intuitive feeling that it is free, and upon the theory that it is so in fact we erect the whole gorgeous structure of civil and ecclesiastical government, but it is not to be forgotten that while our intuition prompts us to believe in this freedom it also warns us that there are narrow limits to it. Even savages — nay, even theologians — , as I was but lately showing, are aware of the warning, and take it seriously. Every one of the factors which condition the operations of the mind must also condition the operations of the will, and to a much greater degree, for the mind can carry on its workings in secret and with something approaching olympian calm, whereas the will commonly shows itself in overt acts, and thus comes into constant and often violent conflict, not only with the passions which beset it from within, but also with the environment which presses upon it from without.

In thinking of other people, we always think of them as more or less bound by that environment. No prudent Southerner would really trust a colored pastor in his chicken-yard, for though the pastor might go over the fence reaffirming the Eighth and Tenth Commandments in a voice of brass, and fully determined to follow them to the last jot and tittle, the presence of the concrete fowl would probably undo him. What is thus true of the pull of environment is true also of the pull of what we call character — a vague but powerful compound of congenital passions and pre-dispositions, remembered precepts and experiences, and physical talents and disabilities. No one expects a known coward to be brave. He may decide, by a purely intellectual process, that a given act of courage is highly desirable, and he may urge himself to its performance with every atom of his will, but the chances will still remain good that he will fail at the last minute. All of our dealings with our fellows are predicated upon an acceptance of just such odds. We estimate their probable behavior — and estimating it is the chief business of everyday living — by trying to interpret their character.

Not a few philosophers, starting from this position, have argued that character and environment between them account sufficiently for the whole behavior of man. As Sidgwick says in his " Methods of Ethics," " we infer generally the future actions of those whom we know from their past actions, and if our forecast turns out in any case to be erroneous we do not attribute the discrepancy to the disturbing influence of free will, but to our incomplete acquaintance with their character and motives." To which George Pitt-Rivers, in his " Conscience and Fanaticism," adds that " the causality involved in human actions would enable anyone who knew perfectly our character and our circumstances to predict our acts." Bergson, in an effort to answer all this on behalf of the libertarians, makes the somewhat lame argument that, in order that A should ever know B so well, A would have to be B. There is no need to go so far; it is sufficient to remember something that Sidgwick and Pitt-Rivers seem to have forgotten: that what we call character also includes will — that will, indeed, is an essential part of it. Thus when we say of a given man that he is of lofty character, and may be trusted at all times to do the honorable thing, what we really say is that, under normal circumstances, his will may be relied upon to save him from whatever temptations to dishonor happen to be thrust upon him by his environment, his passions, or the suggestions of his mind as to his self-interest, or by all three. Here we complete another of the circles that seem to hedge in all discussion of free will. Many more might be followed round. The books are full of them.

What, then, are we to think? What is the truth about the freedom of the will? The answer must be that it is yet undetermined. Perhaps the problem will remain forever unsolved, for there may be infirmities in the human consciousness which make it incurably incapable of comprehending its own nature. Or perhaps the solution is delayed simply because the science of psychology has yet to produce its first genius. But even a genius, I fancy, could not answer with any certainty without having before him more evidence than is now available. The study of the mind and will has been pursued on really scientific principles for little more than half a century; before that, it was only a pastime for metaphysicians, which is to say, for men with no taste for exact facts, but only a desire to transcend and forget them as quickly as possible. Today such facts are mounting up at a rapid rate, accumulated not only by psychologists, but also and more especially by biologists; even the Freudians and the behaviorists, though they are often bad psychologists and worse biologists, have given us some new and valuable information about the operations of the mind and will in the murky region below the threshold of consciousness. But still there are great gaps in what we really know.

All that can be said with any assurance is that the accumulation of facts tends to narrow the field of free will rather than to widen it. The mind, as it is emancipated from the immemorial shackles of vain wishing and romantic believing, takes on a greater and greater freedom, but the will, as we study it, seems to be less and less a prime mover, and more and more a function of forces below the conscious level. To the later Greeks it was pure volition, and hence the peer of the mind, but since Schopenhauer's day it has been only an innate, impenetrable, irrational complex of impulses and reactions, a mysterious *élan vital* whose " abrupt intervention," in Bergson's phrase, is " a kind of *coup d'état*." As such, it is considerably less respectable than it used to be, but on the other hand it has become rather more fascinating, for under it and behind it lurk all the dreadful shapes of the Freudian menagerie. Perhaps we had better let it rest there — dark, puzzling, and not a little terrifying. As a practical matter, we have to assume that it is more or less free — if not quite as free as the mind, then at least sufficiently so to support the work of priest and hangman. This pragmatic doctrine of its freedom, though large doubts may linger, yet undoubtedly *works* better than determinism. For determinism, if it is to have any genuine validity, must exclude free will absolutely, whereas even the most radical libertarianism has room in it for plenty of determinism.

5

The same pragmatic sanction supports the common human belief that there are really such entities as good and evil, right and wrong, and that they may be described and their nature determined. The prevailing concepts of them, to be sure, tend to differ in detail from place to place and from time to time, but such differences are much less serious than they are often thought to be. As I pointed out at the beginning of this essay, all of the simpler acts that the Christian moral code prohibits — murder, theft, trespass, adultery and false witness — are also frowned upon by savages, and some of them even by certain varieties of the lower animals. The apparent exceptions almost always turn out, on examination, to be no exceptions at all, but merely refinements of definition. Is it an act of merit, among the Dyaks of Borneo, to slay and decapitate an enemy? Then it is just as surely a crime to slay and decapitate a fellow tribesman. Do the men of many tribes lend their wives to guests, and even barter them with friends? Then these very hospitable fellows are quite as much shocked as a Christian would be when their wives do the lending on their own motion. I can find no authentic record of a tribe which tolerates murder on *all* occasions, or regards theft as completely virtuous or even as indifferent, or has no notion of adultery. Nor is there any record of one which has no reprobation for the lesser offenses — lying, shirking duty, disturbing the peace, disloyalty to the tribe, and so on. There are, of course, aberrations in all systems of morals, and some of them are of a fantastic eccentricity, but in all the known systems, ancient or modern, civilized or savage, you will find the assumption that certain basic and familiar categories of acts are intrinsically anti-social, and in all of them you will find an unvarying purpose to put such acts down.

We do not know, of course, by any direct evidence, what the moral ideas were that prevailed among the earliest groups of *Homo sapiens,* but as in the case of their religious ideas, we can come to an approximation, probably accurate enough for all practical purposes, by examining the moral ideas prevailing among savages and children. To this material we may add

[89]

something that is not available in the religious field: the apparent practice and inclination of the lower animals, and especially of the so-called social species thereof. What is known in all three areas is mainly very new knowledge, for anthropology as a science scarcely antedates Darwin, and the investigation of the psychology of children and animals was not begun until our own time. Thus it is not surprising to find that the earlier writers on ethics, including even the most learned, started off with premises that are now known to be absurd, and came to conclusions that were even more absurd. In general, they followed Plato in picturing primitive society as abandoned to a sort of moral anarchy, modified only by such prudence as was suggested by the immediate event. Dawn Man, as they imagined him, was almost as unmoral as an idiot. If a neighbor annoyed him he knocked that neighbor in the head — openly and at once if he had the advantage in strength, but in his own time and by stealth if the odds were against him. If he saw anything that he wanted — a club, a woman or a ration of food — he simply took it. If no other victuals were available, he slew and ate his brother, his wife or his child. He was subject to no law save his own will, and saw no distinction between right and wrong.

Obviously, a society based upon such principles must have been very uncomfortable, and even Dawn Man, in his more amiable moments, must have tried to invent something better. The early writers depicted him as seeking a way out by a series of truces. First, he agreed with his wife not to kill her by day if she would agree on her part not to kill him at night, while he slept, and then he made a similar agreement with his brother, and then with his neighbor, and so on until there was a group bound by a treaty of mutual protection and forbearance. Naturally enough, the members of this group would develop varying ideas as to whether certain given acts, falling short of downright murder, were right or wrong, and out of their discussion of the matter there would evolve generally accepted principles, and, in the long run, some machinery for enunciating and enforcing them. Thus moral science arose, and with it law and government. The whole process, as the pre-scientific anthropologists imagined it, is best set forth, perhaps, in Chapter XVII of Thomas Hobbes's " Leviathan " (1651), but the fancied treaty of peace and amity got its name, *le contrat social,* from Jean-Jacques Rousseau (1762), though Rousseau, it should be added, did not believe that primitive man was the bloodthirsty hyena that Hobbes had made him out to be.

The theory died hard. You will find it still offered as gospel in Chapter VII, § 44, of " The Principles of Ethics " (1879) of Herbert Spencer, who held that the origin of all morality lay in " mutual dread of vengeance." Spencer was the chief philosopher of Darwinism in England, but he apparently never accepted Darwin's belief, set forth in " The Descent of Man " (1871), that Dawn Man came into the world a moral agent; on the contrary, he always thought of morality as something invented much later on, at a relatively high stage of human evolution. Huxley inclined the same way. In his Romanes lecture, " Evolution and Ethics " (1893), he granted *Homo sapiens* a certain immemorial " sociability," but he nevertheless saw " self-assertion " as " the essence of the cosmic process," and civilization, with its all-important systems, as no more than " an artificial world within the cosmos."

But though Darwin's two chief interpreters in English, bemused despite themselves by the magic phrases, " struggle for existence " and " survival of the fittest," rejected his concept of man as a congenitally social animal, it got support from two amateur disciples, Henry Drummond in England and John Fiske in America, and was very hospitably received by certain Continental scientists, especially the Russian geographer Prince Peter Alexeyevitch Kropotkin (1842–1921), who developed it at length in two works, " Mutual Aid " (1902) and " Ethics: Origin and Development " (1922). It is one of the ironies of history that Kropotkin is chiefly remembered as an anarchist, and that his memory is thus associated with thoughts of bomb-throwing and other such sanguinary acts. As a matter of fact, he was one of the gentlest of men, and the anarchy that he advocated

had no room in it for violence. He believed innocently
that all force was unnecessary and hence wrong —
that if men were relieved of the oppressions of government their natural sociability and need of one another
would suffice to hold them together in a tolerable society. For preaching this bland and naïve doctrine
he was twice condemned to prison — first in Russia
in 1874 and again in France in 1883. After that he
sought refuge in England, pursuing his professional
studies and hoping for a revolution that would liberate
humanity from the tyranny of the strong. When the
Czar was overthrown he returned hopefully to Russia
after forty years of exile, but his ideas were as ob-
noxious to the new Bolshevik bosses as they had been
to the old régime, and his last years were full of
grievous privation and loneliness. He wrote his
" Ethics " in a small village sixty versts from Moscow,
cut off from books and subsisting miserably on peasants' fodder. The work as it stands is merely a frag-
ment. Kropotkin planned to write two volumes, the
first dealing with the origin of moral codes and their
historic development, and the second attempting to
lay down the principles of a really scientific science
of ethics. But we have only the first volume, and even
that is incomplete.

6

" The Descent of Man " lays the foundation for the
whole corpus of Kropotkin's ideas. In it Darwin starts

off by admitting that " of all the differences between man and the lower animals, the moral sense or conscience is by far the most important," but he proceeds to argue that the rudiments of this conscience are in all animals, and that what nourishes it in man is simply intelligence. Given, he says, " well-marked social instincts, the parental and filial affections being included, any animal whatever would inevitably acquire a moral sense or conscience, as soon as its intellectual powers had become as well, or nearly as well, developed as in man." That such social inclinations are to be found in many animals is a matter of everyday observation. Indeed, the members of every species that show any cognizance of their fellows at all seem to take pleasure in their society, " to feel a certain amount of sympathy with them, and to perform various services for them." Sometimes this sympathy is confined to what Darwin calls " the same association " and Charles H. Cooley " the primary group," and sometimes it is confined to a single family or even to a single individual, but on the other hand it not infrequently extends to all the members of relatively large societies, and even to individuals of other species. The clumsy and repulsive hippopotamus certainly appears to lack social graces, yet it lives habitually in herds of a dozen or more, and the members thereof appear to guard one another against all the enemies of the species. The rhinoceros is even more forbidding, yet it not only loves the company of its own kind, but is also tolerant of the rhinoceros bird, which rides on its back, feasting upon its parasites. Nor is this tolerance of strangers confined to the higher mammals. Snakes of different species, especially rattlers, copperheads and blacksnakes, live together amicably, and so do fish of widely varying kinds. Even among the insects the same taste for mixed society is occasionally observed.

Darwin says that this feeling of pleasure in the presence of other creatures, whether of the same species or some other, " is probably an extension of the parental or filial affections," and that the extension " may be attributed in part to habit, but chiefly to natural selection." The advantage of living in societies is obvious: the individual is better protected at all times than he could conceivably be on his own, especially in immaturity. Thus those individuals who, lacking the full development of the social impulse, essay to go it alone are most likely to die sooner and to leave fewer young. We observe this in civilized man today; in primitive times the penalty of solitariness must have been ten times more certain and disastrous. But by the time man emerged from his ancestral shadows such solitariness was already very rare, and perhaps it was even rare enough to be called pathological. The earliest groups of *Homo sapiens*, born of long ages of natural selection in some pre-human species, appear to have come into the world as social animals, and all that was needed to make them reflect upon the ties which bound them together, and to concoct thereby a theory of right and wrong, was the mere power to think at all.

Once that power awakened, says Darwin, the science of morals was born. Man could then examine logically the results of his acts, and suffer " dissatisfaction or even misery " when he had sacrificed his social instinct " to some other, at the time stronger, but neither enduring in its nature nor leaving behind it a very vivid impression." For of all the instincts, says Darwin, the social instinct is the most durable and, in the long run, the most powerful. Only the instinct of self-preservation offers it continuous challenge, and that challenge necessarily tends to weaken as society provides increasing security for the individual. Thus the social instinct is steadily reinforced, and becomes a habit as well as an instinct. Above all, it is reinforced by public approbation, for the benefits of yielding to it are shared by everyone.

Kropotkin, in general, follows Darwin so far, but on two points he dissents sharply. First, he rejects the Darwinian suggestion that the social instinct " is probably an extension of the parental and filial affections "; second, he holds that the struggle for existence, as an agent of evolution, is comparatively impotent within the species. In support of his first point he shows that there are many highly social species — for example, the ants and bees — in which no sign whatever of the parental and filial affections is to be detected, and that among other species those affections are often plainly subordinated to the social instinct — as, for example, among birds which desert their young in the nest to follow migrations. In support of the second point he argues that the factor which really preserves and develops a species is not the stamping out of the unfit by natural selection, but the practice of mutual aid.

His observations as a geographer in Siberia, he says, convinced him that the struggle for existence within a species is seldom as keen as the early Darwinians assumed it to be — that the real war confronting every individual is " against adverse [environmental] conditions, or against some such enemy as a kindred species," and that in this war mutual aid must necessarily make for success far better than rivalry. By the practice of such aid " habits are acquired which reduce the struggle within the species, while they lead at the same time to a higher development of intelligence." In consequence, one finds that in each class of animals, " the species in which individual struggle has been reduced to its narrowest limits, and the practice of mutual aid has attained the greatest development, are invariably the most numerous, the most prosperous, and the most open to further progress." Nature " has thus to be recognized as the first ethical teacher. The social instinct, innate in men as well as in all the other social animals — this is the origin of all ethical conceptions and all the subsequent development of morality. . . . Society has not been created by man; it is anterior to man."

To the proof of this thesis Kropotkin brings up a formidable mass of facts from zoölogy and ethnology, some of them very persuasive, but others, it must be confessed, somewhat dubious. His cavalier dismissal of natural selection need not be taken too seriously. Obviously enough, the struggle for existence may continue in full blast, even in the presence of the most elaborate mutual aid. It goes on today in civilized societies, despite that vast conspiracy to oppose and obliterate it of which Huxley was so fond of discoursing. No conceivable expansion of mutual aid can ever put the unfit on precisely the same footing with the fit; they are bound, taking one with another, to succumb sooner, leaving the propagation of the next generation to their betters. In the chief countries of Christendom, largely because of the Christian weakness for weakness, the effort to preserve them is carried to fantastic lengths; nevertheless, they go on dying faster than the fit, and so the race maintains a healthy mastery of its environment. Moreover, it is highly probable that the gregariousness on which mutual aid depends, whether it be actually a biological inheritance or only a cultural inheritance, is itself a product of natural selection: one can scarcely think of it originating in any other way without getting bogged in theories of special creation.

But in spite of the difficulties into which Kropotkin's enthusiasm for mutual aids leads him, he yet makes out a very plausible case, and it has been supported by many authorities who stand aside from the romantic political yearnings which colored all his scientific thinking. Among such authorities I need mention only Karl Pearson. The opposition to Kropotkin (and to Darwin) has been carried on mainly by men who admit that a powerful instinct conditions the social behavior of all animals which gather in societies, but are unwilling to grant that it is specifically social. Notable among these opponents are Robert Briffault, S. Zuckerman and Bronislaw Malinowski. Briffault believes that it is actually sexual — that primitive societies are simply arrangements for the facilitation of reproduction — , and Zuckerman, from his study of apes, concludes that it is largely egoistic — that the desire for dominance, rather than any impulse to mutual aid, is what chiefly integrates the anthropoid groups. Malinowski apparently accepts both of these instincts, the sexual and the egoistic, but rejects " any mental phenomena of a collective nature," including even simple gregariousness.

But in all this there is, at bottom, only a flogging of the irrelevant, for the thing itself remains, no matter what it may be called. No one save theologians of the least intelligent sort argues any more that man got all his notions of proper conduct by divine revelation, whether openly inculcated à la Moses, or stealthily insinuated into his psyche à la Kant, and no one save a few die-hard metaphysicians argues that morality is predominantly a matter of logical syllogisms. There is something else — some deep and primitive impulse, some natural and unanalyzable habit, some immemorial reflex, whether pure or conditioned, — which urges man to mingle amiably with his fellows, taking account of their desires and welfare as well as of his own. It is all one whether it be called an instinct or something else, and all one whether it be thought of as a mere corollary to a more fundamental reproductive or self-preservative instinct or allowed to go upon its own. " Social life," says Kropotkin, " — that is, *we,* not *I,* is the normal form of life [in man]. *It is life itself.* . . . The conception of man as an isolated being is a later product of civilization."

7

This conclusion, though many eminent anthropologists oppose it, nevertheless finds some support in their observations among the more primitive races of existing man. The savage thinks of himself as an individual far less than we do: two-thirds of his daily acts are ordered with the group in mind. The popular concept of him as a lawless and immoral fellow is chiefly due to missionaries who put him down as such simply because he is not a Catholic, a Methodist, a Lutheran or a Presbyterian, as the case may be. Actually, he is far more tightly bound by the communal *mores* and what he conceives to be the communal interest than Christians are, and he bears his bondage to his ideal of virtue far more cheerfully. " Everywhere in Africa," says Booker T. Washington in " The Story of the Negro," " where the life of the people has not been disturbed by outside influences, they are governed by law. There is law relating to property, to morality, to the protection of life — in fact, in many portions of Africa law is more strictly regarded than in civilized countries." To this most of the more intelligent reporters from the field bear testimony. In the Ogowe river country of West Africa, says a recent witness, Albert Schweitzer, in " On the Edge of the Primeval Forest," " the legal side of an event is always the important one, and a large part of his [the native's] time is spent in discussing legal cases. . . . It is not mere love of litigation that is his motive; it is an unspoilt sense of justice." In other words, it is a high development of the social sense.

Most civilized men, when either public law or public opinion ventures to invade the area of their private conduct, show a great uneasiness, and not infrequently it leads to open resistance. But the savage commonly submits with good grace, though he also is sometimes guilty, if not often, of what, under his code, is crime. The onerousness of the regulations he submits to is often remarked. His sexual life, far from being without restraints, is commonly cramped and circumscribed in what to us would be a truly intolerable manner, as you will learn by reading Malinowski's two exhaustive works, " The Sexual Life of Savages " and " Sex and Repression in Savage Society," and his control over his private property, even when it owes its existence to his own labor, is rigidly conditioned by tribal custom. He submits willingly to painful mutilations, privations and fatigues, and at the great tribal ceremonies — and especially at that which marks the onset of puberty — his fortitude is pushed to the limit to establish his right to be called a good citizen. The books are full of appalling examples, but I shall content myself with one taken from a paper by a French priest, Father Trilles, quoted by Raoul Allier in " The Mind of the Savage." He is describing the method whereby the courage and resolution of an apprentice sorcerer are tested in the French Congo:

The aspirant leads forward a human victim, generally a woman, though frequently a stolen child. The victim must be suffocated, not bled to death. No sooner has death supervened than victim and sorcerer are closely bound to each other, breast to breast, head to head, and mouth to mouth. Meanwhile, a pit at least three metres deep has been dug, and into it the two bodies are let down, the sorcerer being underneath. The pit is covered with boughs, above which is erected a hut. For three whole days the neophyte will remain in this position. When they have elapsed he is removed from the pit and taken back to his hut, still bound to the corpse. In this position he remains for three more days. During this

*time he is at liberty to eat and drink at pleasure, but in tak-
ing food he must use, not his own hands, but the unbound
right hand of the corpse. A friend will place each morsel in
the hand, and the food will thus be inserted into his mouth.*

In this revolting transaction there is, to the civilized
eye, no ethical element whatever, but that is not saying, of course, that the savage sees it in the same way.
To him the endurance of terror and disgust is just as
praiseworthy as the endurance of pain and fatigue,
and by his standards a dissecting-room *Diener* or side-
show snake-eater might be as much a hero as a champion prize-fighter is to us. Moreover, the idea of service to the tribe undoubtedly gets into his admiration
of such men as Father Trilles's young sorcerer, who
appears to him to be not only a very brave fellow, but
also a model of public spirit. For sorcerers are quite
as necessary in the African jungle as firemen and
traffic policemen are in New York, and they enjoy the
same respect for their willing sacrifice of their private
comfort and security to the common weal. If they
ceased to function the communal crops would never
ripen, the communal nurseries and hen-coops would
be raided by beasts of prey, and there would be no
certainty, satisfying to the Congo mind, of the rising
of tomorrow's sun. Thus they combine the functions
of village priests in Italy, of both philosophers and
diviners in Periclean Athens, of the *posse comitatus*
in rural Mississippi, and of Tammany in New York.

Every savage, in his degree, is similarly a public character, with well recognized duties and responsibilities. He lives out his life with the eyes of his neighbors searching his every act. Of personal freedom in the civilized sense he has next to none. He may not marry any woman who takes his fancy and is willing, but must make his choice in a narrow circle, having due regard for the totemic structure and by-laws of his clan. He must erect his house in a certain place, and according to a certain plan. If he builds a canoe, it is his only formally, for other men have prescriptive rights to its use, and he may not deny them. When he takes fish or game or harvests a crop he must share it with others, designated by immemorial custom. He may not, ordinarily, detach himself from one tribe to join another, and he is forbidden even to travel without the communal consent. The most intimate and sacred transactions of his private life must be carried on according to a pattern, and with constant regard for the rights of others. Even in death he keeps his place in a rigid pattern.

" In the Trobriand Islands," says Malinowski in " Crime and Custom in Savage Society," " there is not one single mortuary act, not one ceremony, which is not considered to be an obligation of the performer toward some of the other survivors. The widow weeps and wails in ceremonial sorrow, in religious piety and fear — but also because the strength of her grief affords direct satisfaction to the deceased man's brothers and maternal relatives. . . . It is her duty toward the surviving members of her husband's clan to display her grief, to keep a long period of mourning, and to carry the jaw-bone of her husband for some years after his death." Nor is this burden undertaken unwillingly and under duress; there is a universal feeling that it is not only polite, but also moral to conform, — that neglecting any part of the business would be a confession of ethical obtuseness verging upon dissoluteness. A widow who dispensed with the jaw-bone would be the equivalent of a widow who, in Christendom, dissected it out and had it made into dice. No one, practically speaking, questions such regulations; they are thought of as necessary safeguards of good order and common decency; their execution is the unquestioned duty of all persons of good repute. " Generally speaking," says Robert H. Lowie in his " Primitive Society," " the unwritten laws of customary usage are obeyed far more willingly than our written codes, or rather they are obeyed spontaneously."

To be sure, there are such persons as lawbreakers in savage society, and occasionally there appears a rebel so pertinacious that he may be almost called an anarchist. Malinowski, in the book I have just quoted, shows that even the most stringent tribal laws — for example, those defining and prohibiting incest — are sometimes violated, and that when the offender happens to be a man of wealth and consequence he may escape without punishment. Punishment among savages, indeed, is not the eager and protean thing that it is in civilized societies. There are no policemen, and the courts are rudimentary. Jails being unknown, the only available overt penalties are death, exile, and the imposition of fines. The first two, by reason of their severity, are reserved, as they are with us, for offenses of the greatest seriousness, and the last collides with the fact that the average savage has very little personal property, and can usually replace what is taken from him without much effort. Thus offenders who, in Christendom, would be punished almost automatically are often permitted to go unmolested, with no penalty save that of public opprobrium. But, as Malinowski says, this opprobrium may place a man " in an intolerable position," so that not infrequently he seeks escape by suicide, or, if he lacks the stomach for that, departs from the tribe and becomes " a hanger-on to some white man." Above all, he is roweled by his evil conscience, for it is seldom that he really questions the wisdom and justice of that obligation to the community which he has flouted. A recreant Ogowe savage, says Schweitzer, " accepts his punishment as something obvious and needing no defense, even when it is, according to our notions, much too severe."

8

This simple feeling of kinship with and responsibility to the group lies deep in every moral system, even the highest. The Greeks of the Fourth and Fifth Centuries B.C. were certainly very far from savages, and yet, as Theodore de Laguna says in his " Introduction to the Science of Ethics," " Plato and Aristotle thought of the individual as, primarily, the citizen. Life meant for them, first and foremost, civic life. Plato's principal ethical work is the Republic, and Aristotle expressly treats ethics as a branch of politics." To which Charles Howard McIlwain adds in " The Growth of Political Thought in the West ": " The state absorbed and included the entire collective activity of its citizens, and was a whole outside of which its members could not even be thought of, much less exist."

As everyone knows, there has been of late a furious effort in some of the great nations of Europe to revive this ancient concept, and the more modern view that every man has rights which not even society may invade is falling into contempt and desuetude. Even in countries which profess to cling to that view the quality called social-mindedness is generally esteemed, and the good citizen is richly repaid for subordinating his private interest and inclination to the common weal. People admire him, and he gains in prestige, authority and other personal enhancement; above all, he is irradiated by the warming glow which always accompanies the satisfaction of a profound impulse. In the earliest races of man that satisfaction must have been the principal if not the only incentive to moral conduct, but on its heels, as Darwin shows, there soon came the reinforcement of public opinion, and the reward of reciprocity. One sees the process in the moral development of children. Their instinctive turning toward and trust in mother and nurse is offered rational support at a very early age by the discovery that it pays to give as well as take — that there is an immediate and certain profit in doing the approved and accepted thing. And the same discovery is made by the more intelligent domestic animals. A dog's natural delight in and eagerness for human society are sufficient in themselves to make him a sort of moral agent, but his progress toward what may be called really civilized habits is always guided and conditioned by the ideas of the concrete men, women and children who surround him.

Thus the sanction of what Darwin calls the social instinct and what the moral theologians call natural law is basic in morals, and even the most refined systems have not outgrown it. It apparently accounts for more moral ideas, even in civilization, than any other sanction, and its antiquity is shown by the universal dissemination of the chief concepts flowing out of it. The sanction of religion plainly arose much later. I have dealt with its probable origin at some length in another work, "Treatise on the Gods," and it is not necessary to go over the ground here. Suffice it to observe that the notion that the gods could have any wishes about the conduct of man had to wait upon their development in nascent theology from mere evil forces — the rain, the lightning, the falling tree, and so on — into definite personalities, with coherent desires and a plausible schedule of rewards and punishments. This development unquestionably took long ages, for even today, among the lowest orders of savages, we find celestial powers which remain only vague congeries of irrational energies, mainly inimical. The concept of the gods as concrete persons who keep a close watch upon human behavior, and regard one act as virtuous and another (perhaps quite as natural) as vicious, had to wait upon the appearance of a class of men generally believed to have some special knowledge of their thoughts and doings.

Such men we now call priests, though when they function among savages the more tender Christian anthropologists prefer to call them magicians. They were, and are, interested parties to all transactions between men and the gods, and the moral doctrines which they invented in the dark backward and abysm of time, when not patent stealings from natural law, were commonly directed to their own advantage. To this day revealed morality gives large care to the welfare of its experts. Among Catholics, as I have heretofore noted, the penalty *post mortem* for a neglect of the believers' so-called Easter duty — *i.e.*, for his failure to report regularly to a priest and take a share in the holy man's support — is actually more severe than that for most kinds of homicide. And among the ancient peoples whose records we can read the duty of the faithful to sacrifice to the gods was hard to distinguish from their duty to victual the gods' earthly agents. When a sheep was slain the priests always got the carcass for dinner. In the same way, among the Fijians of pre-missionary days, the priests shared with the tribal chiefs a monopoly of the usufructs of ritual cannibalism. The gods, of course, had first call upon every rasher of long pig, but they were content, as a practical matter, with its emanation. The actual remains were consumed by their catchpolls, and providing the feast was an act of great merit.

The sanction of religion, when it came in, greatly amplified the general body of moral ideas, but I suspect that very few of its novelties worked any appreciable improvement in human behavior. Practically all of them were grounded, not upon any natural or rational concept of social goodness, but upon private and personal fear. Men were commanded to do this or that, not because it was in accord with their social nature, or because doing it would work any ponderable benefit to their fellow men, but merely because failing to do it would arouse the ire and reprisal of the gods, which is to say, of the priests. In the long run, of course, such acts of virtue, or some of them, began to take on a public aspect, and it was taught that if A offended the gods the penalty would fall also upon $B+C+D+E \ldots +n$. Thus there arose such situations as that which we but lately examined in considering taboo, whereby one man's violation of a forbidden grove, or dinner upon *träfe* fish, or contumacy to a holy personage might expose a whole community to famine and pestilence. But in the main the virtues and vices that originated in religious sanctions remained personal to the believer, and were so rewarded or punished. That is the case to this day, and one of the salient objections to moral theology flows out of the fact, for it inevitably gives the devotee an exaggerated confidence in his own rectitude, and thus makes a pharisee of him, and a bad citizen.

Religion must have made a stout resistance to the first efforts to put morality upon a philosophical basis. To this day, it is instinctively hostile to the sanction of reason, and cries it down whenever the thing can be done with any plausibility. Where the first moral philosophers appeared is unknown, but it was certainly not in Palestine and there is no reason to believe that it was in Greece, as the pedagogues commonly teach. Perhaps it was in Babylonia or Egypt; more likely it was in India, or in Persia, that great reservoir of so-called Greek ideas, especially in the departments of ethics and religion. " Zoroaster, [the ancient Persian law-giver]," says Miles Menander

Dawson in " The Ethical Religion of Zoroaster," " was the discoverer, or at least the uncoverer, of individual morals. . . . His ethics subject all conduct to the acid test, whether or not its consequences, reasonably to be expected, is the weal or woe of men." When this master reformer lived is not known with any exactness, but the authorities agree that it must have been before 600 B.C. He thus antedated Socrates by two centuries, and Confucius and Buddha by more than one. Moreover, what he taught was, in the main, no novelty in Persia; his basic ideas had been accepted there for many years.

By the time the Jews went into captivity to Nebuchadnezzar those ideas were disseminated all over the Near East, and in Babylon the exiles undoubtedly came into contact with them, for one finds references to them in the Old Testament. Every Sunday-school pupil has heard of " the law of the Medes and Persians, which altereth not." The apocryphal Book of Tobit (accepted by the Catholic Church as canonical) is full of borrowings from Persia, and one of its salient characters, " the devil named Asmodeus," comes bodily from the Zoroastrian pantheon. There is some reason to believe that even Satan himself may have first introduced himself to the Jews in the person of the Persian Ahriman, " who is all-death, and counter-created [in opposition, that is, to the good god, Ahura Mazda] the serpent in the river and the Winter, the locust which brings death unto cattle and

[112]

plants, the ants and the anthills, the sin of unbelief, tears and wailing, and the cooking of corpses." But the exportation of such demons was not Zoroaster's great contribution to ethical science; it was the dissemination of the idea that " God reigneth as the Good Mind waxeth," *i.e.*, that man is capable of his own motion of distinguishing between good and evil, and that virtue, like piety, is the product of taking thought.

This doctrine seems to have got a welcome in early Greece, where men were already beginning to examine the fiats of the gods with skepticism. But among the Jews there was a natural resistance, for it was a cardinal article of their religion that Yahweh had revealed to them everything worth knowing, and in consequence they had a somewhat low view of purely human sagacity. They produced no philosophers, but only prophets, which is to say, men who pretended only to transmit the dictates of Yahweh. Even Solomon, their master wiseacre, protested that, in himself, he was without any capacity for moral speculation. " I am," he said, " but a little child: I know not how to go out or come in. . . . Give therefore thy servant an understanding heart, . . . that I may discern between good and bad " (I Kings III, 7, 9). The Jews, in fact, ascribed not only wisdom in the broad sense but also every sort of homely knowledge to divine inspiration, and in Exodus XXXI, 2–11, we find Yahweh condescending to instruct Bezaleel and Aholiab, the contractors for the Tabernacle, in the technique of the goldsmith, the brass-worker, the lapidary, the carpenter, and even the interior decorator. The prophets are full of warnings that the mind of man is only a haunt of follies and delusions: " Let not the wise man glory in his wisdom. . . . There is no wisdom or understanding or counsel against the Lord. . . . Where shall wisdom be found? and where is the place of understanding? Man knoweth not the price thereof; neither is it found in the land of the living. . . . Behold, the fear of the Lord, *that* is wisdom." So in the New Testament: " Hath God not made foolish the wisdom of this world? . . . If any of you lack wisdom, let him ask of God." To Paul there is only one truth, and that is " the truth in Christ," the truth in revelation.

9

But civilized man today is proud of his capacity for the process that he is pleased to call thinking, and such acts as appear to arise from it give him a great deal more satisfaction than those which have any other source, whether lower or higher. The believer who is virtuous simply because he fears the eternal furnaces of a vengeful God is everywhere put on a level below his brother who professes to love righteousness for its own sake, and on purely rational grounds. In the same way the secular philosopher dislikes being told that he is a moral agent because he is a social animal; he prefers to believe that he is so because he is a philosopher. But neither can ever quite emancipate himself from his primordial appetites and aversions, his immemorial character as a marionette on a string, his all-too-human tendency to move first and think afterward. The earliest men must have been conscious of their reflexes and instincts, and therewith of their feelings, long before they were conscious of anything properly describable as thought, and so they must have evolved moral concepts — or, at any rate, moral patterns — before they could give them names, or attempt in any logical way to account for them. " [They] pronounced certain acts to be good or bad," says Westermarck, " on account of the emotions those acts aroused in their minds, just as they called sunshine warm and ice cold on account of certain sensations which they experienced, and as they named a thing pleasant or painful as they felt pleasure or pain." These primary emotions, in Westermarck's view, are still at the bottom of nearly all of our ethical thinking, and we can never hope to get rid of them altogether. They are heritages from the ancient sea-ooze, in which the lowly amœba, coming into contact with something that pleased him, embraced it, and coming into contact with something that hurt him, drew away. " To determine what is to be done, what is not to be done," says H. S. Jennings in " The Uni-

verse and Life," " in other words, to determine right
and wrong, is an insistent problem for all organisms;
it is not something that begins with man."

The factor common to all the moral systems that
we know today, including both the most primitive
and the most advanced, is a general wish, hope and
expectation that every normal individual will act
under given conditions in a predictable manner —
that there will be no great and confusing aberrations
of conduct. The main object of society is to keep
order, and the most powerful of all the rich variety of
human wills is the will to peace. Strange conduct is
not only apt to have dangerous effects; it is disturbing
and unpleasant in itself. The fact accounts for some of
the curious and apparently irrational offenses that are
to be encountered in the moral codes of savage societies, and even in those of civilization. The acts prohibited are regarded with aversion, not because they
really menace life or property, but simply because it
has become the custom to refrain from them, and because any departure from that custom is upsetting.

The thing we call law, indeed, is mainly a device
for enforcing respect for custom, and the moral principles which it relies upon to give it dignity are often
very dubious, and tend to change readily as the folk-
ways change. The early legalists took a loftier view of
it, and the Institutes of Justinian begin by defining it
sonorously as " the knowledge of things divine and
human, the science of the right and the wrong," but a

learned modern judge and legal philosopher, Cardozo, J., does not hesitate to reject all that as hollow highfalutin. Law, he says, is simply " a rule of conduct so established as to justify a prediction with reasonable certainty that it will be enforced by the courts." So much, and no more. To which Morris R. Cohen adds that, in large part, it can never be anything beyond " a special technique for determining what would otherwise be uncertain and subject to conflict. It is socially necessary," he goes on, " to have a rule of the road, but it is morally indifferent whether it requires us to turn to the right or to the left."

Both the civil and the criminal laws of modern states had their origin in a practical desire to promote the public peace by limiting conflicts of will and supplanting private revenge. When machinery is provided for a creditor to recover his debt he is thereby discouraged from taking it out of the hide of his debtor. And when the law seizes upon a murderer and executes him for his crime, it simply usurps the place of the dead man's relatives, who, in primitive society, had a right and perhaps also a duty to butcher him themselves. That right and duty still survive among savages, and even in civilization something analogous to them is recognized in certain situations, as when an injured American husband, taking his wife *in flagrante*, is permitted and even expected to open fire upon her and her paramour. But even the rudest savages, in the interest of the common safety and tran-

quillity, make efforts to limit the field of private revenge, for it is bound to provoke reprisals, and open
the way for a long series of fresh crimes, all of them
highly anti-social. Either the physical punishment of
murder and other such grave offenses is taken over as
a public matter, or the aggrieved are forced to abandon the *lex talionis* altogether and accept some sort
of compensation, usually in goods but sometimes in
services. And when no such surrogate for vengeance
is forced upon them, they are required to do their
retaliating in what is conceived to be an orderly
manner, and in strict accord with custom. Thus, among
the Bedouins of the Libyan desert, though it is the
right of the brother of a murdered man to kill the
murderer, or, indeed, any male member of the latter's
family, he is forbidden to do it openly and face to
face: instead, he must do it by stealth, to avoid a fight.
Moreover, he must make sure that no women are
within eyeshot, for the spectacle would shock them
intolerably, and their uproar would break the public
peace.

Among the ancient Asiatic peoples whose statutes
have been preserved there was only one apparent
theory as to the punitive purpose of law: it was to
make the offender suffer what he had caused some one
else to suffer. Whenever it was possible he had to restore his victim to the *status quo ante,* and in any case
he had to submit to a degree of damage equivalent to
the damage he had inflicted. Thus the penalty for wil-

ful murder, at all events of a free citizen, was invariably death, and that for theft was restitution at least twofold: first enough to reimburse the victim for his loss, and then enough to make the thief savor the full measure of that victim's pangs. This *lex talionis* is writ large across the Covenant Code of the Jews, and one finds it set forth with harsh clarity in Exodus XXI, 23–25: " Thou shalt give life for life, eye for eye, tooth for tooth, hand for hand, foot for foot, burning for burning, wound for wound, stripe for stripe." It is true that the Jews, by the time they framed this code, had also admitted the principle of money compensation into their law, but there were still many situations in which the more ancient law of the talon still prevailed. One of its peculiarities was that it sometimes punished a crime against the person by destroying the member — usually a hand — which had been its instrument. The curious will find an interesting example in Deuteronomy XXV, 11, 12: " When men strive together one with another, and the wife of the one draweth near for to deliver her husband out of the hand of him that smiteth him, and putteth forth her hand, and taketh him by the secrets: then thou shalt cut off her hand."

The Babylonians, as we learn from the Code of Hammurabi, devoted themselves with great ingenuity to making the punishment fit the crime. One who, on being called to help put out a fire, seized the chance to rob the burning house, was thrown into the flames.

One who, by negligence, say in building an unsafe dwelling, caused the death of another's son, was punished by the execution of his own son. One who made a breach in a house wall, planning to enter feloniously, was dispatched on the spot, and his body buried in front of the breach. A wet nurse who substituted a strange baby for one that died in her care had her breasts cut off, so that she could never abuse her trade again. A son who struck his father had his hand cut off; one who denied his father had his tongue cut out. A man who struck a pregnant woman, so that she aborted and died, was not killed himself, but his daughter was: his own life, since he was a man, was apparently rather too much to pay for that of a woman. If a man put out the eye of another man of equal rank, he lost one of his own eyes. If he broke a bone, he had a bone broken in return. If he knocked out a tooth, he had one of his own knocked out. If he struck an equal he received sixty strokes with an ox-whip in public. For assault and mayhem upon slaves and other inferiors, of course, the penalties were milder — mainly modest indemnities in silver. A doctor who, in treating a slave patient, let him die, had to give the owner another slave. If he let a free patient die he lost his own hand. So did a farm laborer who stole wheat from his employer. And so on.

This rough-and-ready system, based upon the idea that the criminal should be made to suffer in kind for his crime, sufficed also for the peoples of classical antiquity, and their philosophers raised little objection to it. Even Plato, though he apparently agreed with Socrates that the truly wise man could do no wrong, and proposed to restrict citizenship in his ideal Republic to wise men only, admitted sadly that men of dubious wisdom would certainly creep in, and was quite willing to punish them for their follies in the forthright Athenian manner. He actually went further than the Athenians, for he proposed to put the sanction of religion beside the sanction of reason, thus converting all crimes into varieties of blasphemy, to be expiated as such by ceremonies of purification, mainly very unpleasant. He even refused to except conscientious unbelievers — necessarily a large party in any really civilized Republic. Plato, indeed, never got rid of a furtive and apparently congenital piety, and in his ethical writings, as in his metaphysics, one finds frequent suggestions of that labored Pecksniffery which has become so familiar in the tracts of the current reconcilers of science and religion.

Aristotle, a far bolder and more original man, was nevertheless content to take the Greek criminal law substantially as he found it. In the Nicomachean Ethics he defined punishment as " a sort of medicine," and pain as its " medium." Its object, he thought, was to so damage the culprit that he would be brought down to the level of the person he had injured. He attempted to distinguish between naturally good men, with " an inborn nobility of character and a genuine love of what is noble," and the common run of humanity: he believed that the former could be kept in order by appealing to their native decency, but that the latter needed stronger measures. " It is the nature of the many," he said sadly, " to be amenable to fear but not to a sense of honor, and to abstain from evil not because of its baseness but because of the penalties it entails." In any case, he held that it was fair and sensible to punish all criminals alike, and on the frank principle of retaliation. " For it makes no difference," he said, " whether a good man has defrauded a bad man or a bad one a good one, nor whether it is a good or a bad man that has committed adultery; the law looks only at the degree of damage done, treating the parties as equal, and merely asking whether one has done and the other suffered injustice, whether one inflicted and the other has sustained damage."

The Romans produced no moral and legal philosophers comparable to Aristotle, nor even to Plato, but they greatly developed law as a practical art, and bred some lawyers whose fame still lives. In their hands legal procedure, in criminal as in civil cases, was rationalized and humanized. They introduced appeals, gave precise definitions to crimes, regularized penalties, and hemmed in the jurisdiction and prerogatives of magistrates. The laws of all civilized countries save Great Britain and the United States are still strongly colored by their ideas, and even in Great Britain and the United States many of their dicta are cherished by judges. In the Law of the Twelve Tables (451–450 B.C.) they had a sort of Bill of Rights, defining their inalienable liberties. Cicero tells us that it was memorized by every schoolboy in his time, though it was then nearly 600 years old. But the Law of the Twelve Tables, on its criminal side, ratified the *lex talionis* — for example, a man who broke another's leg had his own broken in retaliation — , and this principle was seldom challenged in the later and greater days of Roman law, and never quite abandoned. The aim of a criminal statute, as the Romans of the Republic saw it, was not to reform the criminal, nor even (at least primarily) to deter others; it was simply to make him suffer for his offense against private right and the public security, and in strict accordance with its seriousness. Capital punishment was not often inflicted, but the other common penalties were summary and harsh.

As the Republic faded into the Empire the rights of the citizen began to be neglected, and the orderly processes of law yielded, as in the Europe of today, to the evil humors of what finally became an oriental despotism, bloody and outrageous. The courts were intolerably corrupt, the law was changed constantly at the will of the Emperors and their satraps, and the increasing insecurity of the state brought in inevitably the mass persecution of unpopular minorities. It was thus that the early Christians got into the clutches of the Roman Fascisti: the common charge against them was that they were conspirators against the state — what are today called radicals or Reds. The death penalty was inflicted oftener and oftener, and in novel and horrible ways — by decapitation with the ax or sword, by crucifixion (borrowed from the Near East), by drowning in a sack (along with an ape, a serpent and a chicken), by walling up, by burning at the stake, by strangling or stoning, or by exposure to gladiators or wild beasts in the arena. Executions became public shows, and the mob applauded good ones and hissed bad ones. Flogging, branding and mutilation were also common, and the Roman penologists made a notable contribution to their science by inventing penal servitude, usually in the state mines or galleys. The *lex talionis* of the Twelve Tables, in retrospect, began to seem relatively tame, for by now the most appalling punishments were inflicted for the most trivial offenses. Moreover, the old equality before the law was forgotten, and rich and important men, called *honestiores*, were free to commit crimes which brought certain death to *plebeii*.

The influence of Christianity was naturally thrown against all this ferocity, for the first Christians had been among the principal sufferers from it. Nero, as Tacitus tells us, illuminated his gardens at night by clothing them in shirts impregnated with pitch and then setting fire to them. The Stoic philosophers and jurisconsults had long sought to dissuade the Romans from such barbarities, but it was not until after the conversion of Constantine that any serious effort was made to put them down. Constantine, in 325, prohibited gladiatorial shows, abolished the branding of convicts, and made the killing of a slave homicide. That he was prompted to these reforms by his somewhat lukewarm faith is scarcely to be doubted, for they were salient planks in the common Christian platform, and had been advocated for two centuries by the early Fathers. Nor is it to be doubted that the voice of the Christians, growing more resolute year by year, had something to do with the great legal reform of Justinian I (527–65), culminating in the Corpus Juris Civilis, the basis of all the canon law of subsequent ages, and of a large part of the civil law.

Justinian's primary aim was not to formulate any new legislation, but simply to recover the legal principles that had prevailed in the glorious days of Roman jurisprudence, before the disintegration of the state had brought in chaos and oppression. To that end he set a committee of sixteen lawyers to boiling down 2000 law books, running to 3,000,000 lines, and the result was a compact and rational code of 150,000 lines. But even before this it had been found necessary to devise new statutes to meet the rapidly changing needs of the time, and in them the influence of Christian ideas was often manifest. The general tendency of those ideas was to limit the occasions of lawful bloodshed, and in that direction the more earnest Christians went to fantastic lengths. Many of them not only refused to shed blood in person, even as soldiers; they also refused to give testimony in trials for capital crimes. Says Lecky:

The right of sanctuary, which was before possessed by the imperial statues and by the pagan temples, was accorded to the churches. During the holy seasons of Lent and Easter no criminal trials could be held, and no criminal could be tortured or executed. Miracles, it was said, were sometimes wrought to attest the innocence of accused or condemned men, but they were never wrought to consign criminals to execution by the civil power.

10

But when Christianity, once an outlaw in a pagan land, became at last the state faith, and its ministers began to take on the rights and dignities of public functionaries, it quickly abandoned its early effort to engraft the Beatitudes upon Roman law. By the Fifth Century about all that remained of the old horror of shedding blood was the rule that clergymen, as such, should not shed it. But this rule, of course, was easy to evade. When a heretic was taken, or some other culprit was brought to heel by the agents of Holy Church, he was simply handed over to the secular officers of justice with the admonition that he be punished *ut quam clementissime et ultra sanguinis effusionem puniretur* — as humanely as possible, and without any effusion

[126]

of blood. What this admonition amounted to was soon
learned by the almost countless victims who went to
the stake, or were clubbed to death, or drowned in
sacks, or hanged. It should be noted in fairness that
not a few of the early Fathers, and among them some
of the most eminent, opposed this revival of wholesale butchery. Among them were Tertullian (afterward denounced himself as a heretic), Origen, St.
Cyprian of Carthage, Lactantius, St. Hilary of Poitiers
and St. John Chrysostom. (St. Augustine, as usual,
straddled.) But the moderates were opposed vigorously by other great ecclesiastics, beginning with St.
Optatus of Milevis, who flourished in the Fourth Century, and these advocates of force without stint had
the support of the later Emperors, who cherished the
ancient title of Pontifex Maximus and the new one of
Bishop of the Exterior, and greatly enjoyed the sanguinary powers which went with both.

Constantine, by the edict of Milan (313), had de-
creed religious freedom throughout the Empire, but
by the time Justinian's committee of lawyers completed the second volume of his Corpus Juris, in 533,
heresy was again a crime, and they gave a chapter to
it. Christianity, in those days, was in a formative
state, and every third Christian spent a good part of
his time questioning the orthodoxy of his neighbors.
The whole Mediterranean littoral swarmed with the
preachers of heretical sects, and some of them gathered large followings and became serious nuisances.

TREATISE ON RIGHT AND WRONG

The Donatists, at one time, menaced the very security of the Empire, and the Manichæans, who accepted the New Testament but not the Old, were almost as dangerous. Justinian himself, in his old age, succumbed to a heresy — that of the Aphthartodocetists, who taught that the body of Jesus did not decay in the grave. The Council of Nicæa, in 325, had sought to get rid of all these controversies, but they continued for several centuries, and cost a great deal of blood. Whenever a bishop was deposed, which was often, large numbers of his followers were commonly put to death. And when he was restored, which sometimes happened soon afterward, he condoned and even incited the immediate butchery of his opponents. The *lex talionis* was again in full force and effect.

After the Seventh Century there was some abatement in the bloodshed. The same weariness of turmoil and slaughter which, in 800, brought about the formation of the Holy Roman Empire also operated to diminish the professional ardor of theologians, and one by one they submitted to the Pope. But as the authority of His Holiness increased — and before long he was far more powerful than the Emperor — , he revived and sharpened the old laws against heretics. In 1209, in the person of Innocent III, he undertook a crusade against the Albigenses in Southern France, with Simon of Montfort the elder as his commander in the field, and before the fighting was over nearly 50,000 persons, many of them innocent bystanders, had been killed. Innocent, though he is described by the Catholic Encyclopedia as " one of the greatest Popes of the Middle Ages, . . . whose politico-ecclesiastical achievements brought the papacy to the zenith of its power," urged and commanded the secular princes of Europe to put down heresy with the sword, and after the extermination of the Albigenses had showed them the way they proceeded to do so with great diligence. In 1232 one Alberic, a Dominican, was given the title of *inquisitor hæreticæ pravitatis*, and turned loose in Lombardy, and the Inquisition was born. By 1250 it was in full blast throughout Italy, France, Germany, Spain and the Netherlands. Half a century before, in 1205, Innocent III, in his bull *Si adversus vos*, had forbidden lawyers to " assist in any way, by counsel or support, all heretics and such as believe in them, adhere to them, render them any assistance or defend them in any way," and in 1252 Innocent IV, in his bull *Ad exstirpanda*, completed the business by authorizing the use of torture in examining them.

The tale of what followed, in Spain and elsewhere, is too familiar to need retelling. Hiding behind the hypocritical maxim, *Ecclesia non sitit sanguinem* (the church does not thirst for blood), the agents of the Popes, chiefly Dominicans, hunted down thousands of poor wretches with loud hosannas, and handed them over to torture and death. Not all who were accused, of course, were executed. Many were simply thrown into horrible prisons, there to be forgotten. The dungeon of a convicted monk, says the Catholic Encyclopedia, " was euphemistically called *In pace;* it was indeed the tomb of a man buried alive." The secular prisons were even worse. With the principal punishment, whether immolation in such a den or death at the stake, went forfeiture of goods. This forfeiture, at least at the start, was the prerogative of the secular power, and became one of the main sources of income of the collaborating princes. Not even the dead were immune. A man could be accused of heresy *post mortem,* and tried as if he were alive. If the ecclesiastical court found him guilty his property was taken from his heirs. Such confiscations, which were numerous, greatly impeded commerce and industry, for they made capital insecure, and hence timid. Every contract with a heretic was void, and anyone who ventured to make it ran a heavy risk of being accused of heresy himself.

Like the gladiatorial shows of the Romans, nearly a thousand years before, the constant executions filled the populace with a taste for savagery, and when the supply of heretics ran short, which sometimes happened, the jailers and executioners turned their virtuosity upon other unfortunates. In particular, there were recurrent campaigns against witches and magicians, especially in Germany. No man was safe, for any idler could accuse him, and the administration of justice was inordinately brutal and corrupt. The streets of every town ran blood, and the hangman and axman were always busy. As some one has said, it became a salient peculiarity of medieval life that even the most peaceful citizen, leaving his home for a few hours, was bound to see at least one murder, whether judicial or otherwise. The great days of the Universal Church were days of unparalleled crime and disorder, injustice and oppression, outrage and atrocity.

Nor did the Protestant Reformation materially improve matters. The reorganization of Europe upon a rational and civilized basis was the work, not of the Reformation but of the Renaissance, a purely secular movement. The chief of the so-called Reformers — Luther, Zwingli and Calvin — were far more medieval than modern. All three joined St. Thomas Aquinas in holding that the punishment of heresy should be death, and one of them, Calvin, set up a half-secular, half-ecclesiastical tribunal at Geneva which fairly matched those maintained by the celebrated Tomás de Torquemada at Seville, Cordova, Jaén and Toledo. The first efforts to reform the laws did not come from Christian philosophers, but from such skeptics as Hobbes (1588–1679), Grotius (1583–1645), and Pufendorf (1632–94), and it was not until the time of Montesquieu (1689–1755), Beccaria (1738–94), and Bentham (1748–1832), that any really logical theory of crimes and punishments began to be worked out.

Beccaria, who is looked upon as the founder of modern penology, seems somewhat moderate in retrospect, and even timorous, but in his day his ideas were revolutionary. What he pleaded for was a schedule of *fixed* punishments, to be determined, not by judges facing actual culprits but by legislators remote from the passions of the courtroom, and a policy of making those punishments " the least possible in the case given, proportioned to the crime." He was strongly against all the barbaric legal devices that had hung over from the Middle Ages — the use of torture, the admission of secret accusations, the wanton infliction of capital punishment, and the denial of the prisoner's natural right to call witnesses in his defense and to examine those for the prosecution. Beccaria did not reject the medieval theory that the chief aim of a criminal penalty was retaliation, but he protested vigorously against too much severity, and advanced the then novel idea that making punishment certain would be more apt to deter criminals than making it harsh. Neither did he reject Aristotle's doctrine that all offenders should be treated alike — that the nature of the crime was the thing to be considered, not the motives and temptations of the offender — , but he argued that the social damage it had caused should be the measure of the punishment, not the influence and indignation of the complainant. He proposed that the punishment for crimes against property be limited, in general, to fines, *i.e.*, to restitution, and that that for treason be changed from death to banishment. Finally, he criticized capital punishment on the ground (now so familiar) that it left no opening for the rectification of accidental injustice.

Beccaria's book, " Trattato dei Delitti e delle Pene " (Essay on Crime and Punishment), published in 1764, made a great sensation in Europe, and launched reforms in almost every country. Maria Theresa and Joseph II, reading it in Vienna, proceeded at once to amend and civilize the criminal code of Austria, and Catherine the Great was so greatly impressed that she invited the author to St. Petersburg. In England he soon had many disciples, including Bentham, Sir Robert Peel, and the great prison reformers, John Howard and Sir Samuel Romilly. In France his ideas were embodied in the French criminal codes of 1791 and 1810, and in America they strongly colored that general revision of the criminal laws which followed the Revolution. Bentham, like Beccaria, believed that the chief element in punishment was retaliation for the damage done to the public peace and dignity, but he also added the element of dissuasion, and argued that the penalty inflicted should be the least that would convince the offender that the pains of his act outweighed its pleasures. Here he foreshadowed, though without saying so in plain words, the later tendency to differentiate between criminals as well as between crimes, for a penalty sufficient to dissuade a chance offender would be obviously too little to dissuade a hardened professional. Bentham's ideas were immensely influential in England, and probably served more than any other single agency to bring about that radical overhauling of the criminal laws which began in 1820 and culminated in 1861. In the former year there were 222 offenses subject to the death penalty, including all sorts of trivial thefts and trespasses; in the latter there were but three — murder, piracy on the high seas, and treason.

11

Bentham, Beccaria and the German philosopher Feuerbach, who laid down the maxim that there could be " no crime and no punishment without law," are recognized as the chief prophets.of what has come to be called the classical school in penology. In general, though it admits that great severity may be necessary on occasion, it counsels a high degree of humanity in dealing with offenders, and insists that the criminal laws be made known before they go into effect, that they be acceptable as just and rational to a majority of the people, and that they be administered publicly and with strict impartiality. The First, Fourth, Fifth, Sixth, Eighth and Fourteenth Amendments to the Constitution of the United States show plainly the influence of this school. It flourished almost unchallenged until 1889, when the Italian, Cesare Lombroso, published " L'Uomo Delinquente " (The Delinquent Man).

Lombroso's argument, in brief, was that lawmakers had always made a grave mistake by assuming that all criminals were substantially alike, and that the only real differences between them were the differences between their crimes. On this assumption punishment tended to be mere retaliation, adjusted in severity to fit the offense — death for murder, a light fine or short imprisonment for petty theft, and so on. Lombroso believed that this scheme was false and vicious. He argued that in many cases even crimes of great seriousness were mainly accidents of the criminal's environment, and that punishing him severely injured him irreparably without achieving any ponderable social good. On the other hand, he maintained that even the most inconsiderable crime, if perpetrated by an habitual criminal, justified punishing him with such severity that he could never attempt another. For crimes of sudden and irresistible passion, done by men otherwise normal, he believed that the offender's natural remorse was sufficient punishment, but for chronic criminality he was willing to approve life imprisonment, or even death. For the criminally insane he advocated confinement in a suitable asylum until they were cured or dead.

Unfortunately, Lombroso was not content to go so far. In addition, he issued a great deal of solemn nonsense about what he called the criminal type, arguing that it represented a reversion to the unmoral ferocity of primitive man. It was at once pointed out by more competent anthropologists that there was no evidence whatever that primitive man had really been ferocious

— that, on the contrary, he had probably been a mild and highly social fellow. Moreover, when Lombroso began to describe his criminal type with some particularity, it was discovered that the stigmata he listed were quite as common among normal persons as among habitual criminals. Thus all this part of his doctrine ceased to interest scientific penologists, and was relegated to the Sunday supplements of the Hearst papers, where it made an appropriate text for horrifying but wholly fanciful portraits of Neanderthal Man, usually showing him dragging a naked Broadway chorus girl to his cave.

But Lombroso's notion that the punishment should be made to fit, not the crime, but the criminal has had a more prosperous and respectable career. It is an integral part, indeed, of all the varieties of the so-called New Penology, and at the hands of some of the current reformers it has been carried to lengths undreamed of by its author. They propose that the whole of our present system of punishments be scrapped, and that crime be treated, not as an injury to society, but as an injury to the criminal, *i.e.*, as a disease. If they ever have their way the sole function of police, courts and juries will be to ascertain whether a crime has been committed, and if so, by whom. Once so much has been determined, the perpetrator thereof will be handed over to a commission of psychiatrists, who will try to find out what is the matter with him, and to cure it in a suitable hospital. If a cure follows, he will be released at once. But if he baffles their science he will be kept for the duration of his natural life. The nature of his crime, and the social damage issuing out of it, will be immaterial to them.

This somewhat grandiose reform is advocated in the United States, not only by visionaries and enthusiasts, but also by a number of presumably hardheaded men, notably Clarence Darrow, Alfred E. Smith and Warden Lewis E. Lawes of Sing Sing. More, it has got itself translated, at least in a partial and tentative manner, into the legislation of several American States. Simultaneously, the almost century-long struggle between the psychiatrists of the English-speaking world and the lawyers, which began with the ruling of the English Law Lords in McNaughten's case in 1843 (to the general effect that no man may be punished for a crime if his mental state, at the time it was committed, was such that he " could not distinguish between right and wrong with reference to that particular act "), now appears to be going in favor of the psychiatrists. They are called into court more and more often, and if they do not disagree too sharply they are heard with respect. After they have certified to a murderer's moral irresponsibility, even though it be in terms unintelligible to the learned judge, it is most unusual for him to be hanged.

Two considerations impede what otherwise would be the triumphant progress of the New Penology. The

first is that psychiatry is really far less scientific than
its penological fuglemen pretend it is — that both in
diagnosis and in therapeutics it is still almost as em-
pirical, and hence almost as uncertain, as gynecology,
say, was a century ago. It is sound enough in the
region where the symptoms of mental aberration are
gross and obvious, but in that region judges and juries
are also apt to be sound, and since McNaughten's case
even the law itself has been relatively sound. The
moment it launches into the shadowy areas beyond, it
begins to collide with common sense. Common sense
says that any man who performs an anti-social act,
knowing precisely what he is doing, should be punished for it. Psychiatry (I speak of it, of course, only
as it is heard of in the courts) answers that the man
may be impelled to the act irresistibly, even though
he knows that it is wrong. But that answer is manifestly pretty feeble, for there is really no way to tell
with any precision whether a given impulse in a given
man is irresistible or not. If one impulse is, then any
other impulse may be also, and we enter a world
ruled by determinism. For practical reasons that I
was lately discussing, the human race still believes in
free will, and so it views every move toward determinism with suspicion. When a psychiatrist goes on the
stand and testifies that the culprit A, who appears
quite normal to the judge and jury, is suffering from
a psychopathic condition which makes him more
likely than a normal man to rob a filling-station, the

judge and jury are likely to reply that this is precisely the sort of fellow who ought to be in jail.

12

If the psychiatrists could describe the prisoner's psychopathic condition as plausibly as their colleagues of internal medicine describe a case of pneumonia, giving its etiology, its pathology, its probable course, and a plausible scheme of treatment — if this were within their gifts they would convert many more doubters. Unfortunately, it is not. Psychiatry, in so far as it has to do with criminology, remains in the vague and speculative stage of the humoral pathology. But its proponents insist upon plunging ahead, and so they often collide with the prevailing *mores*. Curiously enough, they are most successful in disarming skepticism and hostility at the two ends of the criminal scale. When they undertake to say positively that a given murderer is insane, it is very uncommon, as I have noted, for him to be put to death, and when they declare that a youth caught in some trivial crime is too retarded in mind to be treated as a criminal he seldom goes to prison. But in the wide middle ground, where adults of obvious cunning and daring practise crime as a trade, they are heard much less readily. Common sense revolts against thinking of such criminals as invalids, to be treated in hospitals; it insists that they are criminals, and ought to go to prison.

Here we come to the second consideration which runs against the New Penology. It attempts without sufficient preparation to obliterate the immemorial concept of punishment as retaliation. That the human race, in the long run, will abandon that concept is certainly not impossible, but every reflective man must be well aware that it is not yet abandoned today. We are still too close to the age of private vengeance — much closer, in fact, than most of us generally assume. In England it remained the sole moving force in prosecutions for crime down to 1879, for until that year there was no public prosecutor, and all criminal causes, like all civil causes, had to be carried on by private complainants. An exception was made in the case of murder, on the ground that the complainant, being dead, could not appear in person, and another was made in the case of direct offenses against the King, who could not, without indecorum, plead in his own courts. In the former case the coroner represented the complainant, and in the latter one of the law officers of the Crown. But all other criminal proceedings had to be initiated and maintained by the persons aggrieved, and at their own expense.

In the United States and on the Continent of Europe public prosecutors are rather more ancient officers, but nowhere do they go back more than a couple of centuries. Moreover, they are still urged to action in most instances by what amounts, at bottom, to private vengeance, and when it is lacking its place is often taken by what may be called public vengeance. Every ambitious American district attorney, when he goes to bed at night, prays for the chance to prosecute a conspicuous culprit on the morrow, for he knows that such a chance, if it be seized with sufficient ferocity, makes him popular and opens the road to higher preferment. The list of American statesmen who got their starts in that way runs from Mr. Chief Justice Hughes and Senator Borah to the latest candidates for Congress in Oklahoma and Mississippi. Surely it would be absurd to say that a district attorney, thus leaping to his God-sent opportunity, is animated by any desire to reform and salvage the criminal before him. His one aim is to punish that criminal. And in that aim he is supported very heartily by his public.

Society, indeed, is still too insecure for anyone to view crime really dispassionately. When a house is robbed round the corner no man can help feeling that his own house has been menaced, and when there is a murder he shivers with a sensation of steel at his own throat. It relieves him somewhat to hear that the criminal has been taken, but not enough. He always wants to hear that the criminal has been *punished*, and in a satisfyingly harsh manner — that the pains of fear have been adequately paid for by the pains of ignominious imprisonment or worse. The news that there are men who regard the culprit as merely sick shocks him too much for him to give it any sober consideration: a powerful emotion impels him to reject it as preposterous. " The retributive desire," says Westermarck, " is so strong, and appears so natural, that we can neither help obeying it, nor seriously disapprove of its being obeyed. The theory that we have a right to punish an offender only in so far as, by doing so, we promote the general happiness, really serves in the main as a justification for gratifying such a desire, rather than as a foundation for penal practice." Here law does not deny or dispose of vengeance; it simply provides a formal *katharsis*. It is the last refuge of cruelty in an increasingly tender society. The New Penologists must go a long way before they make a cool and impersonal science of it.

III

Its Varieties

1

The ethical doctrine which now passes under the
name of Christian was mainly formulated, as we all
know, not by Jesus Himself, but by Paul, and Paul in
his muddled way was a very fair precursor of modern
man, for half of his intellectual baggage was borrowed from Asia and the other half from Greece. " I
am debtor," he said in his Epistle to the Romans,
" both to the Greeks and to the barbarians." To this
day we are all half Greeks and half Asiatic " barbarians," at least when it comes to our ideas of good
and evil, right and wrong. From an obscure tribe of
Semitic nomads in the wastes of Asia Minor, occupy-
ing an area smaller than that of New Jersey and so
unimportant to secular history that the ancient records
scarcely mention it, we inherit a body of ethical postulates which, despite frequent and ferocious attack,
show no sign of being abandoned within the day of
any man now living, and from the Greeks we acquire
our apparently insatiable appetite for moral speculation, both as a metaphysical exercise and as an act of
pious merit. In brief, the Jews gave us our axioms in

this department, and the Greeks set us most of our theorems. We have not added many new inventions to the former, and we have yet to digest all of the latter. In detail, of course, there have been changes, but the principles are uniformly old.

Neither the Jews nor the Greeks were originators. Both borrowed heavily, first from the ancient peoples of Mesopotamia and then from the Egyptians. Large numbers of Jews were captives at one time in Egypt and at another time in Babylon, and both times the exiles came home with their heads full of new and exciting notions, in theology, in ethics and in government. But even while all divisions of the tribe dwelt on the soil of their choice they were exposed constantly to the impact of foreign ideas, for Palestine was on the main route between the Tigris and Euphrates valleys on the one side and the Southeastern Mediterranean littoral on the other, and nearly every great Power of antiquity — Babylonia, Egypt, the Hittite Empire, Macedonia, Persia and Rome in turn — made some effort to conquer and control it. All the highways running north and south were commanded by Mount Carmel, and on that low ridge, before the dawn of history, there arose a fortress which the Jews later called Megiddo and the Greeks Armageddon. It was fought for so often and so bitterly that the name of Armageddon came to be the common term for a bloody and decisive battle, and it retains that significance to this day. In Revelation xvi we are told that it is to be the scene of the last great struggle preceding the Day of Judgment, when seven angels will be sent down from Heaven to turn the waters of the seas and rivers into blood, to stoke and heat up the sun, to shake the earth with mighty quakes, and to blast all " the cities of the nations," with their people in them.

Where the Jews came from originally we do not know, but if, as seems likely, they were part of the mysterious Habiru people, mentioned in the Babylonian records, they were roving through Mesopotamia so early as the Twenty-second Century B.C. In his learned treatise on Semitic mythology Stephen Herbert Langdon says that they " served for six centuries as mercenary soldiers and traders among the Babylonians, Assyrians, Hittites, Mitannians and Arameans before they entered and occupied Canaan." This invasion probably occurred during the Fifteenth and Fourteenth Centuries B.C. The land of Canaan, which was roughly coextensive with what we now call Palestine, was peopled very thinly, and by a somewhat confusing mixture of tribes and peoples, ten of which are enumerated in the Old Testament — Amorites, Jebusites, Kenites, Hivites, Girgashites, Hittites, and so on. All of these save the Hittites were of Semitic stock, and the Jews shared with them a legendary *Stammvater*, Shem, the eldest son of Noah. The Hittites, who really belonged to the northward and eastward, in what was later called Syria, were not Semites, but sprang from an aboriginal race that had occupied

Asia Minor before the Semites began to emerge from
their first home, which may have been either Arabia
or Africa. The Jews were better fighters than the other
tribes of their own blood, and so they gradually mastered most of the country west of the Jordan and south
of the Sea of Galilee. But the Hittites, who were very
powerful, stopped them whenever they ventured beyond. Their relations with these formidable *Goyim*
seem, at times, to have been very close, for it was an
admixture of Hittite genes that gave them their characteristic arched nose. The ancient sculptures make it
plain that this Jewish nose is not Semitic at all, but
Hittite. Whether the Hittites bestowed it amicably, by
flustering and wooing the Jewish maidens, or hostilely,
by ravishing them, is not known.

Under Hittite pressure from the north and east the
Jews tended to move into the wild southern part of
Palestine, which marched with Egypt, and presently
some of the more enterprising of them were bulging
over into Egyptian territory, on the prowl for corn for
themselves and grass for their flocks. The Pharaohs
of the time, who were engaged in grandiose building
projects and needed labor badly, promptly rounded
them up and put them to work. Their first great man,
Moses, was born in Egypt during this captivity, probably in the Thirteenth Century B.C. How he liberated
his people from their bondage and led them back to
Palestine is set forth at length in the Book of Exodus,
with many details that lay somewhat heavy burdens

upon faith. Naturally enough, his brilliant success made him the tribal hero, and by an extension as easy then as it is today, the tribal chief and lawgiver.

But Moses himself had not been badly treated in Egypt, save perhaps for a brief period when, after murdering an Egyptian, he was a fugitive from justice. He had been brought up, in fact, as the son of the Pharaoh's daughter, which is to say, as a royal prince, and both in his youth and after his crime had blown over he seems to have had ready access to the Pharaoh's presence. One thing is certain: that he was well educated according to the Egyptian standards of the time, and could read and write — an art that was then very rare among the Jews. And another is highly probable: that he heard and learned a great deal about statecraft, as it was then understood in the world, at the court of the Pharaoh, and scarcely less about theology. For Egypt, in those days, had lately passed through one of the most stupendous politico-religious revolutions ever seen in the world, and every Egyptian must have been full of it. This was the great reform of Amenhotep (or Amenophis) IV (*c.* 1400 B.C.), whose much inferior son-in-law, Tut-ankh-amen, was destined to make a stir thirty-three centuries later by being dug up, a gilded mummy, in the Valley of the Tombs of Kings near Thebes. Amenhotep, in his day, was worth a thousand Tut-ankh-amens, for he was the first skeptic recorded in history. In the end his reform failed — chiefly, it would appear, because it was too radical to be carried out in one lifetime and by one man — but for many centuries after his death it was remembered, and the principles on which it was based seem to have made a lasting impression upon Moses.

2

What Amenhotep tried to do was to calm and consolidate the mighty Egyptian Empire by setting up a simple and relatively enlightened religion for the whole country. When he came to the throne he found Egypt torn between a multitude of cults, many of them purely local and most of them palpably preposterous. Every village had its own outfit of gods, and every god had his outfit of impudent and prehensile priests. All this put a heavy burden on the people, and raised up dangerous enmities among them. Every now and then one of these local gods got a reputation for curing leprosy, or for making women fertile, or for prospering the Nile fisheries, or for some other such marvel, and people would flock to his shrine from near and far, and there would be a great waste of time and money, and the priests of other gods back home would be indignant and full of complaints to the Pharaoh. Sometimes one of these local gods became so popular that he took on the estate and dignity of a national god, but always he had rivals, and his struggles to maintain his hegemony distracted and divided the people and plagued the government. At the time of Amenhotep's birth one Ammon, or Amen, the local god of Thebes, was on top, and the young prince was named after him: Amenhotep meant " Amen is satisfied."

But Amenhotep himself, as he grew up, was far from satisfied. He believed that a great empire, to be really solid and durable, should be burdened with only one god, and that that one should be a great deal more plausible than Amen. So he tore down the temples to Amen at Thebes, moved his capital to Tel el-Amarna in the desert (where gods were naturally scarce), commanded his people to abandon all their local divinities, and ordained that every Egyptian whose piety still needed some stay should worship Aton, the sun-god, who had been much esteemed in Egypt centuries before, but was happily devoid of any great entourage of priests, temple women, tithe takers, and other such expensive parasites. Amenhotep, who simultaneously changed his own name to Ikhnation, meaning " devoted to Aton," prepared a simple form of worship for the new national god, and thought by his reform to get rid of the local rivalries that kept the country in a ferment, and of the huge ecclesiastical budgets that impoverished the people and filled a thousand temples with lazy and seditious priests. We know very little in detail about his theology, but it must have been pretty rational for that time and place, for all the professional theologians were opposed to it. For many centuries after his death, indeed, they continued to depict him as but little better than an atheist, and he was hardly in his tomb before they induced his feeble successors to restore not only Amen, but also a multitude of other gods.

Amenhotep was a great man, and deserves to be remembered better than he is, but he was not great enough to force so sweeping a reform upon a people so conservative as the Egyptians. It was not only too sweeping: it was also too complicated, for there were two distinct parts to it, the theological and the political. Perhaps Amenhotep might have done better with the theological part if he had not failed so badly with the political part. Even so, his failure was very largely due to external circumstances, quite beyond his control. The Hittites, who were rising to power in the country north and east of Palestine, observed his difficulties at home and chose the time to raid his frontiers. The ensuing war went badly and was very expensive, and presently Amenhotep was heavily in debt. This, of course, made an excellent opening for his opponents at home, and he died in the end with the reputation of a bad Pharaoh.

But there must have been many Egyptians among the more intelligent minority who appreciated his virtues and understood his aims, and not a few of them must have belonged to the court circle, for it is hard to imagine even a great King launching such tremendous innovations without some support near at hand. No doubt there were survivors of this faction into the day of Moses, and it is natural to assume that he came under their influence more or less. At all events, he carried away from Egypt a strong opinion that one god was enough for any people, and that concentrating upon the worship of that one god was a very good way to foster a national spirit and put down schism and particularism.

3

When Moses got the Jewish exiles back to what they now regarded as their own country the first big task before him as a practical statesman was to revise and codify their laws, most of which were already ancient and seem to have been common to all the other Semitic tribes of the region and time. There could have been nothing novel, surely, about their prohibitions of murder, theft, adultery, trespass and false witness, nor is it likely that the third and fourth of the ten laws that Moses formulated, forbidding blasphemy and establishing the Sabbath, were his inventions, for both had been in force in Babylonia for at least a thousand years, and the whole of Asia Minor then lay within the Babylonian orbit. The people of Babylonia, who were very pious, had an immense corps of priests to serve their large hierarchy of gods, and where priests are numerous and powerful blasphemy is always under heavy penalties. As for the Sabbath, they had been keeping it for many centuries, first once every lunar month and then four times a month.

Thus the Fourth Commandment, like the Third, could not have been news to the Jews when Moses wrote it down, and told them that Yahweh had ordered them to keep it. Nor could they have been surprised by anything in the Fifth, Sixth, Seventh, Eighth, Ninth and Tenth. If they were astonished at all, it must have been by the First and Second. These, in all probability, were Moses's only actual contributions to their tribal jurisprudence, and both showed a strong Egyptian flavor. Nothing like them was known in Babylon, but the ideas in them had been discussed in Egypt since the time of Amenhotep, and probably since days long before him. According to the most competent scholars, the probable form of the First Commandment, as Moses, acting as amanuensis for Yahweh, wrote it on two tablets of stone, was simply " I, Yahweh, am thy god." And the Second ran " Thou shalt have no other gods." Here was the idea of Amenhotep in brief, with Yahweh substituted for Aton. One people, one god.

There are other unmistakable echoes of the Egyptian captivity in both of the two versions of the Decalogue in the Old Testament (Exodus xx, 2–17, and Deuteronomy v, 6–21). Each starts off with Yahweh announcing sonorously, " I am the Lord thy God, which have brought thee out of the land of Egypt, out of the house of bondage "; and in each there follows, in the Second Commandment, a denunciation of the image-worship that Amenhotep had tried to put down in his dominion. But there the two versions begin to differ, with that of Deuteronomy showing the stronger Egyptian color. Not only does it lay a double stress, in the Fourth Commandment, upon the obligation to let servants rest on the Sabbath, thus recalling the burdens of servitude in Egypt: there is also the curious and apparently quite irrational statement that the Sabbath was instituted in remembrance of the Jews' deliverance from that servitude. I quote Deuteronomy v, 15:

And remember that thou wast a servant in the land of Egypt, and that the Lord thy God brought thee out thence through a mighty hand and by a stretched out arm: therefore the Lord thy God commanded thee to keep the Sabbath day.

It seems plain enough that this version of the Fourth Commandment is later than the version in Exodus, which says nothing about the deliverance from Egypt, but ordains the observance of the Sabbath on the ground that " in six days the Lord made Heaven and earth, the sea, and all that in them is, and rested the seventh day: wherefore the Lord blessed the sabbath day, and hallowed it." Here in Exodus we are plainly facing, not Egypt but pre-Exilic Babylon, and though there is no mention of the Sabbath in the Old Testament until after the escape from Egypt there is every reason to believe that the Jews borrowed it from the

Babylonians, long before any of them crossed the Pharaoh's border, and that they learned about the creation of the world in seven days from the same source. Thus the Exodus form of the Decalogue must be regarded as older than the one given in Deuteronomy, which could not have preceded the Egyptian Captivity. The latter came into fashion in Moses's day, and seems to have remained popular for centuries afterward, but the former was revived as the memory of the Captivity began to fade. Exodus is now preferred by Jews and Christians, Catholics and Protestants alike, and it is the version that boys and girls always memorize in Sunday-schools.

4

When the Jews, having begun to emerge from their primitive barbarism, found it necessary to draw up a code more refined and urbane than the Decalogue, they again borrowed from the Babylonians. This body of laws is given twice in the Old Testament, both times in Exodus. It is called by scholars the Covenant Code, for the shorter of the two forms of it opens with Yahweh ordering the Jews to drive " the Amorite, and the Canaanite, and the Hittite, and the Perizzite, and the Hivite, and the Jebusite " out of the land, and with his promise, if they will agree to refrain from going " a-whoring after the gods " of these neighbors, to take them under his assiduous protection, and to do such marvels for them " as have not been done in all the earth, nor in any nation " — nor, of course, by any other god. The Covenant Code first appears in the Old Testament immediately following the Ten Commandments (Exodus XXI *et seq.*), but it is much later in date, and most authorities believe that it was formulated in the Ninth Century B.C. or maybe a bit earlier.

Its close resemblance to the code of the great King Hammurabi, who had reigned in Babylon more than a thousand years before and was still the Justinian of Babylonian law, is apparent at a glance. It is Babylonian law, indeed, almost as unmistakably as the American Bill of Rights is English law. All of the classical offenses against the social order — murder, theft, false witness, trespass and adultery — are dealt with in the two documents from the same point of view, and in most cases the penalties provided for them are substantially identical. The differences only mark the natural variations between the necessities of a numerous and highly complex society, with wide gradations of rank and wealth, and those of a relatively small and simple one. Thus the Jews did not copy Hammurabi's minute regulations for the pay and punishment of physicians, for professional physicians were scarcely known among them, but in general they followed their Babylonian model very closely, and in particular they seem to have got from it their concepts of the citizen's duty to his neighbors, and of his responsibility for the remoter consequences of his acts. Both codes provide for the composition of unwitting injuries by what amount to merely civil damages, but both assume that negligence has an element of intent in it, and provide heavy penalties for the man guilty of it. Both, *inter alia,* punish injuries to a pregnant woman, whether she miscarries or not, both make a husbandman responsible for damages done by his cattle, and both require him to cultivate his fields in such a way that his neighbor's rights will not be invaded.

The two codes are compared at length and with great learning by Dr. J. M. Powis Smith in " The Origin and History of Hebrew Law." Their differences are almost as interesting as their likenesses. For example, there is no parallel in the Code of Hammurabi to the mandate of the Covenant Code that " he that sacrificeth unto any god, save unto the Lord only, he shall be utterly destroyed." Here the Jews are found arraying their somewhat recent and still more or less shaky tribal monotheism against the expansive polytheism of the Babylonians, but it would be imprudent to argue that the fact shows them to have been the more civilized. On the whole, however, the comparison of one code with the other does them no discredit. They were considerably less lenient with slaves than the Babylonians, but on the other hand they gave more attention to harmonizing the domestic relations, and already had a lofty concept of marital and filial re-

sponsibility. Following the Covenant Code in Exodus
there is a sort of supplement, mainly without any statement of secular penalties. Dr. Smith believes that it is
of later date than the rest of the code. There is in it,
he says, " a deep sympathy with the poor and a distinct effort to protect their interests." The Jew is forbidden to " vex a stranger, or oppress him: for ye
were strangers in the land of Egypt." He may not take
interest upon the debt of a poor man, or keep the raiment of a debtor in pledge beyond the setting of the
sun. If he finds an ox or an ass gone astray he must
return it to its owner. If he builds a fire and it spreads
to his neighbor's field he must make good the loss. He
is forbidden to spread false reports, or " to be an
unrighteous witness," or to " wrest the judgment of
the poor." If, seeking gain, he should undertake to
" afflict any widow, or fatherless child, . . . my
wrath," says Yahweh ferociously, " shall wax hot, and
I will kill you with the sword; and your wives shall be
widows, and your children fatherless."

Altogether, the Covenant Code, despite its occasional outbursts of savagery, reflects an advancing
civilization. The Jews, in the days when it was formulated, were gradually ceasing to be herdsmen and
farmers, and becoming town-dwellers. The time was
one of increasing commercial activity all over the
Eastern Mediterranean, and they shared the general
prosperity. Though they were never to match their
restless northern neighbors, the Phœnicians, as trad-

ers, their geographical situation brought them many chances to drive profitable bargains, and gave them their first taste of riches. As guardians of the caravan routes from Egypt to Mesopotamia they became so important, indeed, that one of the Pharaohs was glad to give their great King, Solomon, a wife from among his own daughters. On the other side they were cultivated politely by Hiram, King of Tyre (which is to say, of Phœnicia), who sent Solomon " cedar trees out of Lebanon " for the Temple, and artificers to fashion them. And from far-away Sheba, which seems to have been in Arabia, came the lovely queen whose portrait still adorns every illustrated Bible, to feast her eyes on David's gorgeous son, and to " commune with him of all that was in her heart." One need not take too gravely the tales of Solomon's magnificence which adorn the Books of Chronicles and Kings, but it must be manifest that he was very far from poor, and that the rest of the Jews of his time were also considerably richer than their fathers had ever been. There was little natural wealth in Palestine, and its people, unlike the Phœnicians and Egyptians, seldom went abroad, at least of their own free will, but they appear to have been very well paid for keeping the trade lines open across their home territory. They thus accumulated money rapidly — so rapidly that their more powerful neighbors were soon viewing it with a covetous eye, and laying plans to seize it.

With this wealth came its inevitable accompaniment: the appearance of classes of men who managed to exist by their wits, and on the labors of the general — public functionaries, lawyers, theologians, literati, and other such prehensile and well-fed ornaments of a rising *Kultur*. Moses, in his day, had been the whole literature of Israel, not to say its whole politics and its whole theology, but after Solomon's time, *c.* 975 B.C., each of these sciences had multitudes of practitioners, some of whom became so eminent that they are remembered even now. The tendency of Christian mythology is to think of the *Geistliche* among them as men of an austere and even ascetic habit, but that error is due, I suspect, to confusing them with the far later John the Baptist, whose raiment of camel's hair and diet of locusts and wild honey are familiar to every Sunday-school scholar. As a matter of fact, the principal prophets of the Old Testament, save maybe Micah, were men of dignity and consequence, and their poverty had only the formal reality of that of a bishop, a Y.M.C.A. magnate or a Harvard professor today. They moved in the best contemporary society, and on the whole they shared its point of view.

The celebrated Jeremiah was the son of a priest (which is to say, of a man of secure position and considerable influence), and the familiar of Kings, and when his noisy defeatism in time of war got him into prison he was delivered by royal mandate. Ezekiel, though he began life " among briars and thorns . . . and scorpions," the ancient Jewish equivalents of the American log-cabin, lived to have a house of his own in Jerusalem, and it was large enough for him to invite all the elders of Judah to come to see him, and he was of enough circumstance for them to come. Daniel, who had been an infant prodigy, " well favored, skillful in all wisdom, cunning in knowledge, and understanding science," was brought up during the Babylonian Captivity at the cost of King Nebuchadnezzar, and in his later years became first president of the Babylonian chamber of princes " in the reign of Darius, and in the reign of Cyrus the Persian." Amos, though he claimed to be, in origin, " a herdsman and a gatherer of sycamore fruit," seems to have become in the course of time a fat canon of the King's chapel, and was accused by a colleague, Amaziah, of yielding rather too much to the luxuriousness of the post. Of the other prophets we know little, but in that little there is nothing to indicate that they were ever on short commons. The Jews, in truth, always treated their theologians handsomely. The trade, of course, had its peculiar hazards, then as now, and a prophet who raised too much goose-flesh was likely to be scourged, jailed or chased into the desert, but it was apparently a settled custom to pardon him before he was seriously damaged. The first of the craft to be put to death was John the Baptist, and he was butchered, not by his fellow Jews, but by the invading Romans.

5

It is a mistake to think that the Jews were the only ancient people to produce great prophets. As a matter of fact, moral and theological exhortation was a favorite theme of the early literati all over Asia, and the Gautama Buddha in India, Confucius in China and Zoroaster in Persia produced masterpieces which are fully worthy to be set beside anything in the Old Testament, and in some ways are far superior. All of these works date from the Eighth, Seventh and Sixth Centuries B.C., which is to say, from the precise time which saw Isaiah, Ezekiel, Hosea, Amos, Jeremiah and Habakkuk in practice among the Jews. The age was one of great change in the world, and of a general overhauling of ideas. Mighty empires were falling and new ones were arising from their ruins. Heroes who still loom large in history heaved and blundered across the stage — Sargon, Sennacherib, Nebuchadnezzar, Tiglath-pileser III, Asshurbanipal, Cyrus, Darius I, and many another. Carthage rose and flourished. Greece approached its Golden Age. Rome began to be heard of. The great empire of Babylonia reached the most dazzling magnificence ever seen on earth, whether before or since, and then succumbed to the Persians. There was a steady development of international trade, both by conquest and by peaceful penetration. The Egyptians raided the territory of

[161]

the Babylonians, and the Babylonians raided the territory of the Egyptians, and meanwhile the enterprising Phœnicians planted their factories in the territories of both. Soon after the opening of the Sixth Century the Phœnicians forced Necho, Pharaoh of Egypt, to let them trade up the Nile valley, and a few years later, if we are to believe Herodotus, they circumnavigated Africa. By the year 500 B.C. the Mediterranean was studded with Greek colonies, trade routes were open across Europe to the Baltic, and the long arms of the Greek, Persian and Phœnician merchants stretched out to India, Arabia and even to what is now Russia.

The Jews, because of their geographical position, met the full impact of this bewildering change and turmoil. Since their land was coveted by all the great Powers, its neutrality was constantly violated, and they were dragged into many dangerous alliances and costly wars. In the year 608 B.C. the aforesaid Pharaoh Necho crossed their territory in an effort to wrest what remained of the ancient Hittite empire from the conquering Babylonians, and the Jewish King, Josiah, foolishly took the field against him. On the ancient battleground of Megiddo, fought over so often in the past, Josiah was beaten and slain, and Necho reduced Judah to the estate of an Egyptian protectorate. But five years later the celebrated Nebuchadnezzar emerged from Babylonia with fresh armies, and gobbled " all that pertained to the king of Egypt . . .

from the river of Egypt unto the river Euphrates,"
including, of course, the entire homeland of the Jews.
They had helped him against Necho, but he remembered the fact so little that he was presently deposing
and imprisoning their new King, Jehoiachin, besieg-
ing and sacking Jerusalem, and carrying off thousands
of their people to captivity in Babylon. Thereafter
Judah was under the Babylonian hoof, with Jehoiachin's uncle, Zedekiah, to govern as Nebuchadnezzar's
agent.

The Jews thought that this arrangement was bad
enough, but worse was to come. For Zedekiah, growing
ambitious, attempted to restore the independence of
their country, with himself as King, and the result
was that Nebuchadnezzar returned, sacked Jerusalem
again, burned the Temple, hauled away all the mov-
able property of the people, including " the pots, and
the shovels, and the snuffers, and the spoons," blinded
Zedekiah, slew his sons, and started back to Babylon
with most of the Jews who had escaped the first time.
Thus began the never-to-be-forgotten Babylonian Exile, which pious Jews still mourn at the Wailing Wall
in Jerusalem, and, indeed, wherever and whenever
they meet to address themselves to Yahweh. How many
of them were rounded up and carried off is not certain, but it must have been a large number, for during
the fifty years of their absence the Southern half of
Palestine was almost a desert, peopled mainly by
wandering shepherds. Nearly all the leading men of

Judah, both clerical and lay, were corralled in Babylon, where, after some preliminary oppressions, they
were well treated, and prospered greatly, at the same
time maintaining the True Faith very sedulously. The
few who eluded Nebuchadnezzar's catchpolls fled to
Egypt, and there launched that melancholy scattering
or Diaspora which has marked the history of the Jews
ever since.

It goes without saying that these stupendous misfortunes made excellent hunting for the professors of
moral theology. In happy and easy times the warnings
and exhortations of such sages are but little regarded,
and this had been the case in Judah from the time of
Solomon to the time of Josiah. Solomon, as every
schoolboy knows, had 700 wives and 300 concubines,
and " loved many strange women "; worse, he allowed
these ladies to " turn away his heart after other gods,"
and we learn from I Kings XI that he once forsook
Yahweh for " Ashtoreth the goddess of the Zidonians
and Milcom the abomination of the Ammonites," and
even went to the length of building " a high place "
for " Chemosh the abomination of Moab " and
" Molech the abomination of the Children of Ammon."
His successors seem to have gone further and worse.
The accounts of them in the Old Testament commonly
close with the sad words: " and he did that which was
evil in the sight of the Lord, according to all that his
fathers had done." Like prince, like people. The Jews

remained, in theory, monotheists, and the great Temple at Jerusalem was dedicated to Yahweh alone, but most of them took their obligations to him very lightly, and forgot a large part of his Law. All during the days of prosperity their prophets howled warnings of the wrath to come, but these warnings, though they seem to have been heard very courteously, were not heeded.

But with the decline in the national fortunes came better days for moral science and its luminaries, and the Babylonian Captivity was a veritable windfall for them. The busiest and most cocksure of the whole fraternity, Jeremiah, lived through both sieges of Jerusalem, and devoted himself assiduously to prophesying disasters of the most appalling character. Indeed, his professional delight, as a herald of the divine wrath, in the cruel woes of his people so carried him away that he actually composed an ode in praise of their enemy, Nebuchadnezzar. During the reign of the unfortunate Josiah the priests of the Temple, eager to turn those woes to account and very probably inspired by Jeremiah himself, announced the " discovery " of a new code of laws in their archives, longer and more drastic than the benign Covenant Code. Josiah, badly scared, ordered this new code — which is now called the Deuteronomic — to be put into force at once, but during the interval of relative peace between the two Babylonian raids the Jews let it fall into more or less neglect, and Jeremiah was moved to issue a violent manifesto in favor of it, calling down curses upon " the man that obeyeth [it] not."

The second siege of Jerusalem gave him his long-awaited chance to alarm and harrow the populace on a really large scale, and he did it to such effect that the commanders of the defending army complained to King Zedekiah, saying, " We beseech thee, let this man be put to death, for he weakeneth the hands of the men of war that remain in this city, and the hands of all the people." The harassed Zedekiah handed him over and he was cast into a dungeon, but soon he was released at the solicitation of Ebed-melech, a eunuch and an Egyptian, and hence a suspicious character. When the Babylonians finally took and sacked Jerusalem, and the captive Jews started off on their long, hot and lugubrious march across the deserts of Syria to Babylon, Jeremiah was treated with significant consideration by the conquerors, and given his choice between going along or remaining in Palestine. He decided to remain, but some time later he was carried off to Egypt by a party of fugitives who had decided to settle there. He continued his horrible prophecies in Egypt, and there is a legend that his fellow Jews finally got so fed up with him that they stoned him to death.

6

The Yahweh whose authority stood behind the Mosaic Decalogue, the Covenant Code and the New Deuteronomic Code had begun his career as an humble rain-god in the desert, and seems to have been shared at the start, though under different names, by all the Semitic tribes. The chief god of any nomadic people is almost sure to be a rain-god, for water is the thing they mainly seek in their wanderings, and hence the thing they mainly pray for. To the Amorites, the next-door neighbors of the Jews, Yahweh was known as Adad or Hadad, but he remained unchanged otherwise. He was, at the start, a somewhat humble personage, as gods go, but when the Jews began to grow in numbers and wealth he took on a rising dignity and largely extended his powers. It seems likely that at one time he was thought of, at least by the country Jews, as the husband of the ancient Earth Mother, and that the two had a considerable family of children — thunder-gods, calf-gods, river-gods, lamb-gods, grove-gods and so on. But this is uncertain. What is better established is that, as more and more Jews settled in towns and began to be aware of the great world, Yahweh was quietly amalgamated with various more sophisticated gods, including especially the splendiferous sun-god, El, who was worshipped under various names all over the Near East, from the Tigris to the Nile. This amalgamation, of course, proceeded fastest in the Northern part of Palestine, where the Jews were in close contact with the Phœnicians and other relatively civilized peoples, and had the best chance to observe El's popularity in the great capitals. He survives somewhat vaguely in the Old Testament under the confusing plural name of Elohim.

The Southern Jews, despite their frequent crazes for strange gods, remained much more faithful to Yahweh, taking one year with another, than their Northern brothers, and preferred him to the sleek and cultured El to the end. One of their main complaints against the Northerners, in fact, was that the latter, yielding to the enchantments of the Phœnician and Babylonian cities, were always forgetting the simple-hearted, horny-handed protector of their fathers, and going " whoring " after more elegant and fashionable divinities, male and female. This difference helped to foment the incessant quarrels between the two halves of the Jewish people, and lay at the bottom of more than one of the civil wars that rural Judah waged against urban Israel, and Israel against Judah. The citified Israelities, I suspect, usually had the better of the argument, theologically speaking, for it was obviously in accord with the advancing civilization of the time to dress up the bucolic Yahweh in the shining garments of the more seemly El, but on the other hand it must be admitted that Yahweh unadorned was very much more Jewish than Yahweh-

El, and hence very much more honest. It is he and not El who survives as the tribal god of the Jews today, and it is he who is followed and adored by the overwhelming majority of Christians and Mohammedans. His moral system is the one we always think of when we think of Jewish Law.

I have spoken of Judah as rural, but that is not quite accurate. The fact is that Southern Palestine, including most of Israel below the battlefield of Megiddo, was not so much a region of peaceful farms as it was a frontier country, wild and even woolly. We are not going to understand the Jews of Judah if we think of them as peasants, or even as small shepherds; they were essentially herdsmen of the open range, inhabiting an often contested and generally lawless country, and they showed all the familiar characters of such adventurers. There has never lived a more warlike people. Though they were small in numbers, and had too little money to buy elaborate military equipment or to hire mercenaries, they never hesitated to tackle even the most formidable Powers of antiquity. Once, as I have just noted, they flung themselves upon the mighty Pharaoh Necho and his Egyptian host, and twice they had the effrontery to challenge the irresistible Nebuchadnezzar, whose armies had beaten off Babylonian rebels and Median invaders, and laid Tyre under siege for thirteen years, and were later on to penetrate to the heart of Egypt.

There was to come a time, indeed, when they would

actually venture to fight the Roman Empire — an enterprise almost comparable to an attack on the United States by Nevada or Arizona. This last most fantastic exploit was destined to finish them as a nation, but while they survived they were truly indomitable fellows, and neither the dull hopelessness of the city proletariat nor the yet more dull helplessness of the tamed yokel was in them. To find a parallel for them in modern times one must think of an amalgam of the Mormons, the Boers of South Africa, and the Irish. Their descendants, dispersed through the world, have changed somewhat, but probably not much. Though they are now largely city men, they still show some of the fierce enterprise and independence of the frontiersman; and nearly all the qualities which their critics complain of in them are identical with the harsh, impatient, cocksure, truculent and alas, somewhat uncouth qualities which won the American West.

If all this be borne in mind it becomes easier to understand the Old Testament, whether as history or as a code of morals. It is, as we have it, a discordant hodge-podge of two distinct sets of documents, thrown together without much skill by the rabbis of the Diaspora, and especially by the rabbis of Alexandria. The one half consists of the relatively naïve speculations and memoranda of the Southern cattlemen and bushwhackers: the other half is made up of Northern refinements which begin by being more Babylonian than Jewish, and end by being more Greek than either. It is the former that constitutes the essential Jewish record, and from it flowers the ethical heritage of Western man. The three codes that we have so far examined — the Decalogue, the Covenant Code and the Deuteronomic — contain the whole essence of the Jewish Law, and it is obviously the law of a simple, hearty, rough and innocent people, willing to accept the dictata of their prophets without any bandying or subtleties, and eager only to get through their devoirs to Yahweh without too much trouble.

Despite the plain traces in it of Babylonian and Egyptian influence, there are two ways in which it differs radically from any code ever heard of in Babylon or Egypt. The first is that it contains no hint of that division of the people into social classes which was so nearly universal in the ancient world, with some told off for power and privilege and the rest doomed to an humble place. The second is that there is very little in it about Kings, priests and other such functionaries, and that that little is mainly devoted to limiting their prerogatives. The Jews, like any frontiersmen, were incurable individualists and, in the best sense, democrats. It was not until two centuries after Moses that they had any King at all, and at no time in their history were they ever really brought to heel by their priests. Their Law was thus relatively simple, and, despite the lingering in it of many barbaric taboos, notably logical and sensible. What it ordained, over and above the immemorial imperatives, was no more than a decent neighborliness, a cheerful acceptance of the so-called social contract. All Jews were equal before Yahweh, and even strangers, if they were well-disposed, shared in his grace. When Jesus, answering the Pharisee lawyer at the door of the Temple, said that the second most solemn commandment was " Thou shalt love thy neighbor as thyself," he was merely repeating what had been standing in the Deuteronomic Code for seven hundred years.

In their later days the Jews were to develop other and more " civilized " codes — some emanating from the sophisticated canon lawyers of the Phœnicianized and Hellenized North, and others confected by the prophets who came back from Babylon after the Exile, their professional emulation aroused by the metaphysical subtleties and enlightened self-interest of the Babylonian priests. These supplemental codes are described sufficiently by the names that scholars have given to them — the Holiness Code, the Priestly Code, and so on. They are full of sacerdotal artificialities, and it is not surprising to hear that, in large part, the Jews of the last two thousand years have disregarded them. In reading the Old Testament one finds it almost as easy to separate the original Law from these hollow bravura pieces of the Jewish decadence as it is to separate the honest, hairy-chested, simple-minded, loud-roaring, sentimental, somewhat vain and wholly human Yahweh of the Southern frontier from the remote and polished Elohim of the recusant North, and the gaseous and *Goy*-ish Logos of the Alexandrine rabbis.

It is a great mistake to think of the Jews as a notably religious people. In the Middle Ages, after they began to be knocked about in Europe, there was an unhealthy flowering among them of that text-chopping, hugger-mugger piety which always flourishes in mean streets, and it survives today, accompanied by the inevitable personal untidiness, among the more stupid fugitives from the Russian pale. But the Jews of Western Europe threw it off as they accumulated civic rights, and so returned to the more rational devotions of their forefathers. Those forefathers, compared to the immensely pious Egyptians and Babylonians, took their faith very lightly, and did not permit it to burden them with too many duties or too large an expense. In this they were rather like the Greeks and Romans, who never had any organized priesthoods, and were generally of a tolerant and skeptical order of mind.

There is little mention in the Old Testament of great virtuosi of virtue; it is filled, rather, with the exploits of bold and spectacular sinners. The Jews never formulated the concept of a saint, and there were no genuine ascetics among them. Even their prophets, as I have shown, were commonly men of easy circumstances and a taste for affairs, with far more of the Church of England bishop in them than of either the Trappist monk or the Methodist parson. If a Jew of unusually tender conscience, overcome by a sense of his recreancy to Yahweh, began to feel that he ought to do something about it, he took the vow of a Nazarite and went into the desert for eight days of meditation, during which he had to let his beard grow and to abstain from wine, but was otherwise free to do pretty much as he pleased. The rules for Nazarites set forth in Numbers vi suggest very strongly that, in many cases, this retreat was simply a convenient regimen for drunkards: certainly it is difficult, on any other theory, to account for the exhaustive list of forbidden beverages in vi, 3. In any case, the Nazarite returned to society after his eight days, and was welcomed with a shave and a stoup of wine.

Pious parents could also dedicate their children to the Nazaritish vocation, apparently for life, but the obligations of these involuntary devotees were very loose, and it is to be assumed from Amos ii, 12, that it was not hard to induce them to eat, drink and be merry. The celibate and vegetarian Essenes of Jesus's time were probably simply Nazarites of unusual austerity, and He Himself, because of His counsel of poverty and humility, was mistaken for a member of the sect (Matthew ii, 23). The Nazarites, by that time, had degenerated into a small and despised body, chiefly resident along the desolate shores of the Dead Sea, and to the metropolitan Jews of

Jerusalem they appeared as repulsive and as ridiculous as a Holy Roller now appears to a High Church Episcopalian of Long Island. The more ignorant of the Jewish cockneys, yielding to what philologians know as the law of Hobson-Jobson, confused Nazarite and Nazarene, to the damage of the folk of Nazareth, a small village in far-away Galilee. It was thus that Nazareth became, to the Jerusalem wits, what we now call a joke town, and it is on this ground that we must explain the silly taunt of Nathanael in John I, 46, otherwise so inexplicable.

7

The question as to how and why the Jews, a small and far from important people, managed to inflict their moral system upon the whole Western world, and with it a large part of their theological system, is one that has puzzled scholars for a great many years. It bristles with difficulties, and down to quite recent times they appeared to be so formidable that most Christian authorities were content to beg the question by saying that God must have been behind the business. Its issue then became a proof of the divine power and wisdom, and so a beautiful circle was closed, and in it the professors of apologetics disported with loud hallelujahs. Even today there is no explanation that has general assent, and some of the scholars who have wrestled with the problem believe that it will probably go unsolved forevermore. Nevertheless, it is still possible, by examining the record without theological bias, to get some light upon it.

The first thing to be remembered is that the constant effort of the great Powers of antiquity to seize the Jews' homeland, beginning in Jacob's time, at the very dawn of their history as an organized people, and going on with scarcely a halt until the fall of Jerusalem in 70 A.D., scattered large numbers of them from end to end of the Levantine world, and thus gave them an excellent chance to spread their ideas. They were not often voluntary travelers, but they were very often fugitives and exiles, and in that character they naturally cherished their memories of the homeland with resolute devotion, and especially their memories of the glorious myths and other consoling arcana that they had learned at their mothers' knees. As exiles, again, they commonly came into contact, not with the more enlightened men among their captors, but with the simpler folk of the lower orders — soldiers, petty functionaries, and so on — and on such levels they found willing hearers for their marvelous tales about the powers of Yahweh and the wonders of his Law. In Babylon, during the Captivity, they carried on a vigorous campaign for Judaism, and made not a few converts. So everywhere else. An intensely self-assertive and truculent people, as indeed all frontiersmen are, they preached whenever it was impossible for them to fight, and even when they were free to fight they commonly did some preaching too. Perhaps if fortune had been more kind to them, and they had ever realized those dreams of empire which enchanted them between invasions, they would have gradually abandoned the Law, or, at all events, greatly modified it. But as misfortunes piled upon them they clung to it with desperate fidelity, and cried it up to whoever would listen to them.

Such listeners must have been especially easy to find during the last centuries of the Jewish commonwealth, for the whole Eastern Mediterranean world was then in violent ferment, and every novelty, whatever its origin, got an eager hearing from the common people. There was a prophet in operation at every street-corner, and all sorts of strange religions were being hawked. What was happening we can now see clearly, with the perspective of the centuries to help us: the old Asiatic system was falling to pieces. That system was based upon absolute monarchy, and under it the individual citizen had no rights whatever, at least as we understand the word today. He often enjoyed substantial privileges, and the government over him was sincerely concerned about his welfare, but in the strict sense he had no rights, and was little more at best than the well-treated slave of the King. He had no hand in making the laws he was forced to obey, and save by the royal favor there was no way for him to rise above the status to which he had been born. This system prevailed in the world for many cen-

[177]

turies, and on the whole it worked very well. Under it the foundation stones of civilization were laid, and the majority of men were content. We owe it a great deal more than we are wont to acknowledge. As Dr. James Henry Breasted reminds us in " The Conquest of Civilization," the culture of which it was the kernel and crown gave us the first architecture in stone, the first poetry, the first history, the first science, and the first efficient government. It gave us the art of writing and the calendar. It gave us the wheel and the arch.

But there came inevitably a time when it ceased to meet the growing needs of mankind. It was too rigid for progress beyond a certain point, and that point had been reached. The King was an impediment to every further advance, for he was thought of as a sort of god, and hence could do no wrong. If he happened to be honest and intelligent, well and good, but if he happened to be stupid and knavish, which was much more likely, he became almost *ex officio* the enemy of every enlightened and reflective man. Such men, it appears, gradually increased in the world. There are dim traces of them in the Babylon of Hammurabi, and they must have been fairly numerous in Egypt in the days before and after Amenhotep. In the Fifth and Sixth Centuries B.C., from Athens as a base, they began to make their influence felt from end to end of the Near East, and there was a widespread movement for the revision of all the old con-

[178]

cepts, both spiritual and secular, philosophical and practical.

What the scattered and cock-sure Jews had to offer fell in with the temper of the time. It was simple, and, for those days, excitingly rational. They had demoted the King to the estate of a mere human being, they had curbed their priests, always eager for power, and they had reduced all the warring and insatiable gods to one, and that one a very simple and even transparent fellow. Moreover, their harsh and somewhat impudent individualism, born of their bitter struggle for existence in what was then, in its way, the Wild West of the world, had caused them to wipe out the old distinctions between man and man, to make all men equal before God, to rid the ancient counsels of conduct of their accumulated extravagances and artificialities, and to bring them into the compass of a few almost self-evident maxims, based mainly on common decency and common sense. If the Jews had been a greater people, and had developed their characteristic ideas notwithstanding, those ideas would have made progress in the world long before John the Baptist and Jesus began to preach them. As it was, they had to wait until the Asiatic system collapsed altogether, and the common man got his chance at last under the eagles of the democratic and iconoclastic Romans.

When that chance came the Jews were admirably situated for seizing it. At home the Law had been

formalized and made odious by the scribes and Pharisees anathematized by Jesus (Matthew xxiii, 2–33),
but it remained a living thing in the Diaspora, and
especially at Alexandria, where there was a large
colony of Jews, including many men of learning.
These exiles, disregarding the Pharisees' insistence
that the Law should not be translated, put it into
Greek, and began to amalgamate it with Greek ethical
speculation. Greece itself, by that time, was already
in decay. Its philosophers had served as shock troops
in the uprising against the Asiatic system, and may
be said to have died on the field. But their ideas survived in Egypt, and there such enlightened Jews as
Philo Judæus tried to reconcile them with the Law.
A convenient bridge was afforded by the so-called
Wisdom literature, which survives in the Old Testament in the Books of Job and Ecclesiastes and parts
of Proverbs, and in the Apocrypha. This Wisdom
literature seems to have been inspired by Babylonian
and Egyptian rather than by Greek influences, for
it was eminently practical and without metaphysical
subtlety, but nevertheless it was close enough to Greek
ways of thought to be interesting to men training in
the Greek schools. It unquestionably had a great
deal to do with founding the Gnostic movement, which
arose before Christianity, and, as the denunciations
of Paul well demonstrate, was for some time a formidable rival to it.

But in the long run the Law got the better of the

combat. For one thing, the Law was much simpler than anything either Greeks or Gnostics had to offer, and less burdened by dilemmas and contradictions. For another thing, it offered a higher degree of personal solace and assurance, and to far larger classes and numbers of men. And for a third thing, and most important of all, its exposition was couched, not in the smart, brittle terms of the academies, but in the lush imagery of the loveliest poetry ever heard of in the world. Many of the systems arrayed against it, whether at home in Palestine, at Alexandria, or around the rim of the Ægean, were more plausible both philosophically and theologically, but, amalgamated gradually with the great fairy tale called Christianity, it prevailed against all of them in the end, for it had something that none of them could match, and that was a gorgeous and overwhelming beauty. Try to imagine two evangelists on a street-corner in Corinth or Ephesus, one expounding the Nicomachean Ethics or a homily by Valentinus the Gnostic, and the other reciting the Sermon on the Mount or the Twenty-third Psalm: certainly it is not hard to guess which would fetch the greater audience of troubled and seeking men.

That the Jews were such incomparable poets is probably due as much to an accident of their environment as to any excess of native genius. All the Semitic peoples run to a kind of eloquence which divides itself naturally into strophes, and Emerson noted long ago that among the Arabs poetry and religion constitute the whole of culture. The Jews were more fortunate than the other tribes of Shem's body in that they came into close contact with the civilization of the ancient East without ever being quite a part of it. Poetry, the most elemental of the arts, always flourishes best under such circumstances: it has a power to move even the most civilized men, but it is produced most copiously by men who are still more or less barbaric — the Greeks of the early wanderings, the Italians of the day when Guelph wrestled with Ghibelline, the English of the Elizabethan epoch. As genuine culture comes in, poets give way to artists of a greater subtlety, practising more formal and exigent arts. There were none of any noticeable merit in Greece after the rise of the philosophers; the last of the royal line, Euripides, died when Socrates was a boy of nine. The French ceased to write poetry with the Seventeenth Century; it could not survive the *éclaircissement* of the century following, which went further in France, and left more lasting effects, than anywhere else. In the same way the Germans abandoned poetry, save as a minor intellectual diversion, as they emerged from their multitudinous Main Streets and began to gather into a homogeneous and first-rate nation: it is, indeed, no wonder that Goethe was hostile to the War of Liberation, for its issue was destined to ruin his trade.

That the Egyptians, back in the twilight of their

history, had poets of high potency is very probable, for traces of their work are to be found in the Egyptian sacred literature of later days, but those poets were forgotten when architects, astronomers and other such practitioners of the more civilized arts and crafts began to appear, as they always do when a culture takes on subtlety and complexity, and the average man fades into the background, and his simple tastes with him. That the Babylonians also had great poets is manifest, for the Jews went to Babylon for many of their most dazzling ideas — the Fall of Man, the Tower of Babel, the Flood, and so on. But Babylonian poetry fell into a decline as the civilization of the Euphrates valley moved toward its stormy peaks, and the masterpieces of its poets survive only in a few hymns and legends, and in the borrowings of the Jews, as the huge polemic of Gnosticism survives only the quotations of its Christian critics.

In our own day and age we are seeing history repeat itself, and perhaps for the hundredth time. There has been no really vital poetry in Europe for a century past, save only in England, a country which, by European standards, has never quite attained to the highest levels of culture. But of late even England has ceased to produce poets of any genuine passion and potency — perhaps a sufficient answer to the alarmists who argue that the civilization of Europe is about to be swallowed up by a new barbarism. These gentlemen would be more persuasive if they exhibited a better acquaintance with *Kulturgeschichte*. Let them show that a dithyrambist comparable to the author of the Song of Songs has appeared of late anywhere in the Western World, and it will be time enough to talk about the liquidation of the Modern Age.

8

The Jews, as I have tried to make evident, were not a notably pious people; compared to the Babylonians and the Egyptians, indeed, they were extremely mercurial in their devotions. That Yahweh, in the long run, prevailed against all his rivals was due partly to the powerful and continuing influence of Moses (whose lightest *obiter dictum* remains law in Jewry after nearly 3200 years), and partly to the ingratiating charm and plausibility of Yahweh himself. The Jews' fidelity to him, such as it was, was plainly beneficial to them, for it saved them the ruinous expense which went with the complicated heavenly hierarchies of Babylon and Egypt, it discouraged the pretension of professional priests (who plainly had no better access to Yahweh, considering his easy simplicity and approachability, than any pious head of a house), and it tended to restrain that natural contentiousness which, if it had not been opposed by a common cultus, might have led them into a civil war to the death.

But the domination of Yahweh also carried serious disadvantages, and one of them was that it dissuaded the Jews from really free speculation on the great riddles of faith and works. Their ethical theory, though it could be modified from time to time by both interior criticism and outside influence, was fundamentally a closed system, for it was based wholly upon the will of their god. In order to make any substantial change in it a revolution was necessary, and in theology revolutions do not come very often. So the Jews, despite their occasional dalliance with heresy, kept the Mosaic Decalogue at the center of their scheme of right and wrong through all the vicissitudes of their history. A great deal, to be sure, was added to it, but what was added never challenged the underlying postulates — that Yahweh was the sole judge of human conduct, that he could not err, and that his views could be and had been ascertained. The Wisdom literature gave evidence that there were Jews who harbored uneasy doubts about these postulates, but they constituted only a small minority of not too reputable intellectuals, and their writings never had any serious influence upon the official doctrine. The chief surviving ornaments of the Wisdom literature, namely, the Book of Job and that of the anonymous Preacher, both close with abject recantations, and fulsome promises to question the jurisprudence of Yahweh no more. The rest of Jewish skepticism faded into the twilight of the Apocrypha, or was forgotten altogether. What was needed, before any honestly realistic examination of ethical ideas could be undertaken, was a clearing off of gods. This was achieved, not by the Jews, but by the Greeks.

The early Greeks were also frontiersmen, but they differed from the Jews in two important particulars. In the first place, they were not the heirs of desert nomads but appear to have descended, at least in part, from the great race that flourished in the Ægean archipelago for four thousand years, and built up there a civilization plausibly comparable to those of the Nile and Euphrates valleys. And in the second place, they were stimulated at frequent intervals, once they were established on the mainland, by powerful invasions from the barbarian wilderness of the North, and showed in consequence, even in the earliest recorded times, the peculiar qualities of restlessness, of iconoclastic enterprise, of wide and dramatic variability that always go with the mixture of virile stocks. Palestine, of course, was invaded too, but its situation was such that an invader who came in at one end usually kept on until he was out at the other, leaving no marks of his passing save a series of burned villages and a host of grieving widows. But when the Ionians, Achæans, Dorians and their like came sweeping down upon the Hellenic peninsula they were hauled up by the sea, and many of them settled down and amalgamated with the peoples they found in the country. Where those earlier peoples came from is still disputed among archeologists, but it seems overwhelmingly probable that a large part of them were colonists from Crete, the center of the Ægean culture. They soon forgot their allegiance, and at some time between the years 1500 and 1100 B.C. they appear to have joined their conquerors in conquering their old homeland, and in fact ruining it. That catastrophe, in its effects upon Western civilization, was almost as disastrous as the fall of the Roman Empire nearly two thousand years later. But like the fall of the Roman Empire, it was not quite complete, for the seeds of civilization survived in Greece as they were to survive in Italy, and in the Fifth Century B.C., there was a Renaissance at Athens that was as magnificent as the Renaissance which began in the Fifteenth Century of our era at Florence.

It was preceded by a long era of commercial expansion, during which the Greeks gradually pushed the Phœnicians out of the Eastern Mediterranean, challenged the Carthaginians in Sicily, and converted all the old outposts of the Cretan dominion, both in the Ægean archipelago and along the adjacent shores of the Ægean sea, into Greek colonies. Athens, in the years of peace following the last barbarian invasion, swarmed with adventurers, and became a thoroughly cosmopolitan city. It not only traded with all parts of the Mediterranean shore; its merchants also penetrated into Egypt, into Asia Minor, and to the line of the Danube. In general, its people showed a strong likeness to the brisk but somewhat raffish fellows who crowded California in the days following 1849, just as the Jews resembled the Mormons who were erecting a Zion in the wilderness at the same time. Every discontented young man in the Mediterranean world, from the pillars of Hercules to the remotest reaches of Syria, must have heard of the town and its brilliant and easy life, and a great many such rebels and misfits made their way to it and were admitted to citizenship. Some of them attained to the highest eminence. Thus Thales, the legendary father of Greek philosophy, was a native of Melitus, on the coast of Asia Minor; Hippocrates, the father of Greek medicine, came from the island of Cos, off the same coast; and Aristotle was born in Thrace. Of the Seven Wise Men, only Solon was born in Athens, and only three of the other six were born on the Greek mainland.

In its early days Athens was far more a camp than a city, and hence overwhelmingly masculine in population, but in the course of time women began to filter in from the murky regions to the northward — not a few of them, I daresay, ladies of easy amiability, like so many of their sisters of early California — , and by the Seventh Century B.C. there was a more or less homogeneous citizenry, and a Greek national spirit began to show itself. That national spirit, for those days, was extraordinarily tolerant and free from chauvinism. The Athenians, like the peoples of the other nascent city-states, were ardent patriots and looked upon whatever was Greek as superior to whatever was not Greek, but they showed little desire to force their

cherished superiorities upon anyone else. Their colonies were loosely governed, and at home they continued to welcome newcomers. In particular, they welcomed newcomers with something strange to tell. In
their mild climate it was pleasant to go downtown of
a morning to hear the latest news and nonsense out of
far places, and their considerable prosperity gave
many of them leisure for the exercise. Thus ideas
came pouring in from near and far — Egypt, Mesopotamia, Persia, the Western Mediterranean, even India
and China — , and were eagerly assimilated and completely naturalized, so that the Western World, in the
centuries to come, could not distinguish readily between those that were native and those that were
imported, but set them all down as Greek.

The lower classes, of course, whether free or slave,
hadn't much time for ideas, but as the plutocracy of
trade and planting developed into something resembling an aristocracy it took to them as a kind of sport,
as other aristocracies have taken to war and the chase,
jobbery and vice. " Young men of the richer classes
who have not much to do," said Socrates in his
Apology, " come about me of their own accord: they
like to hear me cross-examine men who say this or
that, and sometimes they imitate me, and do the cross-
examining themselves." Socrates himself came to grief
by his plainspeaking, but that was most unusual, and
may be laid to his incautiousness in making fun of the
government and so alarming the politicians. In gen-

eral, there was more free speech in Athens than anywhere else on earth. Even so late as the First Century
of our era, as Luke tells us in Acts xvii, 21, " all the
Athenians, and strangers which were there, spent their
time in nothing else but either to tell or to hear some
new thing." Thus it was that Paul was free to preach
his gospel on Mars Hill itself, the official forum of the
city, and to denounce the massed philosophers of
Athens to their faces as ignorant and superstitious. It
was almost as if Mary Baker G. Eddy or Bishop Cannon had been invited to address the Convocation of
Oxford or the College of Cardinals.

9

The inevitable result of all this was a general skepticism, on both the ghostly and the earthly planes. It
showed itself in the theatre, where the writers of the
Old Comedy, led by Aristophanes, poked ribald fun
at everything sacred and profane, and it entered into
daily life and thinking. The educated Greek began to
take pride, not in what he had the stamina to believe,
but in the fact that he was too enlightened to believe
very much. Religion fell out of fashion, and the gods
degenerated into mere literary characters, somewhat
larger in scale than men, but also a great deal less
civilized. In the field of morals the sanction of revelation naturally went with them, and along with it a
good part of the sanction of instinct, leaving only the

sanction of reason. This was a tremendous advance, for hitherto the sanction of reason had got relatively little attention in the world, and from the Jews and other peoples of the nearer East it had got scarcely any. It was Greeks who brought it forward, and showed what great ethical riches were concealed in it, and though they may have got some important suggestions at the start from Egypt, and even from India and China, they developed its possibilities in their own way, and brought a great deal more to the business than they borrowed.

Unfortunately, the enterprise carried its dangers, and they fell into them. It was fatally easy for an ingenious man, trained in the current dialectic, to reduce the whole inquiry to a puerile logic-chopping, with conclusions revolting not only to a sound philosophy but also to the primary instincts of man. That is what was done by many of the sages who performed upon the street-corners of Athens, usually under the name of Sophists, *i.e.*, wise men, clever fellows. Their skill at argumentation was appreciated, but when they essayed to prove, for example, that murder was morally right, and that the common prejudice against adultery was mistaken and even insane, and that a thief was a better man than an honest citizen, many an honest citizen was upset, and began to talk vaguely about calling in the police. Socrates was such a Sophist — the most glorious of the clan, of course, but still a Sophist. No one can read his arguments as they

are reported in the dialogues of Plato without noticing how often he was carried away by his own virtuosity and indulged himself in mere intellectual
gymnastics. When the body corresponding to a grand
jury in Athens brought in a true bill against him there
were a number of far-fetched and even absurd charges
in it, but the charge that he was fond of " making
the worse appear the better cause " was certainly
plausible enough. Socrates, of course, had his categorical imperatives too — indeed, his faith in wisdom,
and in its corollaries, justice, courage and temperance, was almost as complete and touching as Jesus's
faith in love — but, as we see by the case of old
Cephalus in the Republic, his only too frequent dis-
plays of mere smartness had an unhappy way of
puzzling plain men and making them uneasy. When
he brought that smartness to bear against their homely
logic it seemed to them that he was arguing against
the moral postulates they defended, and so it is not
surprising that he became a suspicious character, and
was ripe for a legal lynching.

But even so he succumbed by a very close vote,
and, as I have said, politics entered into it. In general, the Sophists were unmolested, and even the most
extreme skeptics among them were permitted to perform publicly without hindrance. The attack upon their
nihilism, when it came at last, did not come from
plain men but from other philosophers. The chief of
these were Plato and Aristotle. Plato was the pupil,

reporter and biographer of Socrates, and Aristotle was the pupil of Plato, and both owed large debts to the old man, but in their own writings they departed very widely from his programme. In the field of ethics he had been essentially an analyst, picking moral concepts to pieces and trying to find out what gave them plausibility, but Plato and Aristotle were synthesists, and it is from their bold attempts to put together comprehensive and workable moral systems that the Greek element in the ethical thinking of to-day mainly derives. They differed radically in method. Plato, apparently despairing of the men of his place and time, tried to formulate an ideal system of laws and customs for an ideal commonwealth of admittedly impossible citizens. But Aristotle, at once more hopeful and more practical, was content to frame an inductive system based on the actual wonts and wants of decent men, with maybe a few embellishments suggested by their more common failings.

Plato, I confess, seems to me to have been enormously inferior to Aristotle, and on all counts. He was primarily a metaphysician, and hence found it difficult to distinguish clearly between actual ideas and mere words. Fundamentally a religious man, full of thirst for communion with a God he tried in vain to imagine, he provided a great deal of delectable fodder for the early Christian theologians, and it pleased them only the more after it had been half digested for them by his mystical follower, Plotinus.

Out of his Symposium, a banal discussion of the
nature of love, they got what they conceived to be
philosophical support for the simple " Love one another " of Jesus, conveniently forgetting, or perhaps
not noticing, that the Symposium was, in fact, a huge
apology for homosexuality. And out of his Republic,
and especially out of the fifth book thereof, they got
support for that blowsy communism which was the
chief product of their firm belief that the world would
soon be coming to an end. On deeper levels his speculations also provided them with grist for their mill.
The theology of Jesus was too artless for the intellectual snobs who soon appeared among them, and even
that of Paul, though it showed a great deal of Greek
admixture, was still not pretentious enough to stand
up, in their eyes, against such stately rivals as Gnosticism, so they levied upon the murkier, vaguer parts
of Plato's writings, and came close, at one time, to
converting him into a Christian sage. This process
began in the Third Century and reached its climax
with St. Augustine (354–430), who had been a disciple of Plotinus before he became a Christian.

But after the year 500 Aristotle also began to be
heard of in Christendom, and in the long run he was
destined to surpass Plato. At the start, unfortunately,
only one of his works, the Organon, a treatise on
logic, was generally known, and that one only in part,
but in the course of time the Arabs, who had long been
his partisans, began to supply the West with transla-

tions (into Latin from the Arabic, from the Syriac, from the Greek!) of his other works, and by 1250 he was widely studied and esteemed. His impact upon the thinking of the time was terrific. Logician, biologist, anthropologist, physicist, political scientist, economist, moralist, psychologist and critic of the arts, he seemed to the contemporary mind to cover the whole range of secular knowledge, and when it became apparent that this secular knowledge stood at sharp variance, at important points, with the somewhat naïve and misty theology of the medieval church, and the need of reconciling the two became pressing, he was studied with great diligence. The fruit of the attempt at reconciliation was Thomas Aquinas's Summa Theologiæ, the chief text of the Catholic philosophy ever since. It is, in many ways, more Aristotelian than Christian, and so it is a massive monument to Aristotle's persuasiveness, but his success with Thomas was to cost him dear later on, when, in rapid succession, the Renaissance, the Reformation and the Eighteenth Century Enlightenment dealt heavy blows at the Catholic position. It was not until after a fourth and even more profound revolution, the one led by Darwin, that it began to be noticed that this extraordinary Greek of the Fourth Century B.C. had first formulated that conception of a dynamic universe which was to become the fundamental postulate of all modern physical science, and of most modern ethical and theological theory.

His ideas in the field of moral speculation are mainly to be found in his Nicomachean Ethics, a book apparently named in honor of his son, Nicomachus, who fell in battle as a young man. It is the first formal and full-length treatise on morals that we have any record of, and it retains its vitality and interest undiminished to this day, more than two thousand years after it was written; indeed, there are very few later works on the subject that are so well ordered, so clear and sensible, or so plausible. One has got into it no more than a few pages before one begins to realize that Aristotle was essentially a modern man — that his way of facing problems, his definitions of true and false, his views of man and the universe, all his habits of thought, were substantially our own. The book shows no trace of that oriental disdain for mere fact which makes the Bible so gorgeous as poetry and so puerile as philosophy. In his very first chapter Aristotle rejects all *a priori* dogmatizing as unworthy a serious inquirer, and pleads for an inductive study of ethical phenomena, which is to say, for a logical progress from the known to the unknown. He notes that all human activity, whatever its character, is grounded upon some concept of a good to be obtained, and he argues rightly that the central problem of ethics is to separate the goods that are real from those that are only apparent, and to provide convincing reasons for the pursuit of the former. In brief, he contends that this central problem is the problem of values — and in what follows the values that he advocates are almost identical with those that would be advocated by any rational man of today. The highest of them all is wisdom, and its highest manifestation, to borrow a phrase from his latest translator, Harris Rackham, is " the disinterested contemplation of truth." Perhaps contemplation is not quite the word; furtherance would be better. No man of the ancient world would have applauded more gladly the closing words of Huxley's " Science and Morals ": " The foundation of morality is to have done, once and for all, with lying."

But Aristotle was careful to avoid the error of Socrates, who made wisdom almost the whole of virtue, and the attainment of truth the one goal of humanity. He had room in his system for many other goods — indeed, he was enough of the eclectic to discuss soberly some very modest ones, and along with them some far from fearsome evils, including stinginess, shabbiness and vulgarity. His final position, wandering in these mazes, was an eclecticism of another sort: he advocated, not a rigid code of conduct, admitting of no gradations and no exceptions, but a *via media*, a reasonable middle path, a golden mean. There were few virtues, he concluded, which, carried to excess, did not become private curses and public nuisances, and there were few vices that did not have some good in them at bottom. He was for steering between the two extremes — not, to be sure, an easy course, but still the one that most sensible men manage somehow to follow. He was all for temperance, moderation, reasonableness. The ideal world that he envisioned was not peopled by angels, nor even by philosophers, but by healthy, decent, intelligent, fair-minded, honorable men, not greatly differing from the best Greeks of his own time.

But among them, of course, there were gradations, and Aristotle had his own criteria of the good, the better and the best. In the fourth book of the Nicomachean Ethics one finds his memorable portrait of the great-souled or high-minded man. It has been compared very often to the description of " a citizen of Zion " in the Fifteenth Psalm, but a glance is sufficient to show large differences, all of them in favor of Aristotle. The Psalmist is content to praise a good neighbor and an honest man, but the Stagirite tries to trace the moral lineaments of one who is all that, but is in addition something of a scholar and altogether a gentleman. " Honor and dishonor," he says, " are the matters about which the high-minded man is especially concerned. . . . He is open both in love and in hate, for dissembling shows timidity. . . . He cares more for the truth than for what people think. . . . He is fond of conferring benefits but ashamed to receive them. . . . He does not bear grudges, for it is not a mark of greatness of soul to remember things against people. . . . He is haughty toward men of position and fortune, but courteous toward those of modest station. . . . He does not run into danger, and is not a lover of it, but he will face it in a great cause, and be ready to die. . . . He is not prone to admiration. . . . He is no gossip. . . . He will not cry out or ask for help. . . . He likes to own beautiful things, and he prefers those that are useless to those that are useful, for the former better show his independence of spirit." As Mr. Rackham well says, much of this " stands in striking contrast with Christian ethics "; nevertheless, it is almost identical with that concept of the gentleman " which supplies, or used to supply, an important part of the English race with its working religion." The really civilized man of today, indeed, is instinctively, though perhaps unconsciously, an Aristotelian in his canons of conduct. The Jewish code is labored into him in youth, but as he comes to maturity he turns inevitably into a Greek.

10

Aristotle was the last of the royal line of Athenian sages. There were men of wisdom after him, as there were heroes before Agamemnon, but there was never to be another of his immense breadth of interest and magnificent originality. As moralist, of course, he did not invent any new virtues — indeed, all of those that he praised must have been known in the world for many centuries, and not only among the Greeks — , but he at least laid new foundations, solid both in psychology and in logic, under the best of them, and he brought them all together in a coherent and plausible system. His immediate influence was very great, and his ideas are to be found in the tenets of all three of the schools which were to dominate Greek and Roman ethical thought for the next five hundred years. The Stoics rejected his common sense view of virtue and vice as essentially relative values, and would have none of his golden mean, but their austere ideal of conduct showed plain traces of his high-minded man. In the same way the Epicureans, though they rejected his distinction between " good absolutely " and " good for somebody," yet followed him in most of his appraisements of concrete goods, and balanced pleasure against pain in a thoroughly Aristotelian manner. Finally, the Skeptics, though the very nature of their system made it impossible for them to borrow his ethical categories, yet learned a great deal about method from him, and were at one with him in his belief that knowledge and virtue, like life itself, were not static but dynamic, not closed systems but eternal unfoldings.

Next to the Nicomachean Ethics the most notable treatise on morals that the Classical Age produced was the volume of Meditations by Marcus Aurelius Antoninus, Emperor of Rome and Stoic philosopher (161–180). Marcus had a busy time of it as Emperor. He had scarcely come to the office before he faced barbarian uprisings in Germany, in Britain and along the Danube, and later on he was forced to take the field against Roman rebels in Asia Minor. Meanwhile, there were floods, earthquakes and pestilence at home. But in the midst of all these excursions and alarms, he still found time to apply himself diligently to his books, and to set down his reflections about man and the universe. The Meditations were written in Greek, which many of the educated Romans of the time affected, and most of the writing seems to have been done in the field. The work is thus disconnected and indeed somewhat chaotic, but its first section, probably written after the rest, shows a relatively clear design and contains the essence of the whole. It is in the form of a catalogue of thanks to the persons who had been most influential in forming the author's ideas and character, beginning with his grandfather and including various teachers and friends.

To each name is appended a list of the virtues its bearer inculcated. Marcus by no means suggests that he is a practitioner of all these virtues, but we know that he was notable for at least some of them, and they show, at any rate, what an educated, intelligent and highly civilized Roman of the time esteemed. The first that he mentions, kindliness, and the second, good temper, might have been borrowed from Paul's admonitions in the twelfth chapter of Romans, but in a little while we are hearing of virtues that would have been quite beyond Paul's imagination, for example, " to become familiar with philosophy, . . . not to pose ostentatiously as a moral athlete, . . . to look to nothing, not even for a moment, save reason alone, . . . to possess great learning and make no parade of it, . . . to stand free of superstition about the gods." Most of these spacious and noble resolutions Paul would have rejected as heathenish and against Yahweh, as indeed they were. The ethical concepts underlying them had been formulated in the Greece of the great days, and now, in the Second Century of our era, they were cherished by all civilized Romans, but during the next century they began to decline as Rome itself declined, and by the end of the Fourth Century they were to succumb to the *Sklavmoral* of Christianity, by ignorance out of despair, and to pass from the mind of Western man for more than a thousand years.

IV

Its Christian Form

1

Like all other revealed religions, Christianity suffers more or less from an unhappy disparity between the ethical scheme it inculcates and the reported practices of its chief celestial luminaries. Gods always seem to be worse than men, and that is certainly true of the Yahweh of the Old Testament. One finds him engaging in all sorts of bloody brutalities, some of them so revolting that even his own agents, recording them as in duty bound, are moved to something not far from moral indignation. His colleague and *alter ego*, El, always appears as a more seemly fellow, but even El would hardly pass as a good citizen today. As for their Son, he is credited in the New Testament with a long series of acts and sayings that give grave concern to earnest Christians, and still resist the effort of the most ingenious exegetes to explain them away.

Open the Old Testament at random, and you will quickly find examples of Yahweh's generally bad character. In II Kings ii, 24, he sends two she-bears to assault and devour forty-two little children because they have poked some childish fun at the bald head of his prophet, Elisha. In Numbers XXXI he condemns 32,000 innocent Midianite virgins to violation at the hands of his victorious Jewish army, and ear-marks thirty-two for the special use of his high-priest, Eleazar. In Deuteronomy VII, 1–2, he instructs the Jews to massacre the Hittites, the Girgashites, the Amorites, the Canaanites, the Perizzites, the Hivites and the Jebusites, and forbids them " to shew mercy unto them." In II Samuel XXIV he first inspires David to take a census of the Jews, and then proposes to punish it as if it were a crime, and with the utmost fury. With ghoulish cruelty he gives David a choice of penalties: " shall seven years of famine come unto thee in thy land? or wilt thou flee three months before thine enemies, while they pursue thee? or that there be three days' pestilence in thy land? " David chooses the pestilence as the probable least of these afflictions, and is appalled a week later when his agents report that 70,000 Jews have succumbed — more than 5%, according to his census returns, of the whole population of Palestine. His horror, indeed, is so vast that he is moved to remonstrate, saying, " Lo, I have sinned, and I have done wickedly: but these sheep, what have they done? " The answer is not recorded, but the inspired chronicler adds that Yahweh " repented him of the evil."

His occasions for repentance were frequent in those days, for when he was not engaged in such wholesale atrocities he recreated himself with lesser peccadilloes, some of them showing a loutish humor. In Numbers xxi, 6, we find him giving the Jews a great scare by turning snakes loose upon them, and then advising them maliciously to get rid of the nuisance by setting " a serpent of brass upon a pole " and looking at it hard. In Exodus iv he has an unseemly brawl with Moses, and gives him a severe beating. In Genesis xxxii he condescends to a rough-and-tumble wrestling match with Jacob, and throws the poor man's thigh out of joint. In Genesis xxi, 1, he visits Sarah, the wife of Abraham, very mysteriously, and leaves her with child, and in I Samuel he performs a like office for Hannah, the wife of Elkanah. It is commonly argued by Jewish and Christian exegetes that these visits did not involve adultery, but only some sort of gynecological procedure, for both women had been sterile hitherto. But what, then, of the like episode described in Matthew i, 18? Certainly there is no hint that Mary was sterile, and certainly it is plain that her husband, Joseph, viewed the business with grave suspicion and proposed to " put her away privily " as unchaste. Indeed, it took an angel's visit to convince him that Yahweh, in the form of the Holy Ghost, had not done him an unforgivable wrong. The list of divine misdemeanors might be lengthened considerably. In the New Testament Yahweh begins to show a certain elegance, even in his crimes, but in the Old he is frankly a rough character. " He reeks," says Joseph Wheless in " Is It God's

Word? ", " with the blood of murders unnumbered, and is personally a murderer and assassin, by stealth and treachery; a pitiless monster of bloody vengeance; a relentless persecutor of guilty and innocent alike; the most rageful and terrifying bully and terrorist; a synonym for partiality and injustice; a vain braggart; a false promiser; an arrant and shameless liar."

Most curious of all, considering the stress that both Jewish and Christian ethics lay upon the idea of brotherhood, is Yahweh's immense and implacable antipathy to his colleagues in the Great Beyond. The first two of his Ten Commandments, as everyone knows, are drastic prohibitions of any truck with them, and his most appalling penalties are reserved for that offense. In his Second Commandment he goes to the length of threatening to visit the punishment for it " upon the children unto the third and fourth generation," and in almost countless other passages he dwells upon it with great anger. The thing to be remarked here is that, to the Jews, the rival gods they were thus forbidden to patronize were anything but imaginary; on the contrary, they were felt to be very real, and their potency was dreaded. What is more, Yahweh himself appears to have accepted their reality, for his spokesmen represent him more than once as claiming suzerainty over them, or threatening to do injury to them. The word gods, in the plural, occurs in the Authorized Version of the Old Testament more than eighty times, and if the original text were fol-

lowed literally it would occur much oftener. Sometimes, of course, it is used without any apparent acceptance of its transcendental significance, just as we
use it in speaking of the divinities of savages, but at
other times it plainly connotes celestial beings whose
existence is not doubted.

Thus in Exodus XII, 12, Yahweh threatens to " pass
through the land of Egypt this night " and " execute
judgment against all the gods of Egypt," and in Numbers XXXIII, 4, we are informed that this judgment
was duly executed. In Deuteronomy, Joshua, II
Chronicles, the Psalms and Daniel, Yahweh is spoken
of as the god of gods, and in Zephaniah II, 11, he is
said to be ready to " famish " all the others, whatever
that may mean. It is always implicit that these gods,
like Yahweh himself, can work formidable magic,
and their autonomy as moral agents is categorically
admitted in Genesis III, 5. At times, to be sure, they
seem to be confused with their own idols, but that is
not often, and in Deuteronomy VII, 25, and XII, 3, the
distinction is made plain. But Yahweh, though he thus
admits their existence and their powers, never shows
any brotherly feeling for them, such as he so often
orders the Jews to have for one another, and for
strangers; indeed, he is never so much as polite to
them. His conduct toward them is boorish, egocentric
and even megalomaniacal, and we are told in II
Samuel VII, 23, that his motive in wreaking " judgment " upon those who flourished in Egypt, and in

hauling the Jews out of their orbit, was simply a
desire to " make him a name " and get " a people to
himself."

" As nations improve," says Georg Christoph Lich-
tenberg in his *Gedenkbuch*, " so do their gods." That
was surely the case with Yahweh. Starting out upon
his career of world conquest as the blatant ruffian I
have just described, he became, after the Babylonian
Captivity had civilized the Jews, a far more urbane
and seemly fellow, and when, six hundred years later,
he fell heir to Christianity, he began to take on something of the elegance of the Greek Logos and something of the humility and kindliness of Jesus. The
Greek and Roman gods suffered a parallel refining,
until in the end they became, on the one hand, mere
actors in an edifying comedy, suitable for the pious
entertainment of the proletariat, and on the other
hand, a series of metaphysical abstractions, compre-
hended by philosophers but by no one else. The effort
of the early theologians to fit such abstractions into
the homely Christian scheme of things is painfully dis-
played in the Gospel of John, where for the first time
Yahweh becomes the Word (i, 1). A bit later, in the
First Epistle ascribed to the same author, we hear
that he is love (iv, 8). But there is no sign of this God
of love in the Old Testament. Six times Yahweh is
described therein as merciful, and once as " rich in
mercy," but far more often his name is coupled with
the adjectives high, mighty, powerful, fearful, ter-

rible, and glorious. Above all, he is described as jealous and vengeful, both in his dealings with men and in his dealings with other gods. The last word of the Old Testament (Authorized Version) is " curse."

The sorry experience of mankind proves that his punishments and reprisals, if they be actually rational by his own logic and not mere evidences of a savage delight in suffering, go to lengths quite beyond human understanding. Only too often the afflictions that he lavishes upon his votaries have no visible excuse or aim. That this fact was noticed by the more reflective Jews is made plain by the Book of Job, which seems to date from the Fifth Century B.C., soon after the return from Babylon, and probably had a Babylonian prototype. Job is by definition a " perfect and upright " man, who fears Yahweh and eschews evil, and yet Yahweh permits Satan to defame him, and heaps upon him an intolerable burden of woe. His sufferings, if they were not set forth in some of the most gorgeous poetry in the whole Bible, would seem almost comic: he is played with as a cat plays with a mouse. And to what end? To the sole end, so far as one can make out, that Yahweh may have an excuse to boast grandiloquently of his own omnipotence. Translate the tremendous strophes that come out of " the whirlwind " into common speech, and they are reduced to this: " I want to prove to you, Job, that you are only a poor worm. I, Yahweh, really have all power in my hands. I set the stars in their courses, and made the winds, the rains and ' the hoary frost of heaven,' and I can also give you a fine set of boils, and kill all your sheep, and send hypocritical comforters to afflict you, and in general make you miserable and ridiculous. I trust that you are duly impressed, and that the lesson is not lost upon your neighbors."

Here we encounter what theologians call the problem of evil — in Silas K. Hocking's phrase, " the skeleton in the closet of the universe." It has afflicted them ever since their science first emerged from the shadows of legerdemain. Their answers have been various, and usually far from plausible. The Zoroastrians, more logical than the rest, imagine two separate and antagonistic divine powers, Ormuzd and Ahriman, the first told off to do good on earth and the latter to do evil. It is admitted that Ahriman, so far, seems to have the better of it, but it is promised that Ormuzd, in the long run, will overcome and destroy him, and this promise is at the center of the Zoroastrian religion. Some of the early Christian theologians sought to dispose of the problem in the same way, to wit, by setting up Satan as a sort of rival to Yahweh, and ascribing all human wretchedness to him. But the difficulty with this device is that it destroys Yahweh's omnipotence, and in fact makes him a futile and even ludicrous figure, so the powers of Satan have had to be prudently circumscribed, and he is now, according to the best theological thought, no more than a transient rebel against Yahweh's superior authority, whose prerogative is confined to tempting the faithful to sin, and who may be overcome in that field by prayer and exorcism. In the article on evil in the Catholic Encyclopedia, he is not mentioned at all: a significant omission. Instead, we are asked to get whatever consolation we may out of Paul's agnostic exclamation: " How unsearchable are his [Yahweh's] judgments, and his ways past finding out! " (Romans XI, 33), and St. Augustine's not too ingenious begging of the question: " God judged it better to bring good out of evil than to suffer no evil to exist."

The great Catholic philosopher, Thomas Aquinas, grappled with the matter at length, but came to conclusions that are far from convincing. Indeed, his primary assumption — that all the tribulations of man are the penal consequences of violations of the known laws of Yahweh, either by the individual, or, in the form of what is called Original Sin, by Adam — goes counter to common human experience, and is refuted by the salient case of Job. Nor does making it help his subsequent argument, for he is immediately confronted by another hard question: Why did not Yahweh, being omniscient, see that his creatures would abuse the gift of free will, and why, if he foresaw the abuse, did he not surround the gift with appropriate safeguards, or withhold it altogether? Aquinas's answer is that it was impossible for Yahweh to permit any act of his own to be determined or conditioned by the known or probable acts of inferior agents — that so doing (I quote a recent and authoritative gloss) would have "abdicated his essential supremacy" and been "utterly inconceivable." I pass on this explanation for what it is worth: to me it seems suspiciously like nonsense. Nor is there any comfort in the Thomist corollary that the matter is really no one's business save Yahweh's — that he created the world, not for the good of man, but for his own private pleasure. A pleasure it must have been to confect war, poverty, politics, and cancer!

In Moslemism the problem of evil is less difficult than in Christianity, for there is not so much disparity between what it represents Yahweh as doing and what it calls upon the faithful to do. The latter are not bidden to love their enemies but to smite them, and there are no oppressive rules about distinguishing between foes in arms and innocent bystanders. The Moslem theory is that the latter, if they happen to be true believers, will go straight to Paradise and are thus not to be pitied, and that no calamity can be too great for those who doubt. This view of the matter, I suspect, has had a great deal to do with the superior success of Moslemism wherever it has come into competition with Christianity, say in Africa. The savage may not be much of a philosopher, but he is at least a pretty good practical logician. Christianity, as it is preached to him, strikes him as standing in unendurable contempt of the known facts of life, and when he is led into the mazes of its mythology he is sure to note the conflict between the reported conduct of Yahweh and the conduct ordained for Christians. Here even his own theologies, including the most primitive, are less at odds with common sense. The moral schemes that go with them may not be very refined, but they are at least binding on the tribal divinities as well as upon human beings. Nor are savages the only catechumens who afflict Yahweh's propagandists with embarrassing questions. They are heard in American Sunday-schools quite as often as in African jungles, and are just as hard to answer in one place as in the other.

2

The chief peculiarities of the Christian moral system, as it is distinguished from the Jewish and Greek schemes on which it is mainly based, issue from an error in fact made by Jesus, and not abandoned by His followers until it was too late to rectify its consequences. That was the error of supposing that the end of the world was at hand. It is common today for Christian theologians to deny that Jesus believed this, but the texts in point are too explicit to be argued away. They report a conversation with the Disciples in the vicinity of Cæsarea Philippi, and appear in all three of the Synoptic Gospels. In each the prophecy is preceded by the memorable Charge, most familiar as it is given in Matthew:

If any man will come after me, let him deny himself, and take up his cross, and follow me.

For whosoever will save his life shall lose it: and whosoever will lose his life for my sake shall find it.

For what is a man profited, if he shall gain the whole world, and lose his own soul? or what shall a man give in exchange for his soul?

Following comes the flat statement: " There be some standing here, which shall not taste of death, till they see the Son of man coming in his kingdom " (XVI, 28). In Luke IX, 27, the last clause is changed to " till they see the kingdom of God " and in Mark IX, 1, to " till they have seen the kingdom of God come with power," but these variations are plainly immaterial. In Mark XIII, 30, there is the additional assurance that " this generation shall not pass till all these things be done," and in Matthew XXIV, toward the end, the Disciples are commanded to be ready at all times, for people " were eating and drinking, marrying and giving in marriage, until the day that Noe [*i.e.*, Noah] entered into the ark, and knew not until the flood came, and took them all away." In Mark XIII, 32, the Disciples are informed, apparently in response to their natural inquiries, that the precise day and hour " knoweth no man, no, not the angels which are in heaven, neither the Son, but the Father," and there are other cautions to the same purport else-where, but always it is made plain that the time will be in the near future, and in Matthew x the Disciples are sent forth to preach with the assurance that it " is at hand," and ordered to " provide neither gold, nor silver, nor brass in your purses; nor scrip for your journey, neither two coats, neither shoes," and so on. They take all this so seriously that in Mark x one finds two of them, James and John, coming to Jesus privately, and trying to induce Him to promise them seats directly beside Him on the Day of Doom. There is no hint that they expect to die first; on the contrary, it is plain that they are thinking of an event to come in their lifetime, and very soon.

But the denunciation, trial and execution of Jesus seem to have shaken the Disciples' faith in His divine mission, and with it their belief in the cardinal articles of His prophecy, including the imminent end of the world. One of them betrayed Him to the Jewish police, another denied Him, and Matthew tells us (xxviii, 17) that some continued to doubt even when He reap-peared to them after the Crucifixion. According to John, He assured them on His third appearance — " at the sea of Tiberias," seventy-five miles from Jerusalem — that He would certainly return to earth, and bade them " tarry " until then. As a result, " there went this saying abroad among the brethren," that Simon Peter, whom He had chiefly addressed, " should not die." Obviously, this can only mean that the

[215]

Disciples doubted that Jesus would come back to judge the world within the natural lifetime of Simon Peter. They appear to have demanded more light upon the matter, and to have been put off with one of His characteristically cryptic utterances: " If I will that he tarry till I come, what is that to thee? " But as news of the Resurrection spread up and down the Eastern Mediterranean coast, and the first Christian revival got under way, all such doubts were engulfed in a wave of enthusiasm amounting almost to frenzy, and the Disciples, like the rank and file, were ready to believe anything. On the Day of Pentecost, as we learn from Acts ii, they heard a mighty wind roar down from the heavens, saw " cloven tongues as of fire," and began to jabber gibberish in the manner of converts at a Holy Roller camp-meeting. Their preaching to the throngs that crowded about them was thoroughly millennial. They taught that " the last days were at hand," that the appropriate signs and portents were already visible, and that it behooved every prudent man to get rid of his " possessions and goods " and prepare for the reappearance of Jesus, " sitting on the right hand of power and coming in the clouds of heaven " to work the Last Judgment.

Out of all this flowed what the German higher critics call the *Interimsethik,* which is to say, a scheme of stop-gap ethics for the brief interval between an unhappy and hopeless today and a glorious and near tomorrow. It rejected many of the values that mankind had cherished immemorially. Industry, thrift, justice, temperance, and fidelity to family and fatherland were swept away as vain and useless in the premisses, and the new morality counselled instead the giving away of all worldly goods, the abandonment of wife and child, the renunciation of racial and national pride, and the intensive practice of such humble virtues as might be expected to flatter a regal and exacting Yahweh — meekness, self-abasement, patience under injustice, complete chastity, and so on — above all, a simple and grovelling faith. To a large extent this programme was based upon the reported sayings of Jesus, for example, in the Beatitudes, in the denunciation of riches in Mark x, 25 (which so astonished the Disciples), in Matthew vi, 34 ("Take therefore no thought for the morrow"), and in the various categorical prophecies of the early end of the world, already quoted. But there were extensive ratifications by the Disciples in the first days of the infant Church, and many more followed when Paul began his mission. In Thessalonians i he assures his correspondents that "we which are alive and remain shall be caught up together with them in the clouds, to meet the Lord in the air"; in I Corinthians vii and x he gives them warning that "the time is short" and "the ends of the world are come"; and in Philippians iv, 5, he says flatly that "the Lord is at hand." In Romans he returns to the attack, and his famous moral homily in the twelfth chapter thereof is largely an exhortation to the renunciation of worldly values, and to a patient and hopeful resignation to the fast approaching Judgment.

As time passed and it failed to come off there must have been a good deal of murmuring among the faithful, for some of the rigors ordained in preparation for it were not a little onerous. It cost them next to nothing to give away their goods, for most of them were poor, and humility in the face of contumely was natural to them, for they were weak, but no doubt there were many who suffered under Paul's counsel to avoid marriage, and more who found it hard to be " rejoicing in hope, patient in tribulation, and continuing instant in prayer." Their demands for the exact date of their release from these rigors had to be met, and meeting them was not easy. Paul, in his Second Epistle to the Thessalonians, tried to get rid of the question by answering that a great many marvels would have to happen first, including the coming of Antichrist. In this he was supported, though he did not mention it, by Jesus's own prophecy in Mark XIII: " nation shall rise against nation, and kingdom against kingdom: and there shall be earthquakes in divers places, and there shall be famines and troubles." But there must have been many among the faithful who believed that enough woes were already upon the world to justify the immediate commencement of the final catastrophe, and these seem to have been rather pressing in their inquiries. In II Peter III, 8, Simon

Peter is recorded as seeking to put them off by arguing somewhat lamely that " one day is with the Lord
as a thousand years " — an argument that was to be
revived nearly two thousand years later by those
doomed by an unhappy fate to attempt to reconcile
the facts of geology with the cosmogony of Genesis.

It took a long while for hopes in the Second Coming
to die out. There was in them so much consolation for
poor and miserable men, and they were so thoroughly
in accord with the apocalyptic prepossessions of the
time, that they survived long after it must have been
evident to every rational person that Jesus and Paul
had been mistaken. Down through the First Century
there were frequent reports that the great day was at
hand, and after the fall of Jerusalem in the year 70 it
was looked for with new confidence. In the latter part
of the Second Century there was a great revival of
hopes led by one Montanus, a convert to Christianity
from the cult of Cybele, the Great Mother, whom he
had served as a priest in Phrygia. For some unknown
reason Montanus held that the Second Coming would
be in Pepuza, a small town in what is now Turkey,
and thither many of the faithful flocked, to suffer
drought and wait in vain. Later the place designated
was Jerusalem, which was more probable and seems
to have been more persuasive, for Montanus presently
made many converts, including the celebrated Tertullian, the first lawyer of the Church and the author of
the immortal saying, *Credo, quia absurdum* — I be-

lieve because it is absurd. Tertullian was denounced as a heretic, and Montanism began to fade out, but at least one bishop, Cyprian of Carthage, continued to believe in it, and it survived obscurely in some of the remoter backwaters of the East until the Sixth Century, when Justinian finally put it down. The Montanists carried the *Interimsethik* to great extremes. They spurned all worldly goods, refrained from the popular amusements of the time, fasted often and long, frowned upon marriage, and welcomed martyrdom. They produced two women prophets, Maximilla and Priscilla, perhaps the first female divines of flag rank ever heard of in the world. Both claimed to be inspired by the Holy Spirit, which had been joined to the Father and Son but lately, and so did Montanus himself. His preaching was very fiery and alarming, and it was not uncommon for him, when his theme was the impending Judgment, to " fall into a sort of frenzy or ecstasy " and to " rave and babble strange things."

3

The great battle over the nature and attributes of the Trinity, which began toward the close of the Second Century, became so violent during the next hundred years that the theologians of the young Church had little time left to debate the Second Coming, and without doubt most of them were glad to be rid of it. Thus the *Interimsethik* lost much of its force, and the majority of the faithful, led by their pastors, began to show an interest in worldly values. Meanwhile, the Jewish Law, with its burdensome taboos and nationalistic aims, was abandoned as Gentiles made their way to influence in the Church, and the doctrine was invented that all of it was archaic and invalid save the Ten Commandments. The Gnostic sectaries, in fact, rejected the whole Old Testament. In place of these decaying systems there arose a new body of ecclesiastical law, part of it dealing with the duties of the laiety and the rest declaring and determining the prerogatives of the clergy. The latter seems to have interested the theologians of the time more than the former, and by the end of the Second Century they were engaged in a furious controversy over the effort of Victor I, Bishop of Rome, to fix the date of Easter and force all the churches, East and West, to accept it. Each lesser bishop, in his own diocese, made similar attempts to increase his authority, and by the time of the Council at Nicæa, in 325, these pretensions had gone so far that no delegate of less than episcopal dignity was seated, and even the two leaders in the controversy chiefly at issue, Arius and Athanasius, had to content themselves with listening in silence, for the former was only a presbyter and the latter only a deacon. There were plenty of objectors to this aristocratic tendency, and they stood on sound ground, historically speaking, but the venomous debates over the Trinity which went on everywhere and the persecutions which began in the First Century made strong leadership a necessity, and we hear of excommunications and anathemas almost as soon as we hear of bishops.

A moral system shaped by ecclesiastics always shows two salient characters: it lays immense stress upon the virtue of unquestioning faith, and it discovers a special wickedness in acts from which its authors, by virtue of their office, must refrain. The system fashioned by the Early Fathers out of the wreckage of the *Interimsethik* ran true to type. Taking over that covenant with Yahweh which had been the center of the Jewish system, they exaggerated the duty of the believer until it became a slavish and preposterous surrender of will. There was no longer any room left for ethical speculation, nor even for the free functioning of conscience: the only thing to ascertain was what Yahweh ordained. Thus faith in its most naïve sense was elevated to first place among the virtues, and the effort of the Greek philosophers, and specially of the Stoics, to liberate the mind of man was counted as heathenish and even devilish. It was these Stoics who had given the world a rational concept of conscience, and tried to deliver it from supernatural corruptions. The Christians of the first few centuries rejected the idea even when they mouthed the word: their sole touchstone of conduct was the imperious will of Yahweh, as it was revealed from time to time by the expositions and divinations of his appointed agents on earth. Let a man believe without reservation, and he was sure of glory on the Last Day, whether near or far; let him doubt, however politely, and no conceivable secular rectitude could save him from destruction. To this was presently added a parallel and perhaps even more abject surrender to what were accepted as the mandates of Jesus. " Only His disciples," says A. C. McGiffert in " A History of Christian Thought," " only those who acknowledged His messiahship and declared their faith in Him, could hope to share in the blessings of the coming age."

There was, of course, not much true humility here: the early Christians, indeed, were shrinking violets only to the most superficial eye. Their grandiose renunciations had policy in them and demanded an equally grandiose *quid pro quo* — nothing less, in brief, than an eternity of bliss in Paradise, gloating over the agonies of the damned. The homilies of the Christian pastors were largely devoted to limning the delights of this Paradise, and not the least of them was the fact that the happier, more opulent and, above all, better educated and civilized peoples among whom the faithful lived would be deprived of its enchantments. Thus their grovelling before Yahweh, in large part, was no more than a device to gain a vast and unique advantage. They had their eyes fixed ecstatically upon what the immoral I.W.W.'s in the centuries to come were to call, derisively, pie in the sky, and some of their theologians did not hesitate to assure them — for example, Irenæus in his *Adversus hæ-reses*, IV, *c.* 185 — that they would become as gods, with all the high privileges and appurtenances thereto appertaining. This theory survives to our own day in the folk belief (no longer supported by reputable theological opinion) that all true believers, at death, will turn into angels.

Next to the most profound and profuse faith, the virtue held in highest esteem in those days seems to have been chastity. As everyone knows, it had been cried up with almost hysterical eloquence by Paul, who practised it himself, and lamented that so few were as he was. In his Epistle to the Galatians he put " adultery, fornication, uncleanness, lasciviousness " at the head of all sins, even above idolatry and mur-der, and in I Corinthians he actually counselled against lawful marriage, and admitted only reluctantly that it was " better to marry than to burn." To be sure, he allowed bishops and deacons, in I Timothy II, one wife apiece, but those wives had to be " grave " and " so-ber," and it is plain to see that he did not contemplate their use for mere dalliance. With the exception of Clement of Alexandria (*c.* 150–215), who held that marriage was a useful means of afflicting the faithful, and so improving them spiritually, all of the other Christian moralists appear to have followed Paul. Ter-tullian (160–220) was pledged to celibacy by his Mon-tanism, and denounced marriage as next door to for-nication, and St. Gregory of Nyssa (*c.* 375) preached that it was " no part of God's original design that the human race should be continued by sexual union." Though there were many women among the early Christian converts, they and all their sisters were commonly viewed with suspicion. The celebrated Jerome (c. 340–420), the translator of the Bible into Latin, regarded them as " the root of all evil," Tertullian called them " the Devil's gateway," and Augustine (354–430), the real founder of Christian theology as we know it today, expressed his wonder that they had ever been created at all. Even so late as 578 a Council at Auxerre forbade them to take the consecrated bread into their hands, " on account of their impurity."

This, in part, was simply the common opinion of the time, which held women in low esteem, but in part it was probably a reflection of the professional difficulties of the early Christian pastors, who were expected, as clergymen, to practise something at least closely approximating celibacy, and yet were exposed to constant temptation from their female followers. The chastity of a priest, in the Greek world of the first centuries, was as much a part of his technical equipment as his sombre garb and facile smile are today. Even if he served a cult which, on occasion, permitted sexual orgies as a part of its ritual, he was commonly expected to abstain from them himself. This notion that continence belonged especially to the sacerdotal office had come in from the East, and was almost universally accepted in the Mediterranean lands. The

Jews never took it into their moral system, but even to them it seemed somehow proper that a prophet, as opposed to a mere priest, should hold himself aloof from sexual love, and there is every reason to believe that the preaching of Jesus would have been heard less attentively if He had carried a wife on His journeys. So early as *c.* 300 a council held at Elvira in Spain imposed the strictest celibacy on bishops, priests and deacons, and we learn from St. Epiphanius (*c.* 315–403) that in his time a married aspirant could be admitted to holy orders only if he were willing to give up his wife.

But it must have been very hard, at times, for the early bearers of the Word to maintain this chastity, for many of their converts were women of the more ardent and emotional sort, and not infrequently such converts fell in love with them, and proceeded to storm them. How inconvenient such onslaughts could be is amusingly set forth in the Acts of Paul, one of the New Testament Apocrypha. Paul, after his flight from Antioch, went to a little town called Iconium, and there converted a beautiful maiden named Thecla, who was betrothed to one Thamyris. As soon as she was baptized she proposed to renounce Thamyris and follow Paul, and as a result there was a dreadful uproar in the town, and Paul was forced to flee between days, and Thecla narrowly escaped being burned alive. No doubt it was after this experience that Paul formulated the views set forth in I Corinthians VII, 8. Many another holy man must have had the same disquieting experience. The evangelical clergy are under heavy pressure from sirens and vampires to this day, and their frequent succumbings continue to delight the damned. In Apostolic times they faced a world even more ribald than our own, and so it is no wonder that they made a capital virtue of the chastity it enforced upon them, and tried to bring their followers up to the same level of grace. But the thing itself was not their invention. It had been an ingredient of piety in the Near East for centuries.

For the rest, the code of morals that they preached was mainly made up of the peculiar virtues of lowly folk at all times and everywhere. Nietzsche has called it a slave morality, and with plenty of reason. The noble qualities of Aristotle's high-minded man were quite beyond the reach of the early Christians, and even beyond their imagination. Such pride as they had was founded upon the fatuous belief that they would soon be snatched up to Heaven, to lord it over their betters for all eternity; in the common sense, they had next to none. Nor were they capable, in view of their situation, of liberality, of independence, of wisdom, or of any of the higher varieties of courage. They could die for their faith if need be, but what sustained them was not any dignity of soul, but only their hope for a stupendous reward, out of all proportion to their deserving. The moral system that they thus cherished was respectable, but not much more. It was at its best in their first days, when they received it fresh from the hands of Paul. Their later teachers contributed little to it that was new, and nothing that was beautiful. Founded upon the most gorgeous poetry the world has ever seen, Christianity quickly became prosaic and banal. The Early Fathers, after Irenæus, were all predominantly theologians, and thus cared nothing for the sough and sigh of words. They carried on their gory feuds in slipshod Greek and Latin, and seemed to get an actual satisfaction out of writing badly. This was true even of the mighty Augustine, whose " City of God " is almost unreadable. After the Book of Revelation Christianity was doomed to wait thirteen centuries for its next first-rate poet.

The original code of the brethren had to be revised considerably as they got on in the world. It was all well enough for them to be meek so long as the alternative was falling into the hands of the Roman police, and all well enough to be brotherly so long as it could involve no possible condescension, but as the new faith attained to official toleration and then became official itself, and bristling bishops arose to enforce its arcana with loud threats, recalling those of Yahweh, meekness and brotherhood receded into the background, and so did charity. Certainly there was nothing meek or brotherly or charitable about the first Popes, or about the theological bravos who fought to the death at Nicæa in 325. By the middle of the Fourth Century what remained of the Beatitudes was resigned to the care and keeping of special communities of virtuosos of virtue, founded upon Egyptian models and soon scattered over East and West, mainly in remote and uncomfortable places. The Rule of St. Basil was promulgated in 356, and that of St. Benedict a century and a half later. Thus monasticism was born, and there has been a sharp division ever since between the small minority of Christians who really try to follow Jesus, and the great majority who only pass under His name.

This dualism was most marked in the so-called Ages of Faith, when Christianity was triumphant from the Euphrates to the Atlantic, and its great ecclesiastics met the secular rulers of the time as equals, and even pretended to be their superiors. By then all the raucous debates that had torn the early Church were over, and there was universal acceptance of the doctrines which continue to be basically Christian today, though the Twelve Apostles never heard of any of them — the Trinity, the Virgin Birth, the Incarnation, the Atonement, and so on. The disciplinary powers of Hell had been discovered, and the terrors thereof were the chief theme of all preaching and of a large part of popular legend. Once more Yahweh, through his appointed agents, struck his old and simple bargain with his lieges: Believe, and you shall be saved; doubt, and you shall be damned. It was generally taught that the faithful, once safe in Heaven, would be taken on tours of Hell, to enjoy the agonies of its inmates. Thus the appetizing picture is drawn by Cynewulf, an early English bard, in his " Christ " (translated by Dr. Israel Gollancz):

> *In the baleful gloom*
> *The blissful throng shall contemplate the damned,*
> *Suffering, in penance for their sins, sore pain,*
> *The surging flame and the bitter-biting jaws*
> *Of luring serpents, a shoal of burning things.*
> *Then a winsome joy shall rise within their souls,*
> *Beholding other men endure the ills*
> *That they escaped, through mercy of the Lord.*
> *Then the more eagerly shall they thank God*
> *For all their glory and delight.*

The price of this ineffable joy was simply faith — Yahweh's ancient exaction, now put above all other considerations once more. The rest of the Decalogue retreated to the monasteries and nunneries, and along with it all that survived of the *Interimsethik*. There were some who looked for the Second Coming in the year 500 and others who looked for it in the year 1000, but these at best were only faint hopes, and they seem to have had no influence upon human conduct, whether clerical or lay. In the second volume of Lecky's " History of European Morals," Chapter IV, you will find a description of the state of affairs in the Europe of the Sixth and Seventh Centuries. The passage is too long to quote in full, but a few extracts will perhaps suffice:

The mind is fatigued with the monotonous accounts of acts of violence and fraud springing from no fixed policy, tending to no end. . . . All classes seem to have been almost equally tainted with vice. . . . We read of a bishop named Cautinus, who had to be carried, when intoxicated, by four men from the table; who, upon the refusal of one of his priests to surrender some private property, deliberately ordered that priest to be burned alive, and who, when the victim, escaping by a happy chance from the sepulchre in which he had been immured, revealed the crime, received no greater punishment than a censure. The worst sovereigns found flatterers or agents in ecclesiastics. . . . Gundebald, having murdered his three brothers, was consoled by St. Avitus, the bishop of Vienne, who, without intimating the slightest disapprobation of the act, assured him that by removing his rivals he had been a providential agent in preserving the happiness of his people.

The bishoprics were filled by men of notorious debauchery, or by grasping misers. The priests sometimes celebrated the sacred mysteries " gorged with food and dull with wine." They had already begun to carry arms, and Gregory of Tours tells of two bishops of the Sixth Century who had killed many enemies with their own hands. . . . There were few sovereigns who were not guilty of at least one deliberate murder. . . . We read of a Queen condemning a daughter she had had by a former marriage to be drowned, lest her beauty should excite the passions of her husband; of another Queen endeavoring to strangle her daughter with her own hands; of an abbot compelling a poor man to abandon

his house, that he might commit adultery with his wife, and
being murdered, together with his partner, in the act; of a
prince who made it an habitual amusement to torture his
slaves with fire, and who buried two of them alive, because
they had married without his permission. . . .

And yet, adds Lecky, " this age was, in a certain
sense, eminently religious. All literature had become
sacred. Heresy of every kind was rapidly expiring."
The clergy " had acquired enormous power, and their
wealth was inordinately increasing." No wonder hundreds of thousands fled from such scenes to the holy
houses, and there sought to resuscitate and practise
the elemental Christian virtues. The Seventh Century,
in fact, produced more saints than any other, save only
the age of the martyrs. And it saw " several sovereigns
voluntarily abandon their thrones for the monastic
life."

4

It took Europe many centuries to escape from this
wallow: that organized Christianity had anything to
do with its deliverance is at least doubtful. There were,
to be sure, plenty of bishops and not a few Popes
who made heroic efforts at reform, but they were far
outnumbered by those who pulled the other way. A
desperate, bloody struggle for power and dominion
between the Papacy and the secular Kings went on
for year after year, and running parallel to it and

often intermingled with it there was a similar struggle between the Popes and the bishops. The details need not concern us here: they are so notorious and so revolting that even Catholic historians have abandoned all hope of mitigating them, as you may discover by reading the article on Pope Alexander VI in the Catholic Encyclopedia. Alexander was probably the champion scoundrel of his exalted rank, but he had formidable runners-up, and on lower levels there were many even worse. The occasional efforts of good Popes to cleanse the Church went for little. It became almost unimaginably corrupt, and so its moral authority vanished. The Popes assumed the airs and prerogatives of oriental monarchs, the bishops gathered in vast fortunes in land and gold, and the lesser clergy afflicted the people like a plague of locusts. Even many of the monasteries and nunneries, theoretically refuges from the world and its evils, became sewers of intrigue and debauchery. Outside their walls the system of indulgences made a mock of all moral values, and reduced every decent Christian to despair. How it degraded both clergy and people we may learn from the testimony of Thomas Gascoigne, chancellor of Oxford and a faithful churchman. Writing in 1450, he said:

Sinners say nowadays, " I care not what or how many evils I do before God, for I can get at once, without the least difficulty, plenary remission of any guilt or sin whatever

through an indulgence granted me by the Pope, whose writ-
ten grant I have bought for fourpence, or for the stake of a
game of ball"; for indeed these sellers of indulgences run
about from place to place, and sometimes sell one for two-
pence, or a drink of wine or beer, or enough to pay their
losses at gaming, or the hire of a harlot.

Through all this orgy of faith without works the
voice of the Gascoignes was never quite stilled. A
great many of them were proceeded against as heretics and done to death, but enough always survived to
carry on memories of the primitive Christian tradition. In the universities, which began to spring up
in the Thirteenth Century, earnest men devoted themselves to searching the Law with almost Jewish as-
siduity, and the more seemly religious houses were
swept by frequent waves of renewed austerity, the
most notable of which was that which centered at
Cluny in France in the Tenth Century. On April 25,
1475, a young man of Bologna, appalled by the horrors all about him, sought refuge in such a house in
his native city. That night he wrote a letter to his
father, explaining his step. I quote a few sentences
from the translation of Ralph Roeder in " The Man
of the Renaissance ":

I know that you grieve greatly, particularly since I left
you in secret, but I wish you to understand my mind and my
purpose, so that you may be comforted. . . . The reason
that moved me . . . is, first, the great misery of the world,

the iniquities of men, the rapes, adulteries, larcenies, pride, idolatries and cruel blasphemies which have brought the world so low that there is no longer any one who does good. . . . I saw all virtues cast down and all vices raised up. This was the greatest suffering I could have in this world. Answer me, then: is it not great virtue in a man to flee the filth and iniquity of this wretched world, and to live like a rational man and not like a beast among swine?

This was during the pontificate of Sixtus IV, a relatively decent and enlightened Pope who is chiefly remembered because he was opposed to the wholesale butcheries of the Spanish Inquisition. In 1484 he gave way to the more normal Innocent VIII, whose claim to immortality is that he issued a celebrated bull against witches. In 1492, six weeks before Columbus sighted the shores of America, Innocent yielded to the aforesaid Alexander VI, and on May 23, 1498, the young man whose letter I have quoted was tortured and hanged in Florence, and his body burned. He was Girolamo Savonarola. His crime was that he had preached against the evils of the time, and especially against the corruptions of the Church. The charges against him were heresy and sedition.

But it was not the Savonarolas who saved Christendom, for the system they advocated was too naïve and archaic for its expanding needs. Their substitute for the *lex talionis* was, in essence, simply primitive Christianity, with faith as its cardinal article, and peace and brotherhood as its chief worldly values. Many of the sermons of Savonarola himself might have been lifted from the preaching of the *Interims-ethik*, and at his best he was in plain conflict with the practical necessities of an era of rapid change. The moral system that really emerged from the turmoil was in greater consonance with common sense, and if it was wide enough to admit a number of mere taboos on the one side, it was also wide enough to admit the logic of Aristotle on the other. It had its beginnings, as I have said in Chapter III, far back in the abysm of early medieval times, but it did not show any vitality until the Eleventh Century, when Europe began to react to the great adventure of the Crusades.

The crusaders were successful in their first assault upon the Saracen, and Jerusalem fell to them in 1099, but in their triumph they developed a large respect for their enemy, both as a soldier and as a man. He had been depicted to them by Peter the Hermit and the other warlocks of the day as a bloody and intolerable barbarian, almost comparable to the German of American legend in 1917, but what they found before them was a gallant and chivalrous foe, and in the hours of truce, a pleasant and enlightened fellow. Thousands of them were so impressed that they abandoned Christianity forthwith and submitted to circumcision as Moslems — a fact of which Christian historians naturally make as little as possible.

ITS CHRISTIAN FORM

The rest, returning home, brought with them an entirely new view of infidels in general, and of the Saracen infidel in particular, and it clashed inevitably with the central Christian doctrine that only the baptized were children of Yahweh, or could be saved. Moreover, what thus went on among simple soldiers was matched, and in an exaggerated manner, among the learned. It began to be manifest to them that the Saracens, in many a field of useful knowledge, really knew a great deal more than the Christians. For one thing, they were much better mathematicians; for another, they excelled in the art of the physician; for a third, they had a wider and sounder acquaintance with geography, then a novelty among the sciences, and beginning to be held in esteem. Above all, they were full of the fascinating speculations and questionings of the Greek philosophers, taken over from the last Sophists of Byzantium and cherished through the years. The early Christian theologians had either rejected this Greek philosophy outright, as heathenish and devilish, or sought to cry it down by arguing that it represented a sort of third-rate inspiration by the Logos, imperfectly understood and badly recorded. But now, as its arcana gradually filtered back into Western Christendom from the schools of Constantinople, Antioch and Alexandria on the one hand and the Arab colonies in Spain on the other, the learned found that it was full of ideas of a very agreeable pungency, and that many of them were to be sought in vain in Christian literature. Of all the strange authors thus studied, the one who aroused the most interest was Aristotle. In particular, his system of logic made a powerful impression, for it seemed to give the inquiring mind a whole arsenal of new weapons.

The first efforts to reconcile the new ways of thinking with the adamantine certitudes of Christian theology seem to have been made in obscure monasteries by even more obscure monks, but in the course of time the enterprise emerged from that darkness and began to be generally undertaken by the literate. One of the first adventurers to leave his name in history was Rousselin or Roscellius, a canon of Compiègne, born in the middle of the Eleventh Century. This Roscellius tried boldly to reconcile the laws of reason, as set forth by Aristotle, with the murky dogma of the Trinity — to such unhappy effect, alas, that he came near being stoned to death and was forced to flee to England. But other daring and curious men were presently walking in his footsteps, and during the century following some of them attained to a fame which survives to this day — for example, Anselm of Canterbury, Guillaume de Champeaux, and the romantic Pierre Abélard, whose gloomy love affair with the beautiful Héloïse has been the theme of poets ever since. Most of these innovators were led into a kind of rationalism which seemed almost atheism to their ecclesiastical superiors, and so they commonly got into trouble. Abélard thus acquired the enmity of a number of archbishops, and was saved from the wrath of Pope Innocent II only by the aid of Peter the Venerable, the very intelligent abbot of the reformed abbey of Cluny. In accordance with the immemorial pattern of their trade the brethren quickly divided into two metaphysical camps, that of the Nominalists and that of the Realists, and thereafter a large part of their energy was consumed, not in furthering the new enlightenment, but in opposing and traducing one another.

The grand master of them all was Thomas Aquinas (c. 1226–74), now a saint and by long odds the most influential Catholic theologian since Augustine. The task that he undertook was the stupendous one of reconciling Greek philosophy with Christian theology, and so making Christianity respectable intellectually. It had gone on for years as a loose congeries of dogmas, some of them borrowed from the Jews, others invented by Paul or brought in by him from rival religions, and yet others formulated by a long series of Popes and councils. Time and the wear and tear of everyday usage had given the system a certain rough coherence and simplicity on its lower levels, where it impinged upon the common run of the faithful: " Believe or be damned," was its first principle there, and " Obey your lawful superiors " was its second. But higher up the scale, among men of better education, it had less easy sailing. Only a brief glance was needed to show such men that some of its cardinal doctrines — for example, that of transubstantiation — were unfathomable by the ordinary processes of reason, and had to be accepted, if they were to be accepted at all, by a sheer act of faith, with faith defined, in Paul's beautiful but unhappy phrase, as " the substance of things hoped for, the evidence of things not seen." As the new learning, by the heathenry of Araby out of the Greek academies, began to throw a critical light upon this corpus of irrational and often unintelligible ideas, its weaknesses became painfully manifest, and the need of providing it with something resembling scientific support began to press. That need had been recognized for a long while, but now it became exigent.

Aquinas, who was an Italian of noble birth, educated in the best schools of the time, devoted his whole life to the business of redefining Christian theology in rational terms. He was admirably fitted for it, for though he knew no Greek, he had read the Greek authors in Latin translations, and as a theologian he had no better in all Europe. Moreover, he was a man of supple, enterprising and highly original mind, and of such skill in controversy that few dared to stand up against him. Beginning as a follower of Albertus Magnus, the leading Aristotelian of the day, he soon surpassed his master, and was frequented at Paris, Cologne, Bologna, Pisá and Rome by ever increasing bands of eager pupils. The Popes soon heard of him, and deferred to his immense learning. At the age of forty-eight he was summoned by Gregory X to attend a General Council at Lyon, and simultaneously he was offered an archbishopric, which he declined. He died soon afterward but his fame continued to increase, and in less than half a century he was canonized. In 1567 Pope Pius V ordained that on his festal day he should have all the honors hitherto reserved for the four great Latin Fathers, Augustine, Jerome, Ambrose and Gregory, and in 1879 Pope Leo XIII directed that his teachings be accepted as authoritative by all Catholic theologians. His right arm is preserved as a holy relic in the Church of St. Jacques at Paris, and other portions of his earthy frame are similarly venerated at Naples and Rome. Nor is his high and almost singular eminence confined to the precincts of Holy Church. He has of late acquired a substantial following in the outer void also, chiefly among persons who shrink from the harsh skepticism of science, and he is much resorted to by those who seek to fashion a new concordat between science and theology.

His own method of effecting that reconciliation is set forth mainly in his *Summa contra Gentiles*. It consists, in brief, of marking off two quite distinct intellectual realms, that of reason and that of faith. In the former the mind is free to disport as it will with any data that happen to be available, but in the latter its cogitations are confined within the limits of what has been revealed, either primarily to the whole body of the faithful or secondarily through competent authority. There is provision for an exchange of data between the two realms. The testimony of the senses may be accepted to support revelation, and revelation may be counted as an objective fact. There can be no real conflict between the two kinds of knowledge, for both issue from the same Divine Absolute, the same Omniscient God, and so must be in essential harmony. In cases of apparent conflict man must abandon his feeble speculations and take refuge in faith, for it rests on revelation, which is a kind of knowledge that is additional to, and hence superior to any that may be attained by mere reason. It is lawful and indeed meritorious to support faith by the devices of reason, but its definition, in the last analysis, must always be by authority, and the sole repository of that authority is the One Holy Catholic and Apostolic Church. It alone can formulate eternal truths, and when so engaged it cannot err. In particular, it cannot err when it undertakes to separate right from wrong in the great fields of theological dogma and moral science.

That there is in all this a vast begging of the question must be plain to every reflective reader, but such as it is, it has satisfied the intellectual needs of multitudes of men, and will probably continue to do so for ages to come. Aquinas's own age seems to have been completely convinced by his reasoning. He had opponents who disputed this or that detail of his doctrine, but its fundamentals were apparently accepted at once, and by all the faithful, from the Popes down to the meanest monks. Not many, perhaps, understood him clearly, for he wrote in a difficult Latin and made use of a metaphysical vocabulary so formidable that the business of interpreting it is still going on, but enough was grasped to produce a general feeling of relief. Christianity was now safe from attack by skeptical raiders, armed with Aristotle. It had been reconciled with the Greek learning, and given a new start in the world, intellectually speaking. In wide areas the true believer was at liberty to exercise his mind as he pleased, and in the dark woods of theology he had an infallible guide. As time passed and civilization moved on, some of the possessions of theology naturally slipped away, to the enrichment of the domain of free reason. Thus it lost its hegemony over witches when they were proved to be imaginary, and its authority in matters of celestial mechanics at the hands of Copernicus and Galileo, and a large part of its practice as attorney at the throne of grace when men began to abandon prayer and penance for the measures of science. But the movement has not been all in one direction. Revelation has made some conquests too, and is still making them in our time. I need point only to the matter of birth control. There is nothing about it in the New Testament, and next to nothing that is apposite in the Old, and in Aquinas's day it was unheard of, but the Catholic theologians

now lay down the law on the subject with the utmost
confidence, and none among the faithful ventures to
challenge them.

The Thomist system, at more than one point, conflicts with the customary thinking of civilized man
today, and those who cling to it are commonly persons who, by some softness of mind, find that thinking
unendurable. But it would be a mistake to dismiss it
as mere medieval rumble-bumble. Aquinas was actually a philosopher of the first order, and most of his
defects were the defects of philosophy itself, which
wastes itself, at all times and everywhere, on vain
efforts to penetrate the unknowable. As a practical
moralist he was extremely intelligent. Borrowing the
idea of the golden mean from Aristotle, he got rid of
the ages-old conflict between the unhealthy, catacomb-
ish utopianism of the early Church and the everyday
needs and desires of normal men living in a naturally
pleasant world. Even the casuistry which was one of
the by-products of his metaphysics has probably done
a great deal more good than harm, if only by providing a bridge between the impossible and the possible.
The Catholic moral system of today is largely his
handiwork, and it testifies alike to his metaphysical
ingenuity and his shrewdness as a practical psychologist. There are large parts of it that cannot be
defended rationally, and a few of its articles, as I shall
presently try to show, are in conflict with what most
educated men regard as common decency, but it rests

upon a logic of its own and hangs together admirably, and on the whole it seems to fit very well the needs of those whose needs it fits.

5

The authority assumed to lie behind it was thus described by Pope Pius XI in his encyclical, *Casti connubii,* on December 31, 1930:

Christ Himself made the Church the teacher of truth in all matters which have to do with the right regulation of moral conduct, even though some knowledge of the same is not beyond human reason. For just as God, in the case of the natural truth of religion and morals, added revelation to the light of reason, so that what is right and true, " even in the present state of the human race, may be known readily, with real certainty and no admixture of error," so for the same purpose He has constituted the Church the guardian and teacher of the whole of the truth concerning religion and moral conduct. To her, therefore, the faithful should show obedience, subjecting to her their minds and hearts that they may be kept unharmed and free from error and moral corruption.

His Holiness's quotation is from the decrees of the Vatican Council, Session III, Article 2, dated April 24, 1870. Three months later the same council, by a vote virtually unanimous, adopted and promulgated the doctrine of papal infallibility, whereby the Popes are invested with all the authority here claimed by

Pius XI for the Church. In order to exert it, however, they must hold themselves within certain bounds and observe certain formalities. The subject dealt with must concern either faith or morals, and it must be plain that the Pope is speaking *ex cathedra,* which is to say, in his official capacity, and, as it were, with malice prepense. His passing *obiter dicta,* even on matters within his jurisdiction, are not infallible, and on matters outside that jurisdiction his opinions, putting aside the respect naturally due him because of his high place in the world, are worth no more than those of any other man. Thus if a Pope permitted himself to enter the field, say, of medicine, and to recommend aspirin for acute appendicitis, no Catholic would be bound to follow him. He lives, indeed, in a very ceremonious *milieu,* and must follow its rules strictly. There is still dispute among Catholic canon lawyers as to whether Pius X's famous Syllabus of Errors of 1907 has infallibility behind it. It was ratified under his hand on July 4 of that year and ordered to be published, and on November 18 he issued a *motu proprio* prohibiting the defense of the condemned doctrines on pain of excommunication, but the Syllabus itself was not his act, but that of the Holy Office, and so a doubt remains. The faithful, of course, are expected to obey it, but apparently they are still free to question its infallibility without risk of mortal sin, and by the same token the present Pope is free to modify it.

In the primitive Church the laity seem to have had a voice in questions of both faith and morals, and even down to the Middle Ages, at least in some places, they took a hand in the election of bishops, and sometimes of Popes. Until 1904, when the practice was formally interdicted by Pius X, certain of the Catholic Powers claimed the right to forbid the election of any Pope distasteful to them, and in 1903 Austria thus banned Cardinal Mariano Rampolla, the Papal Secretary of State. To this day, by concordat, a few Powers retain the right to pass on the appointment of bishops within their territories. But this control by laymen is only local and never very effective, and the overwhelming majority of Catholic ecclesiastics stand clear of it altogether. Thus the hierarchy is essentially a self-perpetuating body, and its authority cannot be challenged by the faithful. The rights of the latter, such as they are, are swallowed up by their paramount duty to obey. The most heinous of all sins, under the Catholic system, are sins against the faith: as McHugh and Callan say in their " Moral Theology," they are " worse than sins against the moral virtues." And sins against the faith, of course, simply mean doubts about what the Church, through its Supreme Pastor and its other rev. spokesmen, has declared to be true. The first duty of a Catholic is to believe, and his second is to obey. After that, and only after that, come the duties he shares with the rest of us.

It would be hard to find, in civilized history, a

match for the power that thus lies in the hands of the Catholic clergy. Certainly nothing of the sort was visible among the Jews, who kept their priests in subjection and were always willing to listen to amateur theologians, as the case of Jesus exemplifies. Among the Greeks and Romans a priest was simply a minor public official, and as much under control of the government as a soldier or a tax-gatherer. Even in the great Asiatic empires of antiquity the secular arm was always superior to the spiritual arm. But the Popes and their ghostly brethren in descending rank, though they have given up their old claim to direct authority over all temporal rulers and law-makers, still exercise a complete police power over the faithful in matters of faith and morals, and every effort to modify it has been resisted and put down. One must go to Tibet to find a parallel. Theoretically, the Pope could declare cannibalism lawful tomorrow, and even exact it as a duty, and there would be no way for his mandate to be upset, save maybe by the lame process of finding him insane. Not even a general council of the Church could vacate it, for the assertion of his infallibility made in 1870 was, by a universal Catholic assumption, simply the statement of an eternal truth, and eternal truths cannot be changed. That even God Himself could change one, at least without another return to earth, is in doubt, though His continuing capacity to set aside the ordinary laws of physics is a cardinal article of faith.

Obviously, such a system is a formidable impediment to the free functioning of the intelligence. The Catholic is not only forbidden to do any effective thinking for himself on matters of faith and morals; he is also discouraged from speculation in the fields adjacent, which include those of history, anthropology, sociology, psychology, philosophy, and many of the physical sciences. Since the Renaissance, which was basically a skeptical movement, and the Reformation, which was as much a revolt against the fundamental moral authority of the Church as against its administrative corruption, the torch of progress has been carried on mainly by non-Catholics. To be sure, there have been Catholic scientists of high attainments — I need mention only Pasteur and Mendel — and to be sure there is always some dabbling in the safer sciences on the upper levels of the teaching orders, but the fact remains horribly plain that Catholics have contributed a great deal less than their fair share to the increase of human knowledge during the past three or four centuries. In most Catholic countries today the intellectual aristocracy is predominantly agnostic and anti-clerical, and in Protestant countries the Catholic minority, when put to any test of mental enterprise, almost vanishes. In the United States, for example, Ellsworth Huntington and Leon F. Whitney were lately showing, by an examination of " Who's Who in America," that but 7 Catholics in every 100,000 attain to enough distinction to be listed therein, as against 16 Baptists, 18 Methodists, 20 Jews, 31 Quakers, 62 Presbyterians, 115 Congregationalists, 156 Episcopalians and 1185 Unitarians. Only the members of a few bucolic foot-wash sects stand below them. Their generally low economic status may have something to do with this, but such a status is itself a sign of inferiority. The fact that many of them are recent immigrants is also to be considered, but against it may be set the fact that many of the Baptists and Methodists are Negroes. Huntington and Whitney lay the blame largely on sacerdotal celibacy, which bottles up some of the best Catholic stock, and prevents its reproduction.

But the truth is that the Catholic system is in its very essence inimical to intelligence, and commonly either throttles it or drives it out of the fold. The evidence that history offers to that effect is set forth at length in Andrew D. White's monumental " History of the Warfare of Science With Theology in Christendom," and there are fresh additions every day. The Syllabuses of Popes Pius IX and Pius X, binding in conscience upon every Catholic, are full of denunciations of principles that are cherished by all civilized men — for example, that " everyone is free to adopt and profess that religion which, guided by the light of reason, he holds to be true," and that " truth is as changeable as man, because it evolved with him, in him and by him." No Catholic can venture into the physical or social sciences, or into history, or even

into political and economic theory, without watching
his step very carefully: he must always consider, not
only what he believes to be true, but also what he
knows to be official. A Catholic medical man is surrounded by taboos that seem absurd to his non-
Catholic colleagues, and in the field of obstetrics is
forbidden to adopt measures that the overwhelming
majority of them hold to be sound and humane. The
Jesuits, Dominicans and other *Gelehrten* of the Church
confine themselves pretty strictly to such innocuous
sciences as seismology, meteorology, paleography and
philology, and when they venture into biology show
all the caution of Mendel. Relatively little that is of
any value to anthropology has come from Catholic
missionaries, though they were in the field long before
the Protestants, and probably outnumber them to this
day. Let a priest-professor turn to economics and he
must ground his teaching, not on Adam Smith and
Ricardo, but on Leo XIII's *Rerum novarum* and Pius
XI's *Quadragesimo anno;* let him undertake psychology and he must be very wary of the heresies of
Freud, Watson and company. Even members of the
hierarchy, and of the highest rank, are expected to
avoid dangerous thoughts, as Cardinal Gibbons discovered at Rome in 1887.

This draconian system, enforced pedantically,
would have destroyed itself long ago, for all save
the meanest and most abject varieties of men would
have found it unendurable. Fortunately for the

Church, there have been few attempts to apply its full rigors, and all of them, including the Spanish Inquisition, have been transient. The bonds of the faithful, in normal times, are light ones, and the Catholic is actually much less harassed in his daily life than the Protestant of equal piety. So long as he does not talk too much he may harbor all the doubts he pleases without hearing anything more than polite remonstrances from his confessor — here, indeed, the scandal is much worse than the offense — , and so long as he confesses freely and applies himself to his penances he may commit any imaginable secular crime without losing his rank as a child of God. The confessional is not a burden on him but a kind of relief, for it transfers all his worst troubles of conscience to professional shoulders, and purges him at convenient intervals of his accumulated sins.

In theory, he faces the risk of spending eternity in a burning, blistering Hell that is depicted by his pastor in appalling terms, but actually there are more ways to escape it than to get into it, and even the vilest sinner, if he be full of faith, hopes to find one of them. Indeed, the Church itself provides a sort of anteroom in a vague place called Purgatory, and while he is there the sinner may work off his debt, and get help in doing so from the prayers of his pastor, relatives and friends. For infants who die unbaptized, and so approach judgment staggering under their full share of Original Sin, there is another vague place called the Limbus Infantium, or Limbo, where they may be reasonably happy, if not actually blessed. St. Augustine rejected Limbo and taught that unbaptized infants went to Hell, but Thomas Aquinas, a kindly as well as a learned man, restored it. It is now accepted by all Catholic theologians of any authority, and those medieval fathers who sided with Augustine are spoken of contemptuously as *tortores infantium,* which is to say, torturers of infants. But the roasting of these innocents was taken over joyfully by Calvin, and it remained a cardinal article of the Presbyterian theology until only the other day.

In other directions the Catholic system, despite its theoretical ferocity, is equally humane. Its doctors developed the great science of casuistry to get rid of its worst rigors, just as the English lawyers developed the rules of evidence to get rid of the brutalities of the Common Law. As McHugh and Callan say, " the Church does not wish to be unkind, nor, generally speaking, to have her laws applied rigorously for every case." Thus she provides an elaborate apparatus of dispensations and indulgences, penances and absolutions, for the erring, and assumes as a matter of fact, though without saying so categorically, that most of the faithful will escape Hell and go to Heaven, the joys of which are frequently described with great eloquence by Catholic pastors, though perhaps not so often as they describe the pains of Hell. The Church has never laid it down as a fact that the blessed will recognize one another in Heaven, and its spokesmen carefully avoid indicating that this or that person will go there, but sometimes there is a hint in an official act, for it would be hard to imagine an infallible Pope canonizing, beatifying or even praising one whose soul was actually in Hell.

But such supremely virtuous persons, to the Catholic way of thinking, are extremely rare, and though the calendar of saints, to the infidel eye, may look crowded, it really accounts for no more than one Catholic in many millions. The Church, grounding its polity firmly on II Chronicles VI, 36: " for there is no man which sinneth not," assumes that the children of Adam are incurably wicked, and that all it can hope to do with them is to keep them in reasonably decent order. This assumption admits of no exceptions whatever. The Pope on his throne and the most saintly nun in her convent must go to confession as regularly as the most abandoned sinner, and it is taken for granted that they will always have something to confess. " God," said the Council of Trent in one of its decrees, " does not ask the impossible." This frank acceptance and tolerance of the Old Adam is one of the chief sources of the Church's strength, and probably explains more plausibly than anything else its long prosperity in the world. It is spared thereby those moral witch-hunts that have so often disrupted the Protestant sects, it is aided in keeping down the nuisance of spiritual pride, and it is given a firm grip upon the lowly, who are as conscious of their lack of saintliness as they are of their lack of wealth, and are naturally grateful to a vast, lordly and mysterious organization which condescends to them politely, and makes them comfortable. The whip it cracks over them is barbed with the fear of Hell, but the cracking is done with infinite discretion, and a fine understanding of psychology as she blows in the lower IQ brackets. Upon the superior minority — never large — the Church makes play with other weapons, some of them of a great subtlety, but the rank and file are policed by fear alone, and its only administrative reinforcement is a very simple system of obligations and taboos. Make your Easter duty. Avoid meat on Friday. Keep Lent. Marry only in the Church. Bring your babies for baptism promptly, and have plenty of them. Be respectful to your spiritual superiors. Give to the Church's poor. Read no forbidden books. For the rest, do as well as you can, considering the feeble strength that Yahweh hath granted you — and trust Holy Church, which is wise and merciful, to save you somehow from Hell.

6

Unfortunately, the Church is not always happy in its dealings with concrete problems in ethics, and not infrequently its whole moral system is strained by sharp conflicts between competitive values. Such a conflict, as we have seen in Chapter I, seduced it into taking an untenable position on the subject of slavery: with the rights of man pulling one way and the rights of property the other, it yielded imprudently to the latter. It fell into a like costly folly when, alarmed by the Renaissance and the Reformation, it established the Congregation of the Holy Office in 1542, and sought to put down heresy by *force majeure*, relying on the mandate, "Compel them to come in," in Luke XIV, 23; for the only effect of the long and bloody effort was to make the Church itself infamous. Perhaps quite as often it has made narrow escapes. Thus, in 1864, when Pope Pius IX issued his Syllabus of Errors, it came close to the disastrous blunder of denouncing Darwin's "Origin of Species," published only five years before. The majority of the moral theologians in practice at Rome at the time seem to have been in favor of putting the book on the *Index*, but either more intelligent counsels prevailed or there was a saving hint from Omnipotence, for nothing was done. To this day the Church has done nothing, and so the hypothesis of organic evolution is neither true nor false, officially speaking. But though a Catholic, in theory, is thus free to believe in it if he chooses, he must qualify his belief, if he elects it, on a material point, for he must also believe that when man appeared on earth the soul was specially created. Not many Catholic savants are thorough-going evolutionists; nearly all of them hedge cautiously, and are full of rejoicing whenever it is discovered that Darwin was in error in this detail or that. The Dutchman Dubois, the discoverer of *Pithecanthropus erectus* in 1891, was a true son of Holy Church, for when he got back to Holland with his bag of sardonic bones he insisted upon treating them as parts of the earthly matrix of an immortal soul, and caused a great deal of ill-feeling among his agnostic colleagues by refusing to let them share in the autopsy and inquest. The learned abbot, Gregor Mendel, was another, for he confined his investigations to plants, which are safely soulless, and permitted himself no perilous speculations about the bearing of his researches on the biological history of man.

In recent years the Church has got itself into serious difficulties over the highly indelicate and embarrassing matter of birth control, and despite the vast ingenuity of its moral theologians, it seems unlikely to emerge from them without marked damage. There is nothing in revelation to support its violent and uncompromising denunciation of the practice, for the New Testament writers were all for celibacy, which is the natural antithesis of fecundity, and the lone and overworked case of Onan in Genesis xxxviii is hardly in point, for what Yahweh punished Onan for was not his practice of contraception *per se*, but simply his evasion of his fraternal duty, under the Jewish Law, to provide an heir for his dead brother. The statute he violated belonged to the Old Dispensation, and is no more binding on a Catholic of today than the sacrifices

ordained in the Pentateuch. Thus the brethren are reduced to finding arguments against birth control in
the laws of nature, and in that field they make very
heavy weather. For after starting out from the postulate that it is inherently wrong to misuse or pervert a
natural faculty, they are forced at once to admit a
number of misuses or perversions of this one. One is
the resort to dalliance at those times in the cycle of
ovulation when it is known (or, at all events, hopefully believed) that the female cannot conceive. Another is its practice during pregnancy or after the
menopause. Yet another is its continuance after either
party has been sterilized, whether by trauma, by disease, or by surgical efforts to cure either or both. All
of these evasions of parenthood have been approved
by competent Catholic authorities, and yet it must be
obvious that they pervert a natural faculty exactly as
contraception does, and are equally in *genere luxuriæ*.
There is no thought of Christian duty in them; their
aim is purely voluptuous.

When the question first came into consideration,
about a century ago, the moralists of the Church
showed a prudent disinclination to tackle it frankly.
This was during the pontificate of Pope Gregory XVI,
and it was a French bishop, Monsignor Bouvier of Le
Mans, who asked the Sacred Penitentiary for a ruling.
The practice of birth control, he said, was spreading
in France, and he feared that denouncing it as a mortal sin would only keep penitents away from confes-

sion. The Penitentiary replied very cautiously. First, it said, confessors must remember that the consent of but one party is needed for the offense, and that the other, if formally unwilling, has committed no sin. Second, it should be borne in mind that the *debitum conjugale* is a very delicate matter, and that confessors should not concern themselves with it unnecessarily or unduly. But in 1851 the question was raised again by other bishops, and this time Holy Church, speaking through the Congregation of the Holy Office, saw fit to decide more clearly. It condemned contraception unequivocally as " prohibited by the natural law," and denounced the doctrine that " for good reasons " married couples might resort to it as " scandalous and erroneous." A year later it termed the practice " intrinsically evil," and such has been the Catholic position ever since. The Penitentiary issued further decisions on the subject in 1876, 1880, 1886 and 1916, and on December 31, 1930, in his encyclical *Casti connubii,* Pope Pius XI summed up the matter by declaring *ex cathedra,* and hence infallibly, that " any use of marriage whatsoever, if deliberately intended to frustrate its natural power to generate life, is an offense against the laws of God and nature, and those who resort to it are guilty of a grave sin."

This is certainly plain enough, but nevertheless the Catholic moralists continue to debate the question, seeking to find rational support for what they are in duty bound to teach. Some of their difficulties have been stated candidly by Dr. John M. Cooper and Dr. John A. Ryan, both of the Catholic University at Washington. Dr. Cooper wants to know " just precisely how we are going to formulate such a definition of the natural function of the reproductive faculty as will permit relations in pregnancy and sterility and yet bar contraceptive practices," and goes on to say that anyone who argues that " exercising a faculty and at the same time putting obstacles in the way of attaining its natural purpose is always and *in se* mortally sinful . . . will have his hands full for a long time to come." As for Dr. Ryan, after admitting that " many actions are morally lawful, even though they fall under a general category of sins," and that this may be true of " birth prevention in certain restricted cases, say, when the life or health of the wife would be endangered by pregnancy," he proceeds to crawl back under the shelter of *Casti connubii* by arguing that " no community which accepts this practice as morally lawful in exceptional conditions will long restrict it to those conditions " — which sounds suspiciously like the familiar Methodist argument against licensing the sale of alcoholic beverages. The Pope himself listed some licit " secondary " ends of marriage, " such as mutual aid, the cultivation of mutual love, and the quieting of concupiscence (*remedium concupiscentiæ*)," but this simply raised a fresh difficulty for confessors, for it is a practical impossibility for them to distinguish between "the quieting of concupiscence" and mere *luxuria,* and *luxuria* is strictly prohibited. Many of them recommend marital continence, and in *Casti connubii* one reads that "there are no possible circumstances in which husband and wife cannot, strengthened by the grace of God, fulfil faithfully their duties, and yet preserve in wedlock their chastity unspotted." But this is only too plainly the theory of men who have never suffered personally the onerous temptations of connubial intimacy in *déshabillé,* particularly with wives who have read Havelock Ellis. Moreover, they always have to add that if either party refuses to enter upon a pact of chastity, the dissenter retains rights which may not be denied without sin.

Altogether, the brethren appear to be in somewhat warm water. On the one hand there is the draconian mandate of *Casti connubii,* and on the other hand there is the disconcerting fact that a great many Catholics are now practising birth control, and that the more intelligent, opulent and influential they are, the more likely they are to do so. If they are actually guilty of mortal sin, and persist in it contumaciously, then it must be assumed that all of them will go to Hell *post mortem,* which is a doom which no humane confessor, I take it, wants to contemplate for the flower of his flock. In the United States the hierarchy upholds the official doctrine faithfully, but there is murmuring among Catholic laymen, and especially among Catholic laywomen. Some time ago an eminent bishop, engaging upon visiting the Sodalities of the Blessed Virgin in his diocese, permitted himself some loud, blistering denunciations of contraception in all its forms. At once there was a formidable revolt in the *Frauenzimmer,* fomented by tired married women and expectant virgins alike, and in a little while His Lordship was moved to drop the matter. What the end may be I do not venture to predict. Inasmuch as the pronunciamento made in *Casti connubii* is, by its terms, infallible, it would take a long process and an heroic use of casuistry to modify it. But meanwhile, the birth-rate among Catholics in the United States, though it is still higher than among Protestants, is falling steadily, and the returns from the ever multiplying birth-control clinics, as Dr. Raymond Pearl was lately showing, prove that Catholic women resort to them quite as often, proportionately, as any other kind of women.

At the bottom of the difficulty which Holy Church thus faces is an archaic, absurd and essentially obscene view of sex, formulated in an age when the whole civilized world was weary of life and distrustful of it, and fostered through the years by a tortured priesthood. The practical advantages of sacerdotal celibacy cannot be denied, but they have been bought at a very dear price. The Moslems, seeking like ends, adopted the realistic and efficient device of castration, but the early Christians, save for a few extremists, shrunk from it, and as a result every Catholic cleric of today, if he be physiologically normal, is afflicted inevitably by some of the most unpleasant carnivora in the Freudian menagerie. His faith may be sufficient to sustain him against them, and most often it is, but it is not enough to make him really comfortable. In his own private experience the perfectly natural sexual impulse can be nothing save an incitement to mortal sin, and it is thus very hard for him to think of it as anything else to other men. In consequence, the Church's admissions that indulging it can have laudable effects, even within the bounds of holy wedlock, are made only grudgingly, and outside those bounds it grants nothing at all. Standing firmly on the doctrine, intrinsically not unsound, that any rational morality must subordinate the demands of the body to the health of the mind — or, as it says, of the soul —, it overlooks the capital fact that there is immensely more to sex, at least among civilized adults, than mere animal passion. Of all that lies above the belt it refuses to take practical cognizance: it is too busy policing the horrors below. Its constant effort, whether in or out of marriage, is to extend the domain of chastity, and it cherishes celibacy as ardently as Paul himself. Having but small confidence in human perfection, it is ready to forgive almost anything, but what it really understands seems to be very little. Imagine blind men told off to judge a flower-show, and you will have some approximation to its infirmity.

7

With few exceptions, the Protestant moral theologians reject celibacy, whether as actually achieved or as mere ideal, and in other parts of the sexual domain they are a great deal less rigorous than their Catholic colleagues. Obviously, it would be an absurdity and an indecorum for married men to speak up for that chastity in marriage which Pope Pius XI advocates in *Casti connubii*. Even the harsh Puritans in the lower ranks of Protestantism are cautious here. They denounce the scarlet woman with great violence, forgetting John VIII, 11, as facilely as they forget John II, 1–11, and they are strongly against necking, petting and all other such incitements to the young, but most of them tolerate birth control, and not many refuse to solemnize the remarriage of the divorced. In this field, I suspect, they are strongly influenced by lay opinion, which responds to the increasing skepticism of the time. They have no refuge of infallible authority behind them, to retreat to when rebellion threatens them; instead, they must either please their customers, or lose their livelihoods. It is thus most unusual for a Protestant pastor to go counter to what is generally believed in his flock, and what is generally believed is commonly the opinion of a few principal members, male and female. If one of those *prominenti* decides to put away his wife and marry another it is hazardous for the pastor to object, and if either the first wife or the second chooses to practise and preach contraception he must let her have her way. So he confines himself to denouncing the harlots in the shacks down behind the railroad tracks, and to imagining and describing the carnalities that go on in Catholic nunneries.

On these levels, indeed, Protestantism is so corrupted by policy that, in America at least, its moral mandates are no longer taken seriously by any intelligent person. When it thunders against war everyone recalls the sadistic furies of its chief ecclesiastics in 1917, and when it presumes to advocate social justice its long alliance with the cotton-mill sweaters in the South and with similar anthropophagi elsewhere is remembered. Its intimate relations, amounting to those of mother and daughter or pastor and parishioner, with the Anti-Saloon League, the Lord's Day Alliance, the Ku Klux Klan and other such antisocial organizations are notorious, and Walter White has proved in " Rope and Faggot " that wherever it flourishes lynching also flourishes. In the so-called Bible Belt it is the implacable enemy of all rational pedagogy and free speech, and everywhere outside the big cities it is on friendly terms with the lowest sort of professional politicians. For many years past it has produced no leaders of any weight as men. The last of them to be a national figure of importance, the eloquent Henry Ward Beecher, was taken in *luxuria* with a lady parishioner so long ago as 1874, and the whole fraternity has been going downhill, intellectually and morally, ever since. In the cities its members, even the most eminent, are commonly treated by the newspapers as comic characters, and even in the rural sections their influence is declining, and they are coming to be regarded as hardly more than idle busybodies and public nuisances. Obviously, the moral authority of men so widely suspect cannot be large. They enforce their fantastic mandates, now and then, by entering into arrangements with venal politicians, but such leagues seldom last long, and when they break down there is a wild outburst of antinomianism.

The Puritan clergy of early New England, the professional forerunners of these sorry bounders of God, were greatly superior to them both as theologians and as men. Like any other ecclesiastics, they were eager for secular power, and exercised it harshly while they had it, but they were at least decently educated, as education was understood at that time, and their theology, if insane, was nevertheless not ignorant. In truth, their speculations were often read with attention in Europe, and in Jonathan Edwards the elder (1703–58) they produced in their decline the greatest theologian the New World has yet seen. At the bottom of their doctrine was the Calvinist principle that salvation is only for the elect — that a few lucky individuals, chosen by Yahweh, will go inevitably to Heaven, whereas all the rest are just as inevitably doomed to

Hell. This determinism might have easily become fatalism, and led to an acceptance of the counsel of Isaiah xxii, 13: " Let us eat and drink, for tomorrow we shall die." But the Calvinists got rid of that danger by laying heavy burdens upon the faithful, and by hinting that the divine grace, though hard to get, was easy to lose. They invented elaborate tests for its presence, and taught that its possession was uncommon. Not many of the early New Englanders qualified, and in even the most pious communities there were more damned outside the churches than sanctified within them.

It was these damned who, in the long run, saved the whole region from its theocratic Mussolinis. Some of them were Quakers and others were old-fashioned members of the Church of England, but far more were simply skeptics — sailors along the coast, worldly merchants and mechanics in the towns, adventurers on the frontier, and so on. As the Eighteenth Century Enlightenment came in, these unbelievers received a powerful reinforcement, for its bold challenges to the current theology shook even some of the theologians, who by 1725 were engaged in violent controversies over this point or that. In 1732 Edwards began a series of sermons at Northampton, Mass., in defense of Calvinism, and out of them flowed what is known to students of social pathology as the Great Awakening, a huge revival which swept all New England and then devastated the rest of the country, even to the remotest settlements beyond the mountains. It kept up for fifteen years or more, and has been followed ever since, at increasingly long intervals, by similar uproars, with hundreds of thousands leaping for the mourners' bench, and Yahweh speaking thunderously through his inspired Whitefields and Wesleys, Cartwrights and Finneys, Moodys and Billy Sundays.

But the Great Awakening, though it was launched by the greatest of American Calvinists, was ruinous to Calvinism in New England. The more intelligent minority of the people, disgusted by the orgiastic " enthusiasm " which marked the movement, succumbed easily to the Enlightenment and were presently on their way toward Unitarianism. And on the lower levels the multitudes of the " saved," repelled by the cold rigors of Puritan ecclesiasticism, rebounded into the arms of the Methodists, whose agents began to rove and harry the colonies in the 1760's. The revivals following became increasingly Methodistic, and by the end of the century the austere New England divines would have no more to do with them, but retired to that aloof umbilicular contemplation which remains their chief devotion to this day. The center of the hullabaloo thereupon shifted to the Western frontier, and then to the South. There the old Puritanism, degraded to a kind of voodooism, still survives, though it is sick, and there the village pastor, at least in the remoter areas, continues in practice as a general expert in all the arts and sciences, including especially ethics. The Calvinistic doctrine of grace, resolved into an imbecile theory that the sanctified are actually purged of sin, is cherished by the Holy Rollers, who are degenerate Methodists, and by the bucolic Presbyterians, of whom the late William Jennings Bryan was a shining example. But in New England the doctrine of grace is long forgotten, and with it most of the Puritan moral system. When the Boston police proceed against naughty books and wicked plays today it is not the descendants of the early Puritans who urge them on, but the Irish Catholics, who are Puritans of another sort, but on occasion, of scarcely less ferocity.

The neo-Puritanism which prevails in rural America makes a powerful appeal to men at the bottom of the human ladder, for it makes virtues of the abstinences that fate forces upon them, and permits them to feel pleasantly superior to their betters. Thus a Baptist rustic in Mississippi is consoled when he compares his wife to the houris he sees in the movies, or the white mule he swigs behind the barndoor to the hellish wines consumed in New York. His guides spiritual and moral, in the main, are hinds like himself, and have little learning, even in theology. It does not daunt them when their theorizings bring them into plain conflict with the text of Holy Writ, as happened in the case of Prohibition. There are few of them who do not pretend, by inference if not explicitly, to be better than Jesus. What animates them is mainly an insatiable thirst for power: it explains their frequent excursions into politics, and their general lack of conscience. When Bishop James Cannon, Jr., taken in flagrant stock gambling, protested that he had no love for money *per se*, he was laughed at by many, yet he probably told the truth. He wanted money simply to increase and consolidate his already formidable power, both ecclesiastical and political — in his own jargon, to extend the Kingdom. Cadging money from the faithful, among his colleagues of the evangelical sects, is always spoken of as " Kingdom work." No wonder they are all fond (as the bishop himself is) of quoting John Wesley's sermon on money, beginning " Make all you can." For it not only justifies their own insatiable demands for more and more of it; it also gives a flavor of piety to the practices of their chief lay supporters, who are the bankers and industrialists of the Bible country. Whenever there has been a strike of millhands down there the local evangelical clergy have been almost unanimously in favor of the employers, and for a sound reason: the employers build their churches and pay their salaries.

" To escape its miserable lot," said M. A. Bakunin in " Dieu et l'État," " the proletariat has three devices, two imaginary and one real. The first two are alcohol and religion; the third is the social revolution." He forgot poetry, and so did Paul. But the Catholic Church restored it, and keeps it to the fore today, if not as a living thing then at least as a very charming fossil. The fact explains its occasional success among the *intelligentsia*. Certainly it would be hard to imagine such a man as G. K. Chesterton or Hilaire Belloc testifying by affidavit that he believes in the whole body of Catholic doctrine, including all its necessary implications. But to poets, as they are, there is a powerful appeal in the Church's romantic history, and no less in its gorgeous myths and princely ceremonials. The Protestant, save he be a High Church Episcopalian, which is to say, a Catholic in all save a few trivial details, misses all this. The God he approaches is the harsh old Yahweh of the Old Testament, speaking in plain American through the medium of a bustling agent in a business suit; there is no buffer of saints and angels, holy water and incense, Latin and robes of state. To be sure, there is some movement toward ritualism on the higher levels of Methodism, with candles burning and the pastor in something resembling a chasuble, but it is confined to a few churches in the big cities, and is not likely to go far. The rural Methodist must still take the Word in the raw, and in bleeding chunks. The tragedy of him is that, despite its depressing literalness, it is still the best fodder that his imagination ever feeds on. If poetry could be added to it he would undoubtedly be a happier and a better man. And all Christianity, in all probability, would be a gentler and more charming thing if the Early Fathers had only added alcohol to poetry and revelation, for it offers a pleasanter escape from reality than either of them.

All religions are time-binding mechanisms: one of their central aims is to insure a continuity of thought on the matters with which they deal. There are plain advantages in this, for it is human to assume that truth, like wine, somehow improves with age. The Catholic Church, if it had no other claim to superiority, would seem nobler than the Protestant sects simply because of its greater antiquity. But too implacable a fidelity to what is ancient has its hazards in a world of constantly accelerating change, and Holy Church shows the scars of more than one of them. Its insistence that obedience to authority is a moral duty has lost it two-thirds of Christendom since the Middle Ages, and its archaic and unhealthy exaltation of chastity may run it into other heavy losses on some near tomorrow. I tremble to contemplate what would happen if an infidel scientist discovered that conception could be prevented by some indubitably " natural " means, say a manganese-free diet. Or if another, out of inert matter, concocted a living cell in his laboratory. Both of these possibilities have at least as much probability in them today as photographing the skeleton through the flesh had in October, 1895. And there are others that might be thought of. Though authority may have revelation behind it, its vetoes of science become increasingly perilous. There are multitudes of scientists to whom the Church's mandates are only empty words, and they are the scientists who are chiefly attended to.

All the branches of Christianity suffer by the fact that they seem to be unable to take in the greatest contribution of the modern world to ethical theory, to wit, the concept of a moral obligation to be intelligent, or, at all events, to be as intelligent as possible. To this concept the sanction of revelation makes a stout resistance, and no wonder, for every time it yields, however little, its fundamental postulates are shaken, and with them its whole fabric. As I have tried to show, many of the values that it sets up are highly dubious, and by the same token many of those that it opposes are obviously sound. Thus Christianity, gathering unreality, falls out of the world movement, which is predominantly realistic, and for every Chesterton that it intoxicates by its poetry it alienates a hundred better men by its prose. Its moral system remains an easy and grateful refuge for the weak and the sick, the stupid and the misinformed, the confiding and the irresolute, but there is little in it to attract men and women who are intelligent and enterprising, and do not fear remote, gaseous and preposterous gods, and have a proper respect for the dignity of man.

V

Its State Today

1

How long it will take mankind to get rid of the sanction of religion altogether no one can say, and I do not venture to guess. It may very well be many centuries. For the intelligent minority that I was just speaking of is still precariously small, even in the most advanced societies, and its intelligence does not work all the time, but only at irregular and as yet unpredictable intervals, like Planck's quanta. The art of thinking, indeed, is too recent an acquirement of man for him to exercise it continuously, or with anything resembling genuine virtuosity. Especially in the field of morals his attempts to use it encounter difficulties, for there his every thought is likely to come into conflict with an instant and powerful feeling. Back in the Seventeenth Century the philosopher and mathematician Descartes, discerning what grave damage feelings can do, denounced them all as " only false judgments," and proposed boldly to bring them under the heel of reason. But that was before Freud. Today no psychologist would father a project so at variance with the most obvious facts of human nature. It is well settled that the cerebral cortex, though unquestionably admirable as a machine, is hardly a prime mover, and all of us have had personal experience of the havoc that a slight excess of adrenalin can play with its operations. Nor is adrenalin the only poison able to flabbergast it, or the worst. The full list would run the length of the Pharmacopeia, and high on it would be ethyl alcohol and the obscure but immensely toxic emanations that issue from the eyes of a woman not unwilling. Holy Church, which, if it isn't exactly intelligent, is certainly worldly wise, has known all this for many centuries, and now science begins to marshal the proofs.

Most of the changes that have shown themselves in the ethical thinking of civilized man since the Renaissance are probably due to a gradual abatement of one of the fundamental feelings of the race, to wit, fear. Before *Homo sapiens* began to doubt he was in a constant state of alarm, as savages are to this day. Ghosts haunted him, demons dogged him, and over all reigned an inscrutable Yahweh whose playthings were storms and lightnings, wars and pestilences. It was thought to be extremely dangerous to venture upon any criticism, however polite, of this brutal Libertine of the Air. The problem of evil was scarcely a problem in those days: evil was simply a cosmic fact, like the sun. Did Yahweh strike down strong men in their prime, and hatch multitudes of lepers and cripples, and harass and torture the widow and the orphan?

Then the most that man could do was to note the fact
and acquiesce in it: any search for a remedy, or even
any thought of a remedy, came uncomfortably close
to blasphemy. All this must be remembered if we are
to understand the appalling brutalities of the Ages of
Faith, described briefly in the last chapter. There was
plenty of charity, as there had been among the ancient
Jews — indeed, charity was held to rank third among
the virtues. But it was a kind of charity that not only
accepted the most cruel suffering complacently, but
actually counted it as necessary to the salvation of the
faithful. Without the constant presence of the halt and
the blind, the poor and the despairing, there would
have been no incitement to almsgiving — and next to
faith and chastity, almsgiving offered the most trusted
route to Heaven. The fact goes far to explain the medieval hostility to that pressing inquiry into the causes
of things which modern man takes so much for
granted. In the enterprise, then as now, the religious
mind recognized a tacit conspiracy against Yahweh,
and under the shadow of the Universal Church any
such contumacy was dangerous. Today the danger is
only a memory, but the offense itself, in pious circles,
lives on. One of the favorite arguments of the theologians who made the final fight for slavery in the 50's
of the last century was that freeing the slaves would
be an unholy resistance to Yahweh's obvious will that
they keep their chains. And to this day the same idea,
or something very close to it, appears in the Catholic

opposition to birth control. It is not only a sin against nature for a woman to seek to avoid maternity; it is also a gross affront to the Lord God Omnipotent, who has ordained that her dalliance shall have its inevitable penalty in pain, fright and hemorrhage.

Who the first modern skeptics were is not known, for, being intelligent enough to doubt, they were also intelligent enough to keep their doubts to themselves, but I often suspect that Thomas Aquinas may have been one of them. It is, indeed, impossible to imagine a man of his extraordinary logical sense not applying it, in quiet moments, to some of the more flagrant imbecilities of Christian theology. We first hear of skepticism as a going concern in the Italy of the mid-Fourteenth Century, during the exile of the Popes in France, and there is plenty of reason for believing that their absence opened the way for it. It developed rapidly into the tremendous phenomenon called the Renaissance, the essential achievement of which was the liberation of man from slavery to revelation. From now onward purely human values began to be put on a par with the old divine values, and the way was open for that entirely rationalistic attack upon the great problems of being and becoming which still engages the race. Unfortunately, the Reformation, which followed soon afterward, worked against the Renaissance quite as much as with it, for every time the reformers disposed of some article of the Catholic theology they substituted something worse. If they had succeeded in upsetting Holy Church altogether, and managed to agree among themselves, the Western World would have been in for a new Dark Age, with witches and demons restored, all free inquiry prohibited, and the most blatant and ignorant sacerdotal tyranny ever heard of in power. The despotism of Calvin in Geneva and that of the Puritans in early New England give somewhat mild indications of its probable pretensions. But the reformers were presently at such violent odds with one another that the force of the Reformation was dissipated, and during the Sixteenth and Seventeenth Centuries there was a rapid growth of skepticism, and the organized curiosity that we call modern science was born. The way had been prepared for it, during the first days of the Renaissance, by the revival of Greek studies, but in the long run those studies impeded it more than they helped it. Indeed, the authority of Plato and Aristotle, of Hippocrates and Galen, was an even greater obstacle to the New Learning than the authority of Paul and Augustine, and there was no real liberation of the mind of man until it had been thrown off.

The chief heroes of this double revolt, against Christian dogma and Greek dogma, were Michel de Montaigne (1533–92), Francis Bacon (1561–1626), René Descartes (1596–1650), Baruch Spinoza (1632–77) and Gottfried von Leibniz (1646–1716) — two Frenchmen, an Englishman, a German and a Jew. Montaigne played a sardonic hose upon the

Christian system and left it soggy and bedraggled. Bacon spoke out boldly for the observed fact, and against the *a priori* theory. Descartes, Spinoza and Leibniz, rejecting the incredible Yahweh of Judæo-Christian myth, sought to formulate concepts of a Supreme Intelligence that should be at least imaginable to a sane and sober man. There was rapid progress in detail as in gross. Modern medicine was born, the microscope was invented, chemistry emerged from the shadows of alchemy, the range of mathematics was greatly extended, and astronomy was made an exact science. The period swarms with immortal names — Copernicus, Galileo, Tycho Brahe, Giordano Bruno, Newton, Kepler, Harvey, Boyle, Leeuwenhoek, Malpighi, and many another. All the nations of Western Europe were represented in the movement. The common use of Latin, which continued to be the language of the learned down to the beginning of the Eighteenth Century, made for an easy exchange of ideas, and what was discovered or suggested in one country was quickly taken up in all others. Beginning with the invention of the steam-engine by James Watt in 1769, the world was to see an era of even more rapid progress, but it is doubtful if the great innovations of the Nineteenth Century were more revolutionary in essence or of more certain and lasting value to mankind than those of the Sixteenth and Seventeenth. It was then that civilization as we know it today really came to life.

Naturally enough, ethical speculation kept pace with the forward movement in other fields. The Reformation, if it brought in no new ideas here, at least produced a critical reëxamination of those that had prevailed in Christendom for so long, and as theological authority decayed the sanction of revelation decayed with it, and enlightened men looked about them for more plausible support for the ordinances of custom and conscience. A good beginning was made by Hugo Grotius, a Dutchman, in 1625, with " De Jure Belli ac Pacis " (The Rights of War and Peace), an attempt to establish a rational morality in the realm of international relations. But Grotius was not content to write a mere textbook of international law; he also sought to discover the genesis of moral ideas in general, and he found it, as Sidgwick says, in " the essential nature of man, who is distinguished among animals by his peculiar appetite for tranquil association with his fellows, and his tendency to act on general principles." Out of this appetite and tendency, he said, there arise a series of principles which constitute an immutable natural law, and are superior to " the law which God Himself has been pleased to reveal," for the latter " does not command or forbid things which are binding or unlawful in themselves, but only makes them unlawful by its prohibition, or binding by its command." This was bold speaking for a man but recently escaped from a prison to which he had been condemned for life for heresy. But Grotius went even further. In the very first chapter of his book he argued that " the law of nature is so unalterable that it cannot be changed even by God Himself," and a bit later he actually proposed to test the acts of God by its mandates.

Twenty-six years later, in England, Thomas Hobbes published his " Leviathan," an even more radical attack upon the fundamental ethical problem. Hobbes held that the principles of conduct were simple and few in number, and that all of them were based upon self-interest — either the desire to survive or the desire to enjoy some foreseen pleasure. This theory of self-interest, of course, he did not propose as an excuse for moral anarchy; on the contrary, he posited it as the principal prop of government, the aim of which, as he thought, is to enhance the security and happiness of man on earth by curbing his more bellicose enterprises, and protecting him against those of other men. In brief, man must be kept up to his social duties by proving to him that it is safer and pleasanter to observe them than to forget them. Once he accepts this proof he has acquired the virtue of " complaisance," and is in accord with what Hobbes calls " the fifth law of nature," to wit, " that every man strive to accommodate himself to the rest." His accommodation must be accompanied by politeness — a Chinese virtue, here first heard of in the Western World since the days of Clement of Alexandria. He must acknowledge every other man " his equal by nature," and

neither by " deed, word, countenance or gesture declare hatred or contempt for another." Thus Hobbes,
by a circuitous route, arrived at a cautious restate-
ment of the Golden Rule: " Do not that to another
which thou wouldst not have done to thyself." The
judicious will observe that he changed the familiar
text to a purely negative form, and was silent about
duties of omission.

His somewhat hedonistic and over-simple scheme
was attacked promptly by various other moralists,
both in England and on the Continent. Obviously, it
was not purely individualistic, for behind its concept
of self-interest there was also a concept of the common
good; nevertheless, it seemed harsh and immoral to
socially-minded men, and a long succession of them
tried to work out something better. During the Eighteenth Century that effort divided itself into two
branches. On the one hand, David Hume (1711–76)
and his followers endeavored to find a master-sanc-
tion in " public interest and utility," and on the other
hand Immanuel Kant (1724–1804) looked for it in
the intuitive perception of a somewhat vague moral
law, corrected from time to time by the pragmatic
criterion of workableness. It was Kant's idea that the
good man should test his every action by asking himself what sort of world we'd be living in if all men did
the same. Unfortunately, he overlooked the fact that
the judgment of two equally good men might differ —
that one might welcome a world that the other would

find unendurable. What was needed was a less subjective test, and it was presently found by the Utilitarians in "the greatest happiness of the greatest number." This idea was by no means new: it had been adumbrated back in 1672 by Richard Cumberland, an intelligent bishop, in his "De Legibus Naturæ," written against Hobbes, and it had been stated clearly by Francis Hutcheson in 1725 and by Joseph Priestley in 1768, but it remained for Jeremy Bentham to expound it at length in his "Introduction to the Principles of Morals and Legislation," published in 1789.

The Utilitarian gospel fell upon a world prepared for it by the rise of democracy, and for half a century it prospered mightily, especially in England and the United States, with Bentham first, and then the two Mills, James and John Stuart, as its chief evangelists. It appeared to solve the social problem neatly and finally, and was thus grateful to all the concoctors of Utopias, including the Socialists. To this day it is much esteemed by politicians, whose test of right is that sufficient human blanks vote aye, and of wrong that it can muster only the intelligent. The plain man, indeed, is always a Utilitarian — until he is asked to make some sacrifice for what is held to be the common weal: then he becomes a Hobbesian hedonist of the most implacable kind. On higher levels Utilitarianism has fared less well. It got devastating blows from Carlyle in " Past and Present " (" Happy, my brother? First of all, what difference is it whether thou art happy or not?"), from Darwin in "The Descent of Man," and above all, from Nietzsche, who denounced every attempt to further the greatest happiness of the greatest number as a conspiracy against the welfare of the race. The aim of any true morality, argued Nietzsche, must be to safeguard the natural advantage of the strong, the brave, the enterprising, the superior. The slightest departure from that Spartan programme is a return to Christianity, which " has the rancor of the sick at its very core — the instinct against the healthy, against health," and is " the one great curse, the one great intrinsic depravity, the one great instinct of revenge, for which no means are venomous enough, or secret, subterranean and small enough — I call it the one immortal blemish upon the human race."

2

It seems to be generally believed that we are now living in an age of ethical revolution, and one frequently hears, both from alarmed conservatives and from hopeful radicals, that all the old moral values are being abandoned, and that the *Umwertung aller Werte* announced by Nietzsche is in full blast. This, I believe, is an exaggeration. The rapid decay of the sanction of revelation, and the stout competition that the sanction of instinct (liberated by Darwin, and encouraged to do its worst by Freud and company) is offering to the sanction of reason — this double-barrelled process is naturally upsetting a great many earnest people, but I see no evidence of a general departure from the moral norms established on earth since time immemorial. The five basic evils — murder, adultery, theft, trespass and false witness — are still held to be evils everywhere, and the most we are seeing is a somewhat muddled effort to redefine them in harmony with the changing needs of mankind. Outside the Greenwich Villages and Hollywoods of the world no one advocates anything properly describable as amorality; on the contrary, what we mainly hear is the preaching of new virtues, some of them very onerous.

It is significant that all the more recent despotisms — Bolshevism, Fascism, and so on — are intensely moral in pretension, and bristle with harsh thou-shalt-nots. The Russian of today, for example, bears a much heavier burden of duty than he ever bore under the Czars. If, in that almost forgotten era, he was polite to Church and state, no one showed much concern about his conduct otherwise, and he was quite free to harry a Jew at his discretion, to beat his wife, to waste his substance in riotous living, or to get money by almost any device that seemed feasible. Capital punishment was seldom inflicted for ordinary crime, and imprisonment was uncommon: the usual penalty was exile to Siberia, where the condemned had a great deal of freedom, and could bring on his wife and family and pursue his normal trade if he had any. But today, though he has been delivered from the tyranny of Czar and Church, he staggers under an absolutism that is immensely more oppressive. All his property save a few trinkets has been taken away from him, and he can live only at the pleasure of the politicians, and on such terms as they choose to fix. The penalties for resisting them, even *in petto*, are appallingly cruel, and there is no appeal from their mandates. The offsets to this slavery are few and trivial. One is that the Russian may divorce his wife at a few hours' notice and at the cost of a few paper rubles, but that is a boon to a minority only, for the average man, in Russia as elsewhere, does not want to divorce his wife. The wife, in her turn, is free to employ contraceptive devices *ad libitum*, and if they play her false she may resort to abortion without risk of going to jail, but that also is a very small benefit, for contraception is almost universal in Christendom, and it is virtually unheard of for a woman who survives an abortion to be punished. Both husband and wife may now vote — but only if they vote for the reigning politicos.

Various hopeful Western visitors to Russia have come home with the news that these politicos have talked the common people out of self-interest, and convinced them that the highest moral good is serving the common weal, and it is sometimes assumed that this represents a genuine transvaluation of values, affecting a large fraction of civilized humanity. But the revolution thus reported is more apparent than real. One of the most friendly visitors, Miss Ella Winter, opens the chapter entitled " New Incentives for Old " in her book, " Red Virtue," with the significant admission that " the chief incentive to work under a Socialist order is much the same as the incentive to work under other systems: to make a living." There is no evidence save their general non-resistance that the common people of Russia prefer their enforced and regimented labor to idleness, or find any satisfaction in it superior to the satisfaction that goes with earning money and acquiring property. On the contrary, all the available evidence indicates that they would greatly appreciate greater liberty and larger rewards, including a surplus of cash income above their needs; in fact, one of the ways their masters keep in power is by promising them such rewards on some vague tomorrow. Thus there is no more reason for accepting their complaisance as proof of a moral revolution than there is for accepting the complaisance of prisoners confined in an efficient house of correction. Both alike would escape if they could, and escaping, they would resume the ethics of self-interest instantly, and in its most drastic Hobbesian form.

The Fascist system is even less revolutionary, ethically speaking; indeed, the fact that it is actually reactionary is generally recognized. In both Italy and Germany the reigning powers have come to terms with ecclesiastical authority of one sort or another, and so given the sanction of revelation a new lease on life, and everywhere they have sought to make nationalism — which by their definition simply means subservience to themselves — a kind of religion, with a mythology almost as florid and incredible as that of Christianity. The German Nazis have really gone beyond Christianity to Judaism, for their dogma of a Chosen People, despite its quasi-scientific investiture, is a plain echo of Psalms LXXXIX, 3–4, *ibid.*, CV, 6, Isaiah XLIII, 20, and I Chronicles XVI, 13. The notion that nationalism is a relatively modern invention seems to be widely held, and there are authorities who ascribe it to Henry VII of England, to Mercantilism, or to the French Revolution. But it was really very common in ancient times, and the Babylonians, Hittites, Egyptians, Greeks and Romans were almost as chauvinistic as the Jews. This was especially true in the days of their decline — in Greece, for example, after Pericles — , for nationalism is peculiarly the disease of insecure and alarmed nations, just as communism is the disease of doomed ones. It disappeared from Europe with the rise of the Universal Church, which aspired to break down all geographical and racial lines and establish a world empire, but when the Renaissance and the Reformation dissipated that dream it revived promptly, and has been increasing in virulence ever since.

Its ethical evils have been somewhat exaggerated

by the proponents of international Utopias, but that
its effects have been generally bad is plain enough.
It sets up all sorts of meretricious values, and seeks
to enforce them with new sanctions of revelation,
handed down from Sinai by highly dubious Moseses
— Mussolini and Hitler, Beaverbrook and Hearst,
and so on. It has immensely reinforced the power of
professional politicians, few of them of any rational
conscience, and so greatly interfered with the natural
intercourse between nations that the trade of the
world is almost in ruins and war is a daily menace.
It is impossible for any man, however much he may
dissent from the prevailing mandates, to escape their
effects. At home his property is confiscated and wasted
and his common liberties are invaded and made a
mock of, and abroad he finds himself in the unhappy
position of a suspect everywhere. Meanwhile, the
masses are fed with alarms, and an endless succession
of mountebanks, raising bugaboos only to lay them,
passes through all the public offices, including especially that of the official pedagogue. The evil growth
of the more absurd forms of nationalism during the
past century is probably largely due to the spread of
free education. When the pedagogue becomes a public functionary his natural puerility and timidity are
increased, and he is a docile propagandist of any
doctrine enunciated by the politicians. In the United
States, during the high days of the Anti-Saloon League,
he was an ardent Prohibitionist, and at all times he

is full of the kind of patriotism that Samuel Johnson described as the last refuge of a scoundrel. It would be hard to imagine a more shaky guide to sound morals and common decency.

In the midst of this enormous conspiracy to set nation against nation there remain idealists who dream of abolishing war. If, by some miracle, they could get their wish, nationalism would decay, and with it most of its false and demoralizing values, for the fountains of its strength are in fear, and not many men would fear an enemy armed only with justice. But there seems to be little likelihood that war will be abolished until the present historical era fades into another, and that may be many centuries. Man is still too near the nomad to forego, when his blood is up, the pleasurable excitement of pursuit and combat, and the tendency of all the agencies which fashion his thinking is to keep his blood up. The demand for peace, when it issues from governments, is never anything save a demand for advantage. I have, as a journalist, attended three international conferences for the discouragement of war, and that is all I could detect at any of them. After a few days of hypocritical politeness the assembled statesmen settled down to grabbing as much as they could, and when they got home they were all judged, not by what they had yielded to peace but by what they had got for war. The League of Nations began to disintegrate as soon as its real purpose was detected, which was almost immediately after its organization. Despite all the romantic claptrap of the mountebanks who organized it, it was actually set up to safeguard for the victors the spoils of the World War, and it no sooner began to function than those victors were at odds among themselves, seeking to hoodwink and damage one another.

Under all such failures there is a greater one: the failure of man, the most social of all the higher animals and by far the most intelligent, to provide himself with anything even remotely describable as good government. He has made many attempts in that direction, some of them very ingenious and others sublimely heroic, but they have always come to grief in the execution. The reason is surely not occult: it is to be found in the abysmal difference between what government is in theory and what it is in fact. In theory it is simply a device for supplying a variable series of common needs, and the men constituting it (as all ranks of them are so fond of saying) are only public servants; but in fact its main purpose is not service at all but exploitation, and the men constituting it are as little moved by concepts of public duty and responsibility as, say, the corps of advertising agents, or that of stock brokers, or that of attorneys. To this rule there are so few exceptions that when a politician shows signs of developing into what is called a statesman, *i.e.*, an officer of government capable both mentally and morally of subordinating his private interest to the common good, the phenomenon causes general astonishment, and is regarded as a kind of miracle. The overwhelming majority of public functionaries are devoted to the single purpose of holding and improving their jobs. To that end they are willing to make any sacrifice in morals or in honor. They constitute, in fact, a class of professional immoralists, living by preying on the ignorance and credulity, the foolish fears and vain hopes of their victims. In societies organized as despotisms there is literally no limit to their outreaching for power and profit, and even under the most liberal democracies they carry on a bold and unconscionable conspiracy against the common weal.

So far every effort to curb them has failed. The scheme of giving them a professional status and tenure, and so trying to awaken in them a professional pride and dignity, has been almost as ineffective as the scheme of making their tenure short, and so getting rid of them before they can consolidate their power. The first scheme simply converts them into a chartered band of exploiters, protected by an artificial bill of rights against scrutiny and accounting, and the second only sharpens their voracity by limiting its opportunity. Of all the varieties of government it is probably democracy that has fared worse at the hands of these brethren. Knowing very well, as a cardinal article of their art, how little people in general are moved by rational ideas and how much by mere hullabaloo, they make common cause with every pressure group that comes along, and are thus maintained in office by an endless series of public enemies. In the United States it would be hard to imagine any project so lunatic that they would hesitate to embrace it, if only it could make them votes and keep them in office. In my own State of Maryland the majority of professional politicians of both parties were lately conniving at lynching in order to conciliate the Methodist-Baptist vote in a remote and backward but politically important section. If there arose tomorrow a band of fanatics advocating cannibalism that was as daring in political enterprise and as skillful in rounding up morons as the Anti-Saloon League was in 1919, two Congressmen out of three would be converted to its gospel instantly, and three public-school teachers out of four would probably be serving it as evangelists within a month. In the field of government all the ethical sanctions simply cease to be. Every government, as such, is a scoundrel. In its relations with other governments it resorts to frauds and barbarities that were prohibited to private men by the Common Law of civilization so long ago as the reign of Hammurabi, and in its dealings with its own people it not only steals and wastes their property and plays a brutal and witless game with their natural rights, but regularly gambles with their very lives. Wars are seldom caused by spontaneous hatreds between peoples, for peoples in general are too ignorant of one another to have grievances and too indifferent to what goes on beyond their borders to plan conquests. They must be urged to the slaughter by politicians who know how to alarm them. It is one of the imperishable ironies that this urging is always done in the argot of the loftiest rectitude. Thus the men who, taking one with another, are the worst knaves in the world are also the chief repositories of that dismal hypocrisy which mirrors at once man's longing to be good — and his failure.

3

In the moral novelties commonly preached in the world today there is little that is actually new. The demand for a greater measure of what is called social justice is simply a compound of the old Christian gospel of brotherhood and the Humanism of the Renaissance, as anyone may discover by examining critically any of its salient documents, say Shelley's "Queen Mab," Henry George's "Progress and Poverty," or Pope Pius XI's *Quadragesimo anno*. Dr. James Henry Breasted, in "The Dawn of Conscience," says that in all its essentials it was preached in Egypt "around 2000 B.C.," and that at about the same time the Egyptian theologians, falling into accord with the movement, began admitting the common people to "the glorious celestial destiny" that was formerly "the exclusive privilege of the Pharaohs." In late years the theologians of Christendom have combined with the politicians to put down what is left of the law of natural selection, finally and forever — with the perhaps inevitable result that it promises to enjoy a considerable revival in the near future. In this mer-chanting of hope the politicians may seem to be abandoning their usual professional reliance on fear, but that seeming is only seeming, for they sell their Utopias by the simple device of depicting war and famine, chaos and despair as the alternative to buy-ing. The theologians, as I say, have gone with them, but only, it appears, somewhat reluctantly. There re-mains a formidable body of ecclesiastical opinion which holds that social justice is a dangerous rival to *post-mortem* felicity, and hence an enemy to the True Faith. In a really happy world there would be little incentive to piety, which is intrinsically only an exchange of suffering here for bliss beyond. For-tunately for theology, there seems to be little likelihood that social justice will go far enough to cure all the sorrows of mankind. As the example of Russia well shows, even the most furious levelling cannot extir-pate the universal human longing for privilege. All that Bolshevism has really achieved in that direction is to round up the privileges formerly enjoyed by nobles and millionaires, priests and sages, and hand them over to politicians.

In his interesting and ingenious " Preface to Mor-als," published in 1929, Walter Lippmann envisaged a world in which the sheer scope and momentum of events would tend to break down the motive of self-interest and substitute that of social utility. " When," he said, " the machine technology is really advanced — that is to say, when it has drawn great masses of men within the orbit of its influence, when a corporation has become really great — the old distinction between public and private interest becomes very dim." From this he looked for the emergence of a class of great industrial magnates who would think of themselves as, and be in effect, public officials. But that was written in the optimistic days before 1929; since then we have learned a lot about the fundamental psychology of such men, and about their behavior when they actually get into public office. In brief, they simply swap the frank self-seeking of their own class for the hypocritical self-seeking of politicians. Suffice it to recall the case of the lamented Hoover. After starting out in life as a practitioner of enlightened self-interest in its most relentless corporate form, he took to good works in 1914, and was presently hailed everywhere as a champion altruist. But when, in 1921, he got into public office he began to cultivate at once all the slimy arts of the politician and his election to the Presidency in 1928 was achieved in alliance with all the worst professionals in the country, from the Vare gang to the Anti-Saloon League. It turned out in the end that he had no real gift for the elaborate deceits and dissemblings that are the essence of practical politics under democracy, but certainly he had plenty of libido.

[296]

ITS STATE TODAY

In their recurrent battles for social justice politicians commonly take the line of assaulting William Graham Sumner's Forgotten Man — that obscure, decent, uncomplaining good citizen who works hard, obeys the laws, cares for his family, and pays his own way. He is seldom, of course, denounced specifically, for his merits are too manifest, but every variety of New Freedom and New Deal, though it may appear to be levelled at malefactors much above him, really has him for its chief victim. He is the target alike of all the schemes to rob the haves to fatten the have-nots and of all the schemes to set up new virtues by law and inculcate them by force. Of late in the United States he was harassed for thirteen long years in an effort to dissuade him from that mild use of alcoholic beverages which has been one of the most valuable consolations of civilized man since the remotest antiquity. It failed as such imbecilities always fail, but while it was going on neighbor was set against neighbor, hordes of professional thugs and blackmailers were turned loose upon the country, the courts were corrupted and degraded, and crime was so nourished that it became a major industry. Sometimes the thing runs the other way — that is, the effort is not to erect a new virtue, but to upset an old one. There is an example current as I write, to wit, the attempt by the so-called Brain Trust to depict thrift as anti-social, and the man who objects to handing over his property to politicians and their mendicant clients as a scoundrel. It will fail here just as surely as in Russia, and much sooner, for thrift has been increasingly esteemed throughout the Western World since the Reformation and has been a cardinal American virtue since the time of Benjamin Franklin, but while it is going on it will ruin many Forgotten Men, and prosper a great many fools and frauds. Meanwhile, there is not the slightest chance that it will curb the exploitation at which it is ostensibly directed. All it will accomplish in that direction is what has been accomplished in Russia, which is to say, the substitution of a new group of exploiters for an old one.

Through every such enterprise there runs a common psychology. They are all, at bottom, conspiracies of inferior men against their betters. This was manifestly true in the case of Prohibition, which had little behind it, philosophically speaking, save the envy of the country lout for the city man, who has a much better time of it in this world, and is believed in the country to have an even better time than he actually has. It is no less true in the case of innovations of a political and economic character. The reckless fury of the Brain Trusts that afflict humanity from time to time is due mainly to the fact that they are composed of essentially obscure men — Rousseau, the Montagnards, Tom Paine, Feargus O'Connor, Lenin, Trotsky, and so on. Thus the cocksureness that is natural to the evangelists of new gospels is reinforced and made malignant by a yearning to affront and humble superiors, to seize a gaudy place in the sun, to liberate an oppressed and agonized ego. The Brain Trust that began to harass the American people in 1932 was typical. It was composed mainly of minor university dignitaries, a class of men who suffer severely, in ordinary times, from the low public esteem in which they are held, and are especially upset when they contrast it with the relatively high position of their colleagues on the Continent of Europe. Let such men be thrown, by some aberration of politics, into places of authority, and they are certain to react in an extravagant manner. No doubt the performance that was staged in Washington would have been even more extravagant if the chief actors had been, not pedagogues, but persons of a yet more humble and despised station, say advertising agents, chiropractors, or Y.M.C.A. secretaries. To what lengths the downtrodden may go, once they get power into their hands, was classically exemplified by the black-and-tan Legislatures which ravaged the South after the Civil War.

Like the politicians and the theologians, all such revolutionists carry on their business to the tune of moral outcries, and are eager inventors of new virtues and new sins. They show something of the character of the moral reformer, properly so called, and are almost as anti-social. This moral reformer is a creature peculiar to relatively civilized societies; among savages he would be recognized instantly for the public enemy that he is, and disposed of out of hand. He is, of course, profoundly immoral at bottom, and even a kind of criminal. He appeared in perfect flower in John Calvin, in the New England witch-hunters, and again in John Brown. During the Prohibition madness in the United States he flourished in great numbers, bellowing for the pursuit and jailing and even for the murder of all who declined to accept his brummagem gospel. " The spirit in which she condemns evil," said John Burroughs of " one dear to him," " is worse than the evil itself." It would be hard to characterize the professional moralist more aptly. His motives lie in the Freudian depths, and his altruism is palpably sham. In his more extreme forms he is hard to distinguish from the downright insane. Holy Church, always served by shrewd psychological insight, makes a deliberate effort to restrain him. " The scrupulous who are inclined to suspect or see evil where there is none," say McHugh and Callan in their " Moral Theology," " are generally excused from the duty of making corrections." But on the Protestant side there is no such wisdom, and in consequence the countries delivered from Rome are beset perennially by bands of " madmen and women, men with beards, Dunkers, Muggletonians, Come-outers, Groaners, Agrarians, Seventh-Day Baptists, Quakers, Abolitionists " and other such virtuosi, seeking whom they may save from sin and damnation. Nor is the moral virtuoso much more prepossessing when he takes the Devil's side, and howls for license instead of for restraint. The birth controllers, for example, often carry on their indelicate crusade with the pious rancor of Prohibitionists, and the various factions of Communists are all very bellicose fellows, with so vast an appetite for blood that when they can't shed their enemies' they are quite willing to shed their own.

4

The new moralities cried up in the Western World today mainly have to do with sexual relations, and no wonder, for two epoch-making events have greatly changed the common thinking on the subject, and neither, so to speak, is yet digested. The first is the virtual disappearance of the old Christian belief and confidence in Hell, at least among persons reasonably describable as literate. The second is the discovery and general dissemination of relatively reliable methods of contraception, described by George Bernard Shaw, and with no small plausibility, as the greatest invention of the Nineteenth Century. With the lake of brimstone no longer waiting *post mortem* and the fear of pregnancy abating, it is perhaps not unnatural that young females coming under temptation should succumb rather more often than their mothers, and that the more ingenious among them should attempt to rationalize this surrender to their hormones. The actually amoral, of course, do not bother to invent excuses, but those who suffer from whispers of conscience seek justification in the works of such advanced moralists as Ellen Key, Bertrand Russell, the Greenwich Village poets, the Communist metaphysicians, and the various wings of Freudians and *Über*-Freudians. Something else should be added: the wider opportunities for sexual experiment and adventure that issue out of the unprecedented mobility of modern life. The carnal landscape of a generation ago showed little save an occasional uncomfortable haymow, and to the city girl's eyes even so much was lacking, but now good roads run in every direction, and on them are automobiles carrying the young to innumerable convenient bournes, some of them of great luxury and security. Moreover, the general laxness of manners has liberated many ancient incitements to dalliance, including especially alcohol and the dance.

But it is easy to over-estimate the resultant looseness, and not a few writers on the subject, among both the new moralists and the old, do exaggerate it heavily. Their mistake lies in assuming that the lowest dip of their statistical curve touches something on the order of zero — that there was little or no fornication in Christendom before the present age came in. Nothing could be more absurd — as every oldster knows whose memories go back, say, to the nineties of the last century, when the indignant grandmothers of the present youngsters were young themselves, and fevered by the same hormones. The Victorian spirit

must not be taken too seriously. What it frowned on
and what it actually eschewed were two quite different
things. It was much less a scheme of conduct than a
programme of attitudes, and the excessive chastity to
which it pretended had very little psychological
reality. Obviously, any fair study of moral progress,
either up or down, must concern itself with willing
quite as much as with doing, and on that basis the
young of today would probably turn out, if the whole
truth could be known, to be very little more goatish
than the young of yesterday. They discuss their desires
a great deal more openly, but that freedom of speech
is a gain rather than a loss, for it exhausts curiosity
and dampens imagination. The *Backfisch* who reads
the Russells, Freud and Havelock Ellis emerges from
them with a considerably cleaner mind than her grand-
mother who wolfed inflammatory novels surrepti-
tiously. And if, having mastered the current theories
of sex, she decides to resort to the laboratory, she
commonly comes out of it with relatively little damage,
either physical or psychic. One of the really great
advances that we have made in practical morals lies
in the abandonment of the old view of female chastity
as a sort of toy balloon, to be collapsed instantly and
forever by one touch of flame. It is now known to be
a much more complicated structure, with considerable
powers of repair and regeneration, and every person
of any worldly experience is acquainted with more
than one woman who, after a period of experiment

and disillusion, is now a faithful and contented wife. The fact is that centuries of breeding to predominantly monogamous women have made a tendency to monogamy almost a secondary sexual character in the normal human female. Nor is that tendency absent from the male.

The increase in divorce gives a great deal of concern to moralists of the old order, but there is no evidence that it is actually working against the security of monogamous marriage, or that its social effects otherwise are deleterious. The simian phenomena that it gives rise to in Hollywood and among the more vicious groups of idle rich are of little significance, socially speaking. Women of a certain type have made a kind of prostitution of marriage since the dawn of history, and men of a certain type have found them irresistible. But the general effect of free divorce, as opposed to this special effect, is not to make marriage approximate concubinage but to keep the two things distinct. It brings deliverance to multitudes of women who, without it, would be doomed to an unwilling prostitution far more irksome than the voluntary kind I have just mentioned, and it lets multitudes of suffering men out of situations almost as bad. Nor are those who actually escape the only beneficiaries; it also ameliorates the lot of those who go on, if only by relieving them of their feeling of hopeless imprisonment. The theory that every marriage should endure to the end of the chapter, even if it becomes downright unendurable, is the invention of celibate theologians, and hardly deserves serious refutation. It is a peculiarly Christian piece of nonsense, and in late years has been mainly Catholic. It is based upon a plain perversion of the teachings of Jesus, who would have been amazed and horrified by some of its practical implications. It is, indeed, so preposterous that even Holy Church has been unable to maintain it in its pure form, but has had to dilute it with all sorts of evasions, including separation from bed and board, and dissolution on the ground of deceit or mental reservation. The former is flatly called divorce by secular lawyers — *i.e., a mensa et toro* as opposed to *a vinculo matrimonii* — , and the latter seems to be kept as a special favor for the rich and influential, as the Marconi case so embarrassingly showed. Here, as in the matter of birth control, Holy Church runs counter to the movement of civilization, and gets itself into increasing difficulties.

The Protestant theologians, in some cases, hold to the Catholic position in theory, but as a practical matter nearly all of them accept divorce as an inescapable fact, and try to make the best of it. Their yielding is a natural consequence of their generally precarious economic situation, for in most cases they are at the mercy of their flocks, and cannot go counter to what is done and approved by those who pay their wages and are free to dismiss them if they offend. As we have seen, this enforced complaisance is also visible in other fields, and humanlike, they usually try to rationalize it. Thus the Protestant objection to divorce is seldom an objection *à outrance*, but simply a criticism of what are held to be abuses. Some of those abuses are real, but most of them are imaginary. There is little reason to believe that easy divorce has actually diminished the normal proportion of contented and successful marriages. It has provided a humane escape for the victims of errors and deceits, and it has regularized more or less the polygamy of the naturally polygamous, but the fact remains that, even in Nevada, the overwhelming majority of marriages endure on a tolerable basis, and that relatively few persons whose unions have any social dignity or value ever resort to the divorce courts. Both the alarmed guardians of the old order and the more extreme advocates of the new seem to believe that we are facing a general breakdown of marriage, and with it of the family, but neither offers anything properly describable as evidence to that end. Indeed, all the available evidence runs to the contrary. Some of the ancient rigors of monogamy are lessening, but the thing itself appears to be quite as secure today as it has ever been in human history.

The Bible of the iconoclasts is "Marriage and Morals," by Bertrand Russell. It is really a very mild and cautious document — a fact shrewdly noted by one of its chief clerical critics, the Rev. G. E. Newsom, chaplain to King George V, who observes in

"The New Morality" that "the dogmatic tones of prophecy are not used," and that "every forecast is qualified by adverbs such as 'probably' or 'very likely.'" Earl Russell, in fact, offers only one contribution of any apparent novelty to connubial theory, and that is the suggestion that adultery, when it is carried on with reasonable decorum and has no bad social effects, ought to be removed from the catalogue of sins, torts and crimes. But even this is a novelty only in English-speaking countries; in France and elsewhere on the Continent all that the learned and noble moralist asks for has been embedded in law and custom for many years. Indeed, in England itself adultery has gradually shrunk to the dimensions of a minor breach of property right, and in the United States, though it remains a felony in many jurisdictions, its practice is actually dangerous only to notably unpopular persons. Earl Russell, I gather, does not propose to make it a public duty, nor even to throw it open to all; the most he asks for is that it be permitted to the superior couples who enjoy "a feeling of complete equality on both sides, . . . the most complete physical and mental intimacy, . . . and a certain similarity in regard to standards of value." But such couples, obviously, are already quite free to engage in adultery, for if one party is inclined to it then the other, having similar "standards of value," must necessarily acquiesce.

Like all other moralists who concern themselves

with sexual problems, Russell tends to overestimate the horsepower of the sexual impulse. When he says that " love is an anarchic force which, if it is left free, will not remain within any bounds set by law or custom," and that " uninhibited civilized people, whether men or women, are generally polygamous in their instincts," he comes close to the borders of nonsense. Far from being " anarchic," love is actually a kind of restraint — indeed, almost an inhibition — , especially upon the purely biological sexual impulse, and polygamy, save as an occasional day-dream, is hardly an inclination of the majority of civilized adults. Even on the lowly level of fornication it almost always moves toward monogamy. Its continued practice is confined mainly to persons who have failed to find a safe and comfortable monogamous refuge, and their failure is commonly regarded, even by themselves, as a misfortune showing overtones of social inadequacy. The " purely instinctive " and completely " uninhibited " individuals that Russell speaks of are encountered only in lunatic asylums and in the literature of psychoanalysis. The sexual instinct, to be sure, is not in itself very fastidious, but as a practical matter it is always greatly conditioned, at least among adults, by the social instinct, and by æsthetic impulses that are so profound as to be next door to instinctive. Even when it appears to be unbridled, as in cases of what the newspapers call criminal assault, it is almost always found to be limited in its objects. A young

woman of conspicuously aphrodisiacal face and frame
runs some risk of being stormed anywhere, including
even the Halls of Congress and the Harvard Yard, but
an elderly W.C.T.U. worker or other such frump
might tramp the Black Belt from end to end without
suffering any more molestation than a female alli-
gator. Earl Russell's corollary that " the more civilized people become, the less capable they seem of
lifelong happiness with one partner " is too absurd to
need an answer. If it were true, then the high-water
mark of modern civilization would have to be sought
at Hollywood and Palm Beach.

His book is really not half so saucy as second-hand
accounts of it (including this one) make it appear.
He believes, despite the quotation I have just made,
that marriage is " the best and most important relation that can exist between two human beings," and
that " where it is fruitful and both parties to it are
reasonable and decent the expectation ought to be that
it will be lifelong "; all he asks is that they cease to
" regard themselves as each other's policemen." For
the rest, he makes an earnest and effective plea for
ridding the institution of the family of every sort of
tyranny and oppression, whether of parents over children, of children over parents, of husbands over wives,
or of wives over husbands. Here the enlightened
opinion of mankind sustains him, and there is every
reason to believe that the ameliorations already
achieved will be followed by others hereafter. It is

not necessary to agree with August Strindberg that the Victorian family was " the hell of the child and the home of all social vices," but certainly its defects were serious enough. It left the wife in the intolerable legal position of a minor or a lunatic, it burdened both husband and wife with a too onerous care of their children, and it encouraged them to think of those children as chattels. Happiness was possible under this arrangement, and no doubt it was common, but only at the cost of much bitter sacrifice. There has been a considerable liberation in our time. Almost everywhere the wife has been emancipated from her old disabilities, and elevated to the estate of a free partner in the family firm, and meanwhile a great many of the immemorial burdens of parents have been taken over either by the state or by private contractors, especially in the fields of education and physic. The Victorian mother who sat up fourteen nights running to wear out her offspring's croup has been supplanted by a trained nurse, just as she has been supplanted in her rôle of pedagogue by a schoolma'm.

In democratic countries this movement is greatly accelerated by the scheming of politicians, who know the high uses of seeming to offer something for nothing. In most American States today (barring, of course, those already bankrupted by the business), two-thirds of the old duties and responsibilities of parents are now shouldered by public functionaries, supported by the taxpayer. After the head of the

family has performed the trivial physiological ceremony of fertilizing an ovum, he has few burdens that
are really inescapable to a man who knows his rights.
The whole process of pregnancy is supervised by public experts, the lying-in is cared for in a public maternity hospital, and the subsequent feeding and medi-
cating of the child, down to its school days, are
managed at public crèches and clinics. Once it begins
its formal education it becomes the ward of the state
in a wholesale and wholehearted fashion. Not only is it
instructed free of charge, and provided with elaborate
and expensive facilities for recreation; it is also fed if
necessary, and in the near future, no doubt, the peda-
gogical racketeers will be proposing to clothe and
lodge it. In all this there is plenty of absurdity, but
nevertheless a certain rationality lies buried in it.
That rationality, in its turn, is based upon a dawning
realization, unfortunately somewhat muddled, of the
cruelties and inadequacies of the old-time Christian
home. The public functionary, of course, has inadequacies of his own: he cannot, for example, supply
anything properly describable as parental affection,
and his substitutes for it are sometimes woefully
clumsy. But inasmuch as the real thing, in an unhap-
pily large proportion of cases, is mainly only a brutal
and witless variation of the ancient *patria potestas,*
breeding ingratitude, hatred and rebellion, I suppose
that the world will be able to get on without it. In so
far as it is unselfish, and honest, and hence valuable

to the child, it will probably survive any effort by
world-savers to abolish it.

5

How far we'll go hereafter, in this direction or
some other, is beyond the reckoning of any man now
living. It seems to be very likely that, in Christendom,
the breakdown in the sanction of revelation will upset
that mawkish, unhealthy veneration for chastity which
has afflicted the faithful since the days of Paul, and
that there will be increasing freedom in sexual matters, both as to talk and as to acts. But it is easy, on
the one hand, to overestimate the extent, both laterally
and vertically, of the breakdown of revelation, and,
on the other, to forget how ancient in human history
are some of the chief sexual taboos, and how deeply
they seem to lie in the very nature of man. Religion is
sick, but it is by no means dead, and on some calami-
tous tomorrow it may enjoy something of a revival.
That revival, in fact, is constantly predicted by specialists in human stupidity, and though it has not come
so far it may be on us after the next World War. If,
as Oswald Spengler and other such birds of evil tell
us, Western civilization is really in a low state, then
Christianity or something worse will undoubtedly
profit. Meanwhile, let us remember that a man who
casts off his hereditary articles of faith does not be-

come thereby, and at one stroke, a scientist comparable to Darwin or Huxley. Only too often all that is actually religious in his religion remains.

In this field the world has seen many ups and downs. When Puritanism went out in England the antinomian skepticism of the Restoration came in. It seemed a natural and even inevitable reaction, and we have experienced something of the same sort in our own time. But in it there were the seeds of a counter-reaction, which burst into full flower in the Victorianism that we are just recovering from. Here economic considerations always have a great deal to say. A society takes its moral tone from its dominant class. The landed aristocracy that returned to power in England with the Restoration was educated and sophisticated, as such things were defined at that time, and thus had no taste for theology; in consequence, the century following was an era of doubt and deviltry, and on the lower levels it took thousands of hangings to keep the populace in reasonable order. But when the Industrial Revolution set up a new aristocracy, mainly recruited from the ignorant and timorous burghers of the towns, the newcomers brought their tremors with them, and England became once more a pious and moral country. In Russia we are seeing the familiar process once again. There the old aristocracy of princes and soldiers, landlords and bankers, has been displaced by a new one of politicians and doctrinaires. That a moral revolution is in progress is manifest, but it is hard to say where it will arrive in the end. All we can be sure of is that the new values it promulgates will be enforced, at least so long as the new aristocracy hangs on, quite as ferociously as the old values of Christianity. The world is yet very far from that calm, scientific approach to morality which Dr. H. S. Jennings describes in " The Universe and Life " and Dr. H. M. Parshley advocates with so much eloquence in " Science and Good Behavior." It will probably come in soon or late, but surely not yet. For another age or two human beings will continue as in the past to follow instinct and self-interest rather than pure reason, at the same time keeping a wary eye on whatever gods there be.

As I have said in Chapter I, § 8, the ethical movement of the past two centuries has run against the exercise of irrational and oppressive authority and the infliction of needless pain. " The only sin which seems to us more sinful than it did to our fathers," says Aldous Huxley in " Texts and Pretexts," " is cruelty. We feel for it an abhorrence which would have seemed incomprehensible in the days of torture and public executions." This feeling is a heritage from the Humanism of the Renaissance, much augmented by profitable reinvestment, and it is now almost universally dispersed in the civilized world. In war even the most violent *Schrecklichkeit* has behind it the virtuous purpose of reducing the sum total of human

agony, and in peace the same purpose informs the
most sanguinary enterprises of political reformers.
Both Bolshevism and Fascism, in so far as they are
philosophical systems and not mere political dodges,
are fundamentally humanitarian in aim: if they are
cruel to the few it is only to be kind to the many. To
achieve that end, of course, they must have wide and
despotic powers, and in consequence they must be
careless of that large political liberty which has been
talked up by Western man since the Eighteenth Century. But there is little evidence that he really resents
losing it. On the contrary, he is always willing to
trade it for privilege — and it is as privileges that
his new boons appear to him. Once he has them, he is
at liberty to flout priests, Jews, nobles, bankers, or
some other group that enjoyed or seemed to enjoy
valuable immunities and superiorities in the past, and
the fact soothes his ego and makes him forget conveniently that his new superiors stand quite, or almost,
as far above him as his old ones. Indeed, he does not
forget it, strictly speaking; he simply denies it. It is
possible that, in the long run, he may turn out to be
right. That is, it may turn out that he has made a profitable exchange of the old equality between men, always
in conflict with elemental biological law, for a new
and far more real equality of opportunity. Unfortunately, the history of the world teaches us that equali-
ties of whatever sort are always more or less illusory.
The classical example is that equality before God

which the early Christians borrowed from the Jews, and the Jews, if Dr. James Henry Breasted is to be believed, from the Egyptians.

Every such effort to shift the ethical basis of society causes a great wastage of energy, and brings in a multitude of injustices. In order to abolish slavery in the United States a good third of the country had to be doomed to poverty and imbecility for a whole generation, and it was precisely the part that, in its day, had been the most wealthy and intelligent. In order that women may cease to be ruined for one banal indiscretion, we are now asked to abandon not only the idea of chastity but also that of fidelity to contract. And in order that a few Wiggams and Mitchells may be mulcted of their excessive gains millions of the hardworking and thrifty must be mulcted of their small ones. But that, alas, is the way humanity moves on. There are fearsome bumps along the road, and many weary halts and slippings back. Pessimists greet every such obstacle as a signal of disaster, but the event always proves them wrong. The human race, in fact, has a stupendous capacity for taking punishment. Over and over again it has been through such perils and agonies as would have sufficed to exterminate even the race of cockroaches, and yet it has emerged from them triumphantly every time. Indeed, it seems to thrive on adversity, and every era of calamity and despair has been succeeded by an era of abounding health and fresh hope. The late World War was really a trivial episode, compared to like events of the past, and the *Katzenjammer* issuing out of it is far more theatrical than pathological. Certainly it is hard to imagine Christians taking the breast-beating of the current Spenglers gravely, with so many far more eloquent and convincing prophecies of doom spread before them in the inspired textbook of their faith. If they actually believe, as they pretend, in the inevitable advent of the horrible monsters described in the Book of Revelation, then there is no excuse for them being alarmed by a few Nazis and Bolsheviks.

The great failure of civilized man, I repeat once more, is his failure to fashion a competent and tolerable form of government. Most of our worst vexations are not in the field of morals, properly so called, but in that of law. If the ingenuity and good sense that go into making a Ford, or cutting off a leg, or getting out a newspaper, or navigating an ocean liner could be applied to the common business of society the rate of real progress would be immensely accelerated and most of the more familiar varieties of bogus progress would be avoided. During the historical period government has always been costly, inefficient and oppressive; at all times and everywhere it has been little more than a device for exploiting the masses of men to the gain and glory of special classes — kings, priests, nobles, capitalists, military adventurers, lawyers, politicians, doctrinaires, and what not. More than once, in desperation, idealistic men have proposed that it be abolished altogether — that mankind un-horse and butcher its oppressors in one universal up-rising and return to a theoretical state of nature, rely-ing on common decency for order and on the law of natural selection for progress. It was an idea of this sort, I daresay, that lay at the bottom of Nietzsche's demand for a liberation of the primeval blond beast — brutal but honest, stupid but brave. He spoke too hopefully and too late: the blond beast actually joined the woolly rhinoceros and the sabre-toothed tiger in Valhalla ten millenniums ago. Man, the first mammal to be domesticated, has been a docile member of so-ciety since the Pliocene: it is now too late for him to behave as anything else. Save as an occasional aber-ration, recognized as such, it is in fact simply impos-sible for him to think of himself as standing alone. He is the social animal *par excellence,* and he is incurably resigned to enduring whatever goes with that character, the bitter along with the sweet.

Naturally, he tries to rationalize his resignation, and to make it something rather more grand and noble than it really is. He calls it, for example, obedience to the will of an omnipotent and omniscient God. Or duty, public spirit, patriotism. Or sacrifice to an idea, an ideal, usually obscure and often unintelligible. Out of such concepts arise moral systems. What is sound in them I have tried to show: it is mainly a simple response to a kind of instinct, shared with the ants and the bees. But what is false is still not unimportant, for out of it has flowed a great richness, an immense enhancement of the human spirit. Man is the only animal who yearns to be a part of something larger than himself, to lift himself beyond his nature, to transcend himself. His efforts to that end usually fail, and sometimes they are tragically ridiculous, but not always. There is, in fact, such a thing as progress, and many of the new values that it brings in are authentic and durable. The problem before mankind is to discover trustworthy criteria for separating those that have truth in them from those that are mere appearance. That is not a job for the priests and politicians, the lawyers and metaphysicians who have bungled it in the past; it is a job for honest and sensible men.

BIBLIOGRAPHICAL NOTE

The literature of ethics, like that of religion, is so vast that no reader, however diligent, can hope to go through all of it, nor even the half of it. The most comfortable guidance through its mazes, perhaps, is to be found in the Encyclopædia of Religion and Ethics, edited by James Hastings. This monumental work, first published in 1908 in thirteen volumes, and now reissued in seven, is reasonably impartial and very well-informed, and its arrangement is such as to make consulting it easy. The American edition is published by Scribner and may be found in all public libraries of any pretensions. Two other encyclopædias that are useful are the Catholic and the Jewish. The former, of course, emphasizes the Catholic point of view in all controverted matters, but its articles are fairly written, and the objections of Protestant and other opponents are usually stated. Unfortunately, the work was completed so long ago as 1907, and shows some signs of dating: for example, there is no article on birth control. No doubt the subject will be discussed at length in the next edition. Meanwhile, it has produced a large literature. Good examples on the Catholic side are " Judgment on Birth Control," by Raoul de Guchteneere (New York, Macmillan,

1931), and " Birth Control," by Dr. John M. Cooper (Washington, National Catholic Welfare Conference, 1923). Many translations of Pope Pius XI's encyclical on the subject, *Casti connubii,* have been published since the original was issued on December 31, 1930. The best is probably that of Sheed & Ward, New York, with a commentary by Father Vincent McNabb, O.P. The Catholic case for chastity is set forth at length in " In Defense of Purity," by Dietrich von Hildebrand (New York, Longmans, 1931). The literature on the other side is fast growing. Its chief luminaries are Margaret Sanger in America and Dr. Marie Stopes in England: both have printed many books and pamphlets. A more moderate statement of the case for birth control is in " Marriage, Children, and God," by Claude Mullins (London, Allen, 1933).

There are many general texts on ethics, some of them designed for school or college use. One of the most popular is " Ethics," by John Dewey and James H. Tufts, first published in 1908 and extensively revised in 1932 (New York, Holt). Others of merit are "Introduction to Ethics," by Frank Thilly (New York, Scribner, 1900); " A Manual of Ethics," by John S. Mackenzie (London, Clive, 5th ed., 1920); " General Introduction to Ethics," by William Kelley Wright (New York, Macmillan, 1929); " The Elements of Ethics," by John H. Muirhead (London, Murray, 3rd ed., 1910); " The Moral Self," by Charles L. Sherman (Boston, Ginn, 1927); " Problems of Ethics,"

TREATISE ON RIGHT AND WRONG

by Durant Drake (Boston, Houghton, 1921); "Ethics," by Frank Chapman Sharp (New York, Century, 1928); "A Handbook of Ethical Theory," by G. S. Fullerton (New York, Holt, 1922); "Introduction to the Science of Ethics," by Theodore De Laguna (New York, Macmillan, 1914); and "Ethics," by G. E. Moore (New York, Holt, n.d.). The last belongs to the admirable Home University Library. To these, many more textbooks might be added, but those that I have listed cover the ground adequately.

Of histories of ethics, one of the most useful, considering its small scale, is that of Henry Sidgwick (New York, Macmillan, 6th ed., 1931). It gives special attention to the development of ethical theory in Great Britain. For the early Christian period the best text remains W. E. H. Lecky's "History of European Morals from Augustus to Charlemagne" (New York, Appleton, 2 vols., 1877): it is somewhat diffuse, but it is full of very interesting stuff, and some of Lecky's judgments have passed into the common stock. "The Classical Moralists," by Benjamin Rand (Boston, Houghton, 1909), presents well-selected extracts from the writings of forty-five ancient and modern writers, beginning with Socrates and ending with James Martineau. In "Five Types of Ethical Theory," by C. D. Broad (New York, Harcourt, 1930), there are elaborate summaries of the views of Spinoza, Butler, Hume, Kant and Sidgwick. Edward Westermarck's large work, "The Origin and Development of the Moral

Ideas " (New York, Macmillan, 2 vols., 1908), is worth reading, if only for its rich amassing of anthropological data, but some of its conclusions are to be received with caution. The same thing must be said of " The Dawn of Conscience," by James Henry Breasted (New York, Scribner, 1933), which offers a good conspectus of the growth of moral theory in the Near East, but perhaps lays too much stress on the Egyptian contribution. " The Evolution of Ethics," by E. Hershey Sneath (New Haven, Yale University Press, 1927), has for its sub-title " As Revealed in the Great Religions," which sufficiently describes its scope. " Men and Morals," by Woodbridge Riley (New York, Doubleday, 1929), covers both moral theology and secular ethics, and is shrewdly written and very entertaining. " A History of Ethics," by Stephen Ward (London, Oxford University Press, 1924), is short but useful.

There are many treatises in special fields. The reader interested in the origin and development of Christian ethics will find much to his taste in " The Origin and History of Hebrew Law," by J. M. Powis Smith (Chicago, University of Chicago Press, 1931); " The World of the New Testament," by T. R. Glover (New York, Macmillan, 1931); " The World of Jesus," by Henry Kendall Booth (New York, Scribner, 1933); " Early Christianity and Its Rivals," by G. H. Box (New York, Cape, 1929); " The Ethics of Paul," by Morton Scott Enslin (New York, Harper, 1930);

" A History of Christian Thought," by Arthur Cushman McGiffert (New York, Scribner, 1932); " The Religious Background of American Culture," by Thomas Cuming Hall (Boston, Little, 1930); " Piety versus Moralism: the Passing of the New England Theology," by Joseph Haroutunian (New York, Holt, 1932); " The Inquisition," by Hoffman Nickerson (New York, 1923), and " The Greek Tradition," by Paul Elmer More (Princeton, N. J., Princeton University Press, 6 vols., 1933). I mention only a few recent works; the literature on the subject is almost endless. As correlative reading I suggest Andrew D. White's monumental " History of the Warfare of Science with Theology in Christendom " (New York, Appleton, 2 vols., 1896); Joseph Wheless's two volumes, " Is It God's Word? " (New York, Knopf, 1926) and " Forgery in Christianity " (New York, Knopf, 1930); " The Martyrdom of Man," by Winwood Reade (New York, Dutton, new ed., 1926), and " The Antichrist," by F. W. Nietzsche (New York, Knopf, 1918). To these " The History of Christianity in the Light of Modern Knowledge," by twenty-two English and American scholars (New York, Harcourt, 1929), may be very well added.

The classical moralists, *i.e.*, the Greeks and Romans, are all to be had in good translations in the Loeb Library (New York, Putnam, v.d.), and those of the modern era, especially the English, are nearly all in Everyman's Library (New York, Dutton, v.d.). An exhaustive examination of Aristotle's ideas, as set forth in the Nicomachean Ethics, is in " Aristotle's Theory of Conduct," by Thomas Marshall (London, Unwin, 1909), and the same service is done for Plato in " Plato's Theory of Ethics," by R. C. Lodge (New York, Harcourt, 1928). Two books that throw much light on the general Greek position are " The Greek Skeptics," by Mary Mills Patrick (New York, Columbia University Press, 1929), and " Greek Byways," by T. R. Glover (New York, Macmillan, 1932). In late years there has been a tendency to push ethical inquiry back into primitive times, and to seek light upon the subject by studying the ideas of living savages. Westermarck's large work in two volumes I have just mentioned. Another on a big scale is Robert Briffault's " The Mothers " (New York, Macmillan, 3 vols., 1927), which also appears in a briefer form (New York, Macmillan, 1931). Bronislaw Malinowski is the author of various books on the subject, including " Crime and Custom in Savage Society " (New York, Harcourt, 1926), " Sex and Repression in Savage Society " (New York, Harcourt, 1927), and " The Sexual Life of Savages " (New York, Liveright, 2 vols., 1929).

Other volumes that will be found interesting and valuable are " Primitive Religion," by Robert H. Lowie (New York, Boni, 1924); "Are We Civilized? " by the same author (New York, Harcourt, 1929); " The Primitive Mind and Modern Civilization," by Charles Roberts Aldrich (New York, Harcourt, 1931); " Anjea," by Herbert Aptekar (New York, Godwin, 1931); " The Mind of the Savage," by Raoul Allier (New York, Harcourt, n.d.); " Faith, Hope and Charity in Primitive Religion," by R. R. Marett (New York, Macmillan, 1932); " Coming of Age in Samoa," by Margaret Mead (New York, Morrow, 1928), and " At Home With the Savage," by J. H. Driberg (New York, Morrow, 1932). " The Moral Judgment of the Child," by Jean Piaget (New York, Harcourt, 1932), is also worth reading. Kropotkin's " Mutual Aid " (London, Heinemann, 1907) is out of print, but copies are not hard to come by. His " Ethics: Origin and Development " is still in print (New York, MacVeagh, 1924). I assume that everyone interested in moral speculation will want to read Darwin's " The Descent of Man," obtainable in many cheap editions; Huxley's " Evolution and Ethics " (New York, Appleton, 1894); and Herbert Spencer's " The Principles of Ethics " (New York, Appleton, 1893). There is also useful matter in " Source Book in Anthropology," by A. L. Kroeber and T. T. Waterman (New York, Harcourt, 1931); " The Science of Society," by William Graham Sumner and A. G. Keller (New Haven, Yale University Press, 4 vols., 1927), and " The Natural History of Our Conduct," by William E. Ritter (New York, Harcourt, 1927).

On the ethical systems promulgated by the chief non-Christian religions, the best recent texts that I

BIBLIOGRAPHICAL NOTE

have encountered are: for Mohammedanism, " Islam: Beliefs and Institutions," by H. Lammens, S. J. (London, Methuen, 1929), and " Mohammedan Law," by Seymour Vesey-Fitzgerald (London, Oxford University Press, 1931); for Confucianism, " Confucius and Confucianism," by Richard Wilhelm (New York, Harcourt, 1931); " Mencius," by Leonard A. Lyall (New York, Longmans, 1932), and " The Wisdom of Confucius," by Miles Menander Dawson (Boston, International Pocket Library, 1932); and for Zoroastrianism, " The Ethical Religion of Zoroaster," by Miles Menander Dawson (New York, Macmillan, 1931). " The Meaning of the Glorious Koran," by Marmaduke Pickthall, an English Moslem (New York, Knopf, 1930), is a new translation of the Koran with a brief commentary. It is much better than the older translations.

Rather curiously, there are not many books, at least in English, dealing with moral science from the specifically Catholic and Protestant points of view. The most complete recent statement of the Catholic position is in " Moral Theology," by John A. McHugh, O. P., and Charles J. Callan, O. P. (New York, Wagner, 2 vols., 1929). Another large work is "A Manual of Moral Theology for English-Speaking Countries," by Thomas Slater, S. J. (New York, Benziger, 2 vols., 1908). This last is of English provenance, but there are American notes by Michael Martin, S. J. A useful small treatise is " The Elements of Ethics," by Charles

C. Miltner, C. S. C. (New York, Macmillan, new ed., 1931), another is " Catholic Teachings," by Thomas C. B. Healy (New York, Macmillan, 1931), and a more advanced work is " Ethics General and Special," by Owen A. Hill, S. J. (New York, Macmillan, 1928). Of the Protestant texts, those that I have found the most interesting are " Christian Ethics and Modern Problems," by W. R. Inge (New York, Putnam, 1930); " The Philosophy of the Good Life," by Charles Gore (London, Murray, 1930); " Moral Theology," by Francis J. Hall and Frank H. Hallock, an exposition of the High Church Episcopalian view (New York, Longmans, 1924); and " The Problem of Right Conduct," by Peter Green (New York, Longmans, 1931).

As I have said in Chapter V, the Bible of the New Morality is " Marriage and Morals," by Bertrand Russell (New York, Liveright, 1929). But Earl Russell has also written other books and pamphlets on the subject, and the literature has been further embellished by his wife, Dora Russell. J. M. Guyau's " Esquisse d'une Morale sans Obligation ni Sanction " (1885) is almost forgotten now, but it had a wide influence in its day, and the English translation by Gertrude Kapteyn, " A Sketch of Morality Independent of Obligation or Sanction " (London, Watts, n.d.), is still worth reading. So is " Morals in Evolution," by L. T. Hobhouse (London, Chapman, 1906). Other books of interest and value are " Love and Ethics," by

BIBLIOGRAPHICAL NOTE

Ellen Key (New York, Huebsch, 1911); "Ethical Relativity," by Edward Westermarck (New York, Harcourt, 1932); "Science and Good Behavior," by H. M. Parshley (Indianapolis, Bobbs, 1928); "Intellectual Crime," by Janet Chance (London, Douglas, 1933); "A Preface to Morals," by Walter Lippmann (New York, Macmillan, 1929); "The Freudian Wish and Its Place in Ethics," by Edwin B. Holt (New York, Holt, 1915); "The Theory of Ethics," by Arthur Kenyon Rogers (New York, Macmillan, 1922); "Red Virtue," by Ella Winter (New York, Harcourt, 1933); "The Ethics of Hercules," by Robert Chenault Givler (New York, Knopf, 1924), an attempt to discover a biological basis for moral ideas; "Right," by Wyatt Tilby (London, Williams, 1934), another in the same direction; "The Twilight of Christianity," by Harry Elmer Barnes (New York, Vanguard, 1929), and "The Universe and Life," by H. S. Jennings (New Haven, Yale University Press, 1933). The chief counterblast of the Christian moralists is "The New Morality," by G. E. Newsom (London, Nicholson, 1933). In "Jesus or Christianity," by Kirby Page (New York, Doubleday, 1929), there is an eloquent plea for a return to the ethics of Jesus, long since abandoned in Christendom.

There is a large library of books dealing with special problems in ethics, and they show widely varying points of view. A work that has been much discussed of late is "The Protestant Ethic and the Spirit of

Capitalism," by Max Weber, translated from the German by Talcott Parsons (New York, Scribner, 1930). Others that will be found interesting are " The Lawful Pursuit of Gain," by Max Radin (Boston, Houghton, 1931); " The Doctrine of Sin," by Reginald S. Moxon (London, Allen, 1932); " Gambling and Christian Ideals," by Cecil H. Rose (London, Epworth Press, 1930); " God and Mammon," by J. A. Hobson (London, Watts, 1931); " The Ethics of Business," by Edgar L. Heermance (New York, Harper, 1926); " The Ethical Basis of the State," by Norman Wilde (Princeton, N. J., Princeton University Press, 1924); " Work," by Adriano Tilgher (New York, Harcourt, 1930), which covers the ground of the Weber book aforesaid and is more readable; " The Nature of Evil," by Radoslav A. Tsanoff (New York, Macmillan, 1931); " Divorce," by J. P. Lichtenberger (New York, McGraw, 1931); " Social Control of Sex Expression," by Geoffrey May (New York, Morrow, 1931), a useful historical summary; and " Sin and Sex," by Robert Briffault, a very iconoclastic work (New York, Macaulay, 1931). The best short treatise on free will that I know of is " Free Will and Human Responsibility," by Herman H. Horne (New York, Macmillan, 1912). Another of some value is " Freedom of Will," by N. O. Lossky (London, Williams, 1932). Henri Bergson's " Time and Free Will " (New York, Macmillan, 1910) scarcely needs mention. A well-informed discussion of legal punishments,

BIBLIOGRAPHICAL NOTE

strongly reformist in tendency, is in " The Story of Punishment," by Harry Elmer Barnes (Boston, Stratford, 1930). A more cautious work is " Conflicting Penal Theories in Statutory Criminal Law," by Mabel A. Elliott (Chicago, University of Chicago Press, 1931). Others of interest are " The Personality of Criminals," by Albert Warren Stearns (Boston, Beacon Press, 1931), and " The Morality of Punishment," by A. C. Ewing (London, Paul, 1929).

Soli Deo gloria!

INDEX

INDEX

18, 23, 48, 54, 74, 77, 83, 107, 121–122, 132, 188, 192, 193, 194–200, 227, 236, 238, 243, 244, 278; *and see* Nicomachean Ethics

Arius, 221

Arizona, 170

Arkansas, 11

Armageddon, *see* Megiddo

Ashtoreth, 164

Asmodeus, 112

Asshurbanipal, 161

Assyrians, 56, 145

Athanasius, 221

Athens, 103, 121, 178, 187, 188, 190, 191, 192, 199

Aton, 149, 152

Atonement, 229

Augustine, St., 24–25, 39, 64, 71, 72, 127, 194, 211, 225, 228, 239, 241, 253, 278

Austria, 33, 247

Authority behind moral ideas, 8–10; *and see* Instinct, Reason, Revelation

Auxerre, Council of, 225

Avitus, St., 231

Babylon: and slavery, 34, 35; and first moral philosophers, 111; captivity of Jews in, 112, 144, 160, 163, 166, 168, 176, 208; criminal law in, 119–120;

influence on Jews, 151, 153–154, 155–156, 171, 180, 183, 209; wars of, 161–163, 165, 166, 169

Bacon, Francis, 75, 278, 279

Bakunin, M. A., 270

Ballantine, 37

Baptists, 60–61, 250, 269, 293, 300

Barron, J. T., 58

Barton, R. F., 66

Basil, St., 229

Beatitudes, 8, 18, 59, 126, 217, 228–229

Beaverbrook, 289

Beccaria, 131–133, 134

Bedouins, 118

Beecher, Henry Ward, 265–266

Behaviorists, 83, 251

Belloc, Hilaire, 271

Benedict, St., 229

Benezet, Anthony, 41

Bentham, Jeremy, 131, 133–134, 283

Bergson, Henri, 76, 77–79, 85–86, 87

Berkeley, 76

Bezaleel, 113–114

Bible, 4, 19, 45, 57, 59, 60, 196, 209, 225, 269; *and see* New Testament, Old Testament, Pentateuch, *and titles of various books*

Bible Belt, 265, 270

[ii]

INDEX

[iii]

INDEX

INDEX

[v]

INDEX

INDEX

INDEX

INDEX

INDEX

[x]

INDEX

[xi]

INDEX

INDEX

INDEX

INDEX

INDEX

[xvi]

INDEX

INDEX

INDEX

Wisdom: as supreme good, 6–7, 9; virtue as function of, 8–9

Wisdom literature, 180, 185

Wisdom of Amenemope, 21

Witchcraft, 17, 59, 130

Wollstonecraft, Mary, 50

Women: emancipation of, 45–52, 301–304; attitude of early Christians to, 225

Work, 19–21, 23–29

World War, 291, 316–317

Yahweh, 17, 46, 52, 202, 228, 268; as tribal god of Jews, 9, 10, 20, 53, 113–114, 152, 154, 163, 164, 165, 176, 184, 185; nature of, 13, 157, 167–173, 203–213, 217, 275; and blasphemy, 15; as father, 54; and slavery, 60; and revelation, 222–223; and faith, 229, 230; and baptism, 237; and Onan, 257; and predestination, 266; modern Protestant conception of, 271, 276, 279

Zaccheus, 21

Zedekiah, 163, 166

Zell, Theodor, 2

Zeno, 80

Zephaniah, 207

Zoroaster, 111–112, 113, 161

Zoroastrians, 210

Zuckerman, S., 99

Zwingli, 131